DECENTRALISAT
DEMOCRACY
Localising public services

Edited by
PAUL HOGGETT ROBIN HAMBLETON

Occasional Paper 28

UNIVERSITY·OF·BRISTOL

SCHOOL·FOR·ADVANCED·URBAN·STUDIES

The School for Advanced Urban Studies was established jointly by the University of Bristol and the Department of the Environment in 1973 as a post-experience teaching and research centre in the field of urban policy. In addition to the dissemination of material in courses and seminars the School has established three publications series: **SAUS Studies, Occasional Papers and Working Papers.**

SAUS is open to the submission of manuscripts from outside authors within its areas of interest.

General enquiries about the School, its courses, research programme and publications may be addressed to the Publicity Secretary.

School for Advanced Urban Studies
Rodney Lodge
Grange Road
Clifton
Bristol BS8 4EA

Telephone: (0272) 741117

Director: Professor Murray Stewart

SAUS is working to counter discrimination on grounds of gender, race, disability, age and sexuality in all its activities.

CONTENTS

NOTES ON CONTRIBUTORS

Peter Arnold is Senior Lecturer in Social Policy at Humberside College of Higher Education

Charlie Barker was Team Manager for Elderly Services, Social Services Department, Birmingham City Council and is now Assistant Director (services for elderly people) with the Social Services Department, Tameside

Danny Burns is a Research Associate at the Decentralisation Research and Information Centre, School of Planning, Polytechnic of Central London

Ian Cole is Senior Lecturer in Housing at Sheffield City Polytechnic

Robin Hambleton is Special Lecturer/Administrator at the School for Advanced Urban Studies, University of Bristol

Edmund Heery is Research Fellow at the Department of Industrial Relations, London School of Economics

Margaret Hodge is Leader of Islington Council

Paul Hoggett is Lecturer at the School for Advanced Urban Studies, University of Bristol

Tim Kendrick was Research Associate at the Decentralisation Research and Information Centre, School of Planning, Polytechnic of Central London and is now Project Development Officer at the Safe Neighbourhoods Unit

Edward Pilkington was also a Research Associate at the Decentralisation Research and Information Centre, School of Planning, Polytechnic of Central London and is now working in Nicaragua

Andrew Puddephatt is Leader of Hackney Council

Adrian Rivers is Training Officer for the Housing Department, London Borough of Newham

ACKNOWLEDGEMENTS

As editors we would like to thank all the people who have contributed to this collection by giving their time, energy and ideas to this enterprise. We hope that they feel the effort was worthwhile.

In terms of formal acknowledgement we wish to thank the Economic and Social Research Council (ESRC) for financing our research on decentralisation in Birmingham which is reported in Chapter 5 and also drawn on in Chapter 4. The full research report to ESRC is: **Hoggett, P. and Hambleton, R.** (1985) Decentralisation in Birmingham. A study of developments up to March, Final Report, May.

We also wish to thank the Decentralisaton Research and Information Centre, School of Planning, the Polytechnic of Central London for permission to reproduce in the Annex to this Occasional Paper their Update survey of local authority decentralisation programmes, August, 1986. This survey can be purchased separately from the Centre and copyright remains with the Centre.

Finally, we would like to thank the research secretaries and publication staff at SAUS who have shown remarkable dedication and patient attention to detail in producing this finished document.

Paul Hoggett and Robin Hambleton

December 1986

INTRODUCTION
Robin Hambleton and
Paul Hoggett

This collection of papers is a follow up to The politics of
decentralisation: theory and practice of a radical local government
initiative produced by SAUS in December 1984.[1] Whilst we wish to
preserve the same style as the previous publication - a balance
between case study and theory, between advocacy and criticism - a
number of changes have occurred within the 'decentralisation field'
over the last 18 months or so which we seek to document and
analyse in this new collection.

The first point we would wish to make is that we are now
convinced that decentralisation is not some kind of passing fad.
We say this for a number of reasons. Most immediately, this kind
of innovation has now become widely adopted within British local
government itself. So much so that it is, for instance, now quite
difficult to find a public sector housing department with a stock of
more than 20,000 properties which is not engaged in a
decentralisation initiative of some kind.   Wherever one looks,
whether it be major cities (like Manchester, Birmingham,
Edinburgh or Leeds) or smaller local authorities (like Rochdale,
Norwich, Halton or Greenwich) officers and councillors will insist
that they are busily engaged in new initiatives related to
decentralisation. Indeed, as supported by the evidence set out in
the Annex to this book, we estimate that some 40 authorities are
developing or implementing single or multi-service forms of
decentralisation. Nor is decentralisation, considered as a political
project, any longer simply a property of the Labour left.   In
London, for example, recently elected Liberal controlled Tower
Hamlets, Richmond and Kingston-on-Thames are all embarking on
experiments in various forms of local democracy.   And a recent
Green Paper published by the Social Democratic Party advocates
the creation of a totally new tier of community council at sub-
local authority level to 'represent local feelings and reflect local
anxieties and concerns'.[2]

A second point to note is that decentralisation is fast becoming managerially attractive. Many of the recommendations made by the Audit Commission in its handbook on 'Economy, efficiency and effectiveness' point towards more decentralised forms of management.[3] Central in this is the idea of defining 'cost centres' well down the organisational hierarchy over which local budget managers can exercise considerable discretion. Probably the most talked about example of this approach in British local government at present is the development of decentralised school-based budgeting and financial management by Cambridgeshire County Council.[4] More generally, much of the public sector is still reeling under the weight of books, seminars and training events which have been prompted by the publication of the seminal In search of excellence by the American private sector consultants Peters and Waterman.[5] These authors stress the importance of getting 'close to the customer':

> The excellent companies are better listeners. They get a benefit from market closeness that for us was truly unexpected - unexpected, that is, until you think about it. Most of their real innovation comes from the market.[6]

A number of efforts are now being made to translate some of these ideas into the public sector. Within the health service, for example, there is a great deal of debate about 'quality assurance' and the need for a 'consumer orientation'.[7] And within local government Michael Clarke and John Stewart are attempting to stimulate similar rethinking by arguing that management should take service for the public as its key value.[8]

This brings us to a third and, perhaps in the long run, most important factor - within the private sector itself organisational decentralisation appears to be emerging as the new 'corporate form' for the coming decades.[9] Such developments owe much to the technological revolution taking place around us, a revolution which not only affects the way in which goods and services are produced but, more crucially, the way in which control over such production is exercised. The possibility that Fordist principles of production are, through our present economic crisis, giving way to altogether new sets of principles which are now also beginning to inform how the state organises its production, is considered in our concluding chapter.

Finally, when one looks across the Channel to the welfare state in Europe, as we do in Chapter 3, one is again struck by the depth and

2

breadth of decentralisation initiatives currently taking place. Certainly, compared with Sweden and Italy, developments in Britain seem small scale and immature.

For all these reasons we now feel that decentralisation should now be considered a trend rather than a fad. Certainly in some areas, perhaps particularly some London boroughs, there has been a 'flavour of the month' approach to decentralisation, but such political faddism should not obscure the much more deep-seated trend towards decentralised arrangements which now appear to be on the agenda. But, and this is a point made repeatedly throughout this collection, if decentralisation as a political and organisational innovation has gained widespread popularity there can be no doubt either that its nature has become much more diffuse. For one thing it has become clear that organisational decentralisation often has little or no relevance to the democratisation of public services. It is quite possible to engage in a radical decentralisation of office arrangements whilst centralising power and authority and reducing the accountability between the organisation and the people it serves. For this reason we seek to make a sharp distinction, one which was still obscure to us 18 months ago, between the decentralisation and the democratisation of services. We feel that the distinction is important enough to be featured in the title of this current collection of papers; in particular we note that, whereas rapid advances have been made in terms of organisational decentralisation, progress towards greater local democracy has been faltering indeed.

Decentralisation and democratisation

We suggest in Chapter 1 that the decentralisation and democratisation of public services are expressions of two parallel but distinct approaches to the reform of the welfare state. One approach we regard as essentially 'consumerist' in form, the other as essentially 'collectivist'. Consumerist approaches clearly resonate with and draw upon many of the developments within the private sector, hence their attractiveness not only to all shades of political opinion but to public sector managers also. By focusing upon the efficiency and effectiveness (ie responsiveness and accessibility) of services they tend to use the 'neighbourhood concept' as a vehicle or catalyst for bringing about greater managerial delegation, a reintegration of divided service functions, improved management information systems and more consistent client or customer awareness. As such they do provide the basis for more local and extended forms of accountability but the one

3

need not necessarily follow from the other. Crucially a shift to new forms of local accountability requires a strong commitment of political will.

We need, then, to distinguish between service responsiveness and service democracy. It is quite possible for a service providing organisation to be highly responsive (and hence successful) but quite undemocratic - look at Sainsbury's supermarkets or International Business Machines (IBM) for example. Research on local government initiatives with area management and neighbourhood decentralisation in both Britain and America in the 1970s showed that, whilst they undoubtedly improved service responsiveness, they did little to strengthen local accountability.[10] On the other hand it is perfectly possible for a service providing organisation to be highly democratic (with worker/consumer management boards etc) and yet lack organisational structures and procedures which would enable it to respond effectively to concerns and needs. This, of course, has been an issue in some radical collective and feminist organisations in recent years.[11] Sheila Rowbotham, in her reflections on the libertarian movement of the early 1970s, whilst being keen to stress the importance of learning through doing and on the need for experience to be the source of theory, was well aware of the disabling effect of extreme forms of democracy:

> This led to the assertion that .... there should be no hierarchy, no elites, no chair, no committees, no speakers and even no meetings in some cases .... The stress on total solutions and the fears of co-option could give way to despair and disillusion .... The conviction that organisation should carry the future, breaking down all hierarchy and denying all skills, could become an inturned and moralistic network which excluded people.[12]

Many of the subsequent chapters are concerned to explore ways of making public services more responsive and more democratic. Given the nature of many local government services, and particularly the fact that many of them are consumed collectively, we suggest that the two aims of decentralisation and democratisation are inextricably linked.

4

Bringing about change

We feel it is important not to underestimate the radical nature of the critique of present forms of welfare organisation implied by the consumerist approach to reform - let alone by some emerging collectivist approaches outlined in Chapters 4 and 10. If one thing has become clear over the past five years or so it is that, even leaving aside questions of accountability and democracy, local government organisations have found it exceedingly difficult and painful to change themselves in a direction which is qualitatively more consumer oriented. In particular we assert that there is a real 'failure of courage' by many local government managers to pursue change which amounts to more than a simple amendment to existing unsatisfactory organisational forms. Indeed because of such managerial temerity it has often required councillors to 'come in from outside' as it were and shake up organisations in a way that makes a real difference. In Chapter 8 we chart some of the ways in which change has been fudged by managers and list some general strategies for managing significant change. In Chapter 9 Adrian Rivers amplifies this discussion by providing a case study of his own role as trainer in the facilitation of change in the London Borough of Newham's housing department.

Another major difficulty which emerged, particularly in the period 1984/1985, related to conflictual relationships between decentralising local authorities and their trade unions. Disputes in Hackney in 1983 were followed by disputes in St. Helens, Sheffield and Islington the following year.[13] Many of these conflicts raise important issues, not just practical ones relating to the negotiation of decentralisation but theoretical ones also - relating to the nature of public sector white-collar trade union militancy and the potential contradiction between traditional 'wages and conditions' trade unionism and the requirements of a properly responsive and democratic public service. These and other issues are addressed in Eddie Heery's reflective case study (Chapter 11) on the attitude and behaviour of trade unions towards Islington's decentralisation initiative and the GLC's equal opportunities strategy. They are also touched upon in Chapter 10 by Andrew Puddephatt in the course of his reflections on the boundary between state and community considered in the light of the London Borough of Hackney's recent turbulent history.

To conclude this introduction we would like to re-emphasise how many important developments have got underway since our last collection of papers was produced. Some of these we attempt to document in earlier chapters in this collection. In Chapter 2 Margaret Hodge, Leader of Islington council since 1982, provides an overview of the many developments in Islington, a local authority which has not only been the major innovator in terms of decentralising and democratising its own services but has also been in the forefront of the struggle against an autocratic and centralist Conservative government. In Chapter 5, with the assistance of Charlie Barker, we provide a case study of decentralisation in Birmingham over the last couple of years, a case study which illustrates many of the themes we have already referred to - the ambiguity of decentralisation, competing political and managerial interpretations, competing notions of the 'neighbourhood office concept' and so on.

In Chapter 6 Edward Pilkington and Tim Kendrick survey and attempt a preliminary evaluation of attempts to decentralise local authority housing repairs and maintenance services - services now widely acknowledged as being amongst the most poorly managed in all of local government. In the following chapter Ian Cole and Peter Arnold draw on their own experience as researchers and consultants and on a small national survey conducted by Sheffield Polytechnic to attempt an initial appraisal of developments in housing and social services departments. From this they conclude that current initiatives appear to be increasingly managerialist in conception, that questions of democracy and power tend to be taking a 'back seat', and that surprisingly little evaluation of any of these initiatives has so far taken place.

Inevitably there are gaps in our coverage. Emerging forms of decentralised professional practice - community architecture, community social work - have received scant attention, though clearly the recent book by Beresford and Croft addresses the latter.[14] We have paid virtually no attention to the practical issues of installing forms of new technology - specifically decentralised information systems - which are almost certainly necessary to make neighbourhood structures work effectively. Most local authorities we know of have encountered tremendous problems here both in terms of hardware and software. Nor are we able to deal in any detail with devolved forms of budgeting and financial control - for example, cost centres, area resource analyses, estate and neighbourhood budgets, and so on. Progress here (excluding the formation of cost centres) has been extremely slow, yet fundamental change surely hinges upon such developments. Finally, although we have made a start on documenting and analysing some of the recent experiments in service democratisation, we are aware that far more detailed analyses and case studies need to be provided - perhaps this will be a theme for a future volume!

Notes and References

1. **Hambleton, R.** and **Hoggett, P.** eds (1984) <u>The politics of decentralisation: theory and practice of a radical local government initiative</u>, Working Paper 46, School for Advanced Urban Studies, University of Bristol.

2. **Social Democratic Party** (1985) <u>Decentralising government</u>, Green Paper No 3, p 51.

3. **Audit Commission** (1983) <u>Improving economy, efficiency and effectiveness in local government in England and Wales</u>, An Audit Commission Handbook, November. (Please note that updates to this handbook have been published since 1983).

4. **Burgess, T.** (1986) 'Cambridgeshire's financial management initiative for schools', <u>Public Money</u>, June, pp 21-24.

5. **Peters T.J.** and **Waterman, R.H.** (1982) <u>In search of excellence. Lessons from America's best-run companies</u>, New York: Harper and Row. See also **Clutterbuck, D.** (1984) <u>The Winning Streak</u>, London: Weidenfeld and Nicolson.

6. Ibid, **Peters and Waterman**, p 193.

7. For a useful collection of articles on this, see 'Consumerism in the NHS', pull-out 8 page feature in <u>Health and Social Services Journal</u>, 30 May, 1985.

8. **Clarke, M.** and **Stewart, J.** (1985) <u>Local government and the public service orientation: or does a public service provide for the public?</u> Local Government Training Board, August.

9. **Murray, F.** (1985) 'Bennetton Britain', <u>Marxism Today</u>, November, pp 28-32; **Hoggett, P.** (1985) 'A long wave to freedom', <u>Chartist</u>, October/November, pp 25-28.

10. **Hambleton, R.** (1978) <u>Policy planning and local government</u>, London: Hutchinson. (This contains an appraisal of decentralisation in five cities: Stockport, Liverpool, Boston, New York City and Dayton).

11. The issues are helpfully reviewed in: **Landry, C., Morley, D., Southwood, R. and Wright, P.** (1985) What a way to run a railroad. An analysis of radical failure, London: Comedia.

12. **Rowbotham, S.** (1979) 'The women's movement and organising for socialism' in Rowbotham, S., Segal, L. and Wainwright, H., Beyond the fragments. Feminism and the making of socialism, London: Merlin Press, p 30 and 31.

13. **Wolmar, C.** (1984) 'Divided we stand', New Socialist, December, pp 13-15; **Darke, J. and Gouly, K.** (1985) 'United we stand', New Socialist, February, p 8; **Sharron, S.** (1985) 'Overcoming trade union resistance to local change', Public Money, March, pp 17-23.

14. **Beresford, P. and Croft, S.** (1986) Whose welfare? Lewis Cohen Urban Studies Centre, Brighton Polytechnic.

PART 1
SETTING DEVELOPMENTS
IN CONTEXT

1

BEYOND BUREAUCRATIC PATERNALISM

Robin Hambleton and Paul Hoggett

Introduction

Our starting point is that local government is in crisis. It is possible to see how this crisis in local government reflects wider tensions in our society - in the economy, in culture and, above all, in politics. During the 1980s new patterns of political alignment, new types of political organisation, and new sources of political conflict have emerged.

In a recent and helpful overview of these developments, which is focused mainly on the national level, Dearlove and Saunders highlight: the erosion of the two-party system; the fact that both the major parties have (in their different ways) come to reject many of the basic principles by which governments have attempted to run the country since the Second World War; the growth of social protest (from riots in the inner cities through to the long and weary vigil of the women camped outside the Greenham Common airforce base in opposition to the deployment of Cruise missiles under the control of the American Government); and the constitutional strains arising from the growth of nationalist movements in Scotland, Wales and Northern Ireland as well as the increasing influence of European community institutions in British affairs.[1] These authors suggest that, in the present turmoil of British politics, democracy itself is being questioned from a number of different quarters.

We are in broad agreement with this analysis and believe that these various trends are having and will continue to have a major impact on British local government. In this book we aim to explore some of the implications of these developments for local government by focusing on a single theme: the decentralisation and democratisation of public service. We see the book as a follow up

9

to our earlier Working Paper, The politics of decentralisation, which examined and offered reflections on a number of decentralisation initiatives.[2] We are adopting a similar approach in this volume with case study chapters documenting examples of practical experience set alongside a number of chapters which attempt to locate and/or evaluate these various initiatives. Whilst our earlier Working Paper referred fairly extensively to issues of accountability and local control we feel that this remains an under developed area in ongoing debates about decentralisation - hence our desire to give democratisation more attention now. As suggested in the introduction to this book our perception is that, whilst a growing number of local authorities are decentralising their services, far fewer have made significant progress in democratising public services.

In our view democratisation involves accepting that local government is more a political than an administrative system. This is a crucial distinction. We explain this argument later in the chapter when we outline a conceptual map for understanding emerging patterns of relationship between local authorities and their communities. First, however, we provide a context for that discussion by outlining two key trends which are currently challenging established views about the nature and role of local government: the politicisation of local government and the continuing central government attack on local government. Readers familiar with these developments should skip to the next section.

Two key trends in local government

At risk of some over simplification we suggest that just two trends explain much about what is happening in British local government in the 1980s: the increase in the polarisation of political activity and the continuing Whitehall attempts to centralise financial and policy control over local government. The major research effort associated with the Widdicombe Inquiry lends support to both these claims. Thus, the report suggests that politicisation is 'here to stay'[3] and also asks 'whether the cumulative effect of centralism is eroding local government to such an extent that it no longer possesses the attributes on which its case depends'.[4]

Some might suggest that we are exaggerating the significance of these two trends. For example, the Chairman of the Widdicombe Inquiry suggested that 'there is a solid basis of normality in local government'.[5] Whilst our experience of training and development work with many local authorities around the country gives some support to this 'normality' position we believe it is an interpretation which fails to recognise the dynamics of what is happening in local government, the significance and power of some of the forces at work and the pace at which politically driven change can take place. Let us now consider the two trends in a little more depth.

First, we are witnessing an <u>unprecedented politicisation</u> of local government. Before 1980 local government politics was (notwithstanding the historical research done for the Widdicombe Inquiry) largely non-ideological in form. The coming to power of the new urban left in many city councils in recent years has provided a severe case of 'culture shock' for all of those who had become used to established local government practices and procedures:

> Councillors in jump suits and jeans; clenched fist salutes in the council chamber; the singing (and flying) of the Red Flag .... disdain for many established practices and procedures; a frame of reference which gave party and ideology pre-eminence over professional considerations: such phenomena and the reactions to them of some local government officers were a measure of the gap between them and their new political masters on the left.[6]

A growing number of left councils have been actively developing new policy initiatives relating in particular to employment and economic development, women, race and equal opportunities in general.[7]

However, it is not only the radical left that has provided a challenge to traditional approaches to running local councils. The radical right views local government (indeed government as a whole) as a 'parasite'. Its central claim is that the growth of the public sector, rather like the growth of a parasite, causes chronic problems for the organism on which it feeds (which, in this analogy, is the economy). The growth will lead to economic problems, and ultimately economic disaster. Whilst there is now a good deal of evidence which undermines this position[8] this has not discouraged a number of radical right councils from pursuing vigorous programmes of privatisation. Typically these initiatives have focused on cleaning, catering and maintenance services - for example refuse collection, street cleaning and provision of school

11

meals. However, some councils are keen to extend competitive tendering into other areas which, traditionally, have been provided in-house by local government - for example, pest control, housing caretaking, public conveniences and some aspects of social services.[9] As with the radical left initiatives, privatisation programmes have a strong ideological component. We touch further on privatisation later in the chapter.

Meanwhile in addition to the initiatives of the left and the right we should note the growing influence of the Alliance parties in local government. Until recently in most local authorities the majority party took control and, with clear party discipline, gave stability to the management of the authority. Whilst there have always been a few hung authorities (on which there was no clear majority for one party) it is only in recent years that a significant number of the larger authorities have become hung. Indeed, in May 1985, counties where no party had overall political control became the norm rather than the exception.[10] The Alliance parties see hung authorities as a desirable state of affairs and in many counties it represents the achievement of their aims. However, in some authorities the Alliance has taken overall control and is pursuing its own ideas on radical reform - for example, the Liberal administration in Tower Hamlets elected in May 1986 is in the process of establishing a system of powerful neighbourhood committees reminiscent of the smaller borough councils that operated before the reorganisation of London local government in 1963.

A second major trend which sets the context for our discussion concerns the <u>central government attack on local government</u>. It would be wrong to imply that the efforts to centralise financial and policy control over local government began in 1979. The 1974-79 Labour government had itself embarked on a strategy of expenditure cuts and controls encouraged by the International Monetary Fund. In 1976 the Layfield Committee on local government finance recommended a strengthening of local authority responsibility and the introduction of a local income tax.[11] The Labour government refused to accept such a localist approach and argued instead for a 'partnership basis between central and local government'.[12]

However, having made these points about the record of the last Labour government, there can be no denying that the incoming Thatcher government of 1979 has produced a major shift in the balance of central/local relations. This is not only because of the disproportionate impact of public expenditure reductions on local government, but also because of the introduction of a stream of legislation to control local spending, to determine council policies and even to abolish certain local authorities altogether (the GLC and the metropolitan counties). Since the key features of the unfolding central/local conflict are documented elsewhere - see, for example, Newton and Karran[13] - we will not run through them here.

The different analyses of these developments are, however, of interest. Some writers argue that the key theme is that the government's initiatives represent an attack on local democracy, defined as the right of local people to choose their own levels and forms of service provision.[14] Others argue that this focus on local democracy obscures the fact that the measures represent an attack on the welfare state - on education, housing and social services.[15] Bramley argues that the Thatcher government's policies on local government finance are less a case of radical reform in line with carefully considered analysis and more a process of costly and destabilising incrementalism. The fact that the changes have been partial and erratic reflecting the pressure of current events and the influence of different pressure groups 'has produced outcomes which would be very hard to defend as desirable from almost any perspective'.[16] There is evidence to support all three of these analyses and it is clear that a combination of forces is at work.

Recent research by one of the editors of this volume draws particular attention to the damaging impact of central interventions on local authority policy planning.[17] This analysis shows how, quite apart from expenditure cuts and restrictive legislation, the 1980s have witnessed change in the detailed arrangements for the planning of local authority (and health) services which have worked against local initiative and have extended central government policy control. This is shown to be the case across a wide range of policy sectors from housing through the urban programme to (extending beyond local government) arrangements for planning and managing the health service. The study shows, however, that there are limits to central government policy control of local government. Despite the constraints considerable opportunities for developing new strategies and policy initiatives remain at local level - and these opportunities are being taken up by a number of councils. Indeed many councils argue that it is only by developing new initiatives which attempt to transform local service provision that local government can mount an effective resistance against central intervention and this is a theme which is picked up in subsequent chapters. Within this context of increasing politicisation of local government and continuing central/local conflict we would now like to return to our theme of decentralisation and democratisation of public service by developing a conceptual map of emerging patterns of relationship between local authorities and their communities.

A conceptual map

In a paper we prepared earlier this year for the local authority associations' study of the future of local government we were asked to examine 'emerging patterns of relationship between local authorities and their communities'.[18] At risk of considerable over-simplification we chose to identify a few terms (labels if you like) to highlight the key characteristics of the 'old solutions' and the 'new patterns' which are now emerging. The phrase <u>bureaucratic paternalism</u> succinctly describes the old solutions which have become today's problems in local government. The last five years have not only seen a crisis in these old solutions, but the emergence of two major alternatives. The first alternative, usually associated with the radical right, seeks to challenge the very notion of collective and non-market provision for public need. Centring upon the strategy of <u>privatisation</u> it seeks to replace public provision with private provision. The second emerging alternative aims to preserve the notion of public provision, but seeks a <u>radical reform</u> of the manner in which this provision is undertaken. Thus it seeks to replace the old bureaucratic paternalist model with a much more responsive and democratic model. This latter approach to reform appears to have two central variants, the one being essentially <u>consumerist</u>, the other being essentially <u>collectivist</u>. The old and new solutions are schematically outlined in <u>Figure 1</u>.

Figure 1: <u>Emerging patterns of relationship between local</u>
<u>authorities and their communities: a conceptual map</u>

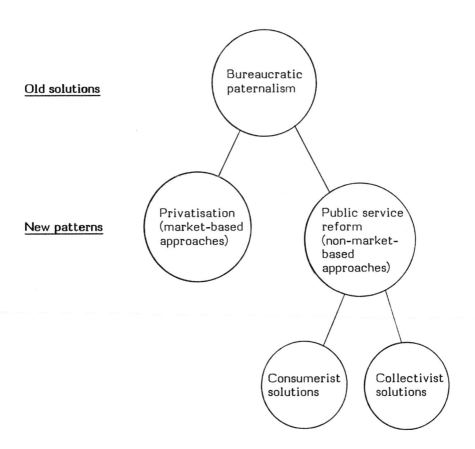

Old solutions

Bureaucratic paternalism

New patterns

Privatisation (market-based approaches)

Public service reform (non-market-based approaches)

Consumerist solutions

Collectivist solutions

Having provided an overall map we can now fill in a few more details. There are two developing critiques of the old solution. First, there is the political critique of massive, alienating public bureaucracies. This analysis suggests that the Thatcher government has cashed in on the paternalism and inadequacies of the welfare state and that the response must go beyond defending existing forms of service to develop new ways forward which will win popular support. David Blunkett, for example, takes this view:

> We must start debating as a movement our values and the ways in which we will extend democracy, participative democracy, as well as defending what we've got; because it is partly the inadequacy of, and the alienation from, the way in which the system is worked that has enabled Thatcher to take the steps she has with such success.[19]

Second, there is the management critique of inward looking organisational cultures - the widespread failure in the private as well as the public sector to put the 'customer' first. The critique has been developed in popular form by Peters and Waterman in their book In search of excellence.[20] On the basis of their research they identified eight criteria which characterised the 'excellent' companies. Inter alia, these companies:

(1)   enjoy a bias for action;

(2)   recognise that employees are the source of quality and productivity;

(3)   have a clear basic philosophy (almost an ideology); and

(4)   listen intently and regularly to the customer.

We shall return to these ideas shortly. The point we wish to stress here is that both the political and the managerial critiques suggest that radical rather than marginal change is needed.

The privatisation option takes several forms ranging from selling off assets (eg council house sales) through rights to private substitution (eg the right to repair) to contracting out services to the private sector (eg refuse collection). From the point of view of this discussion the contracting out of public services to the private sector is potentially the most significant. Supporters of this approach believe that private contractors can often provide a more efficient service due to the nature of competition within the commercial sector and superior resource management. Opponents argue that contracting out leads to a less effective service as a result of short-term profit considerations and the incentive to cut costs. There are, in fact, sound reasons for the rise of in-house public services which are discussed in a forthcoming book.[21]

(1)   Confidentiality Many public services involve the collection of personal information and it may be essential that this information remains confidential.

(2)   Fairness Public services must be provided fairly and equitably to all users. Such an obligation does not exist in the commercial world where suppliers are able to discriminate among, and negotiate independently with, individual clients.

(3)   Fail-safe standards High levels of risk may be involved in the failure to provide adequate standards of public service. Regular refuse collection is necessary to minimise health hazards; frequent social service visits can be critical to the well-being of children, families and older people. While delays in provision of goods or services to commercial firms can have a detrimental impact on sales and profit, the impact upon 'clients' is much less dramatic than it is in the public sector.

(4)   Difficulty in specifying output Few public services lend themselves to easy quantification. While outputs associated with a service like refuse collection are relatively easy to specify, those relating to areas like education and personal social services are not.

It would, however, be difficult to argue that in-house public service provision is right for all situations. There is international experience to show that some services we think of as essentially public are adequately run by the private sector elsewhere, eg the Falck Company provides emergency fire services to nearly half the population of Denmark and there is extensive use of the private sector to provide refuse collection services in the United States. It is also true that the popularity of contracting out as an alternative means of public service delivery has grown considerably over the last five years in Britain. The implications for the town hall-public relationship of these developments are difficult to assess. It is important to recognise, however, that even in its more radical

17

forms contracting out does not signify an end to local authority involvement and control. Local authorities continue to bear responsibility for contracted out services - indeed it is they to whom the private firms must report directly. Often overlooked in debates about contracting out is the fact that the obligation and definition of the state as service provider to the public does not change.

As previously mentioned the option of public sector reform appears to have two basic forms. The first form, which is essentially consumerist in its orientation, gives primary emphasis to enhancing the responsiveness of local government service provision. In contrast, the second form, which can be thought of as collectivist, gives primary emphasis to the democratisation of local government service provision. Clearly there are very close links between the responsiveness and the democracy of public service. Nevertheless it is quite possible to distinguish between local authorities (such as Walsall and East Sussex) whose primary concern has been to make local government more responsive but who have made few efforts to tackle the problem of who controls the planning and delivery of services, and local authorities (such as Islington) where the question of public control has been placed much more firmly on the agenda alongside concerns relating to responsiveness.

Clearly both the emerging consumerist and collectivist solutions require fundamental changes in terms of the relationships between local authorities and the communities that they serve. However the consumerist approach is essentially concerned with the reform of local government considered as a productive and administrative system, whereas the collectivist approach essentially seeks to reform local government considered as a political system. It is important to recognise that there is a tension between these two approaches. In a sense, Walsall's very success has proved part of its failure. Precisely because it has created a set of very responsive local government services (through the creation of 32 neighbourhood offices), demand has increased enormously. As a consequence the decentralised staff find that they are responding to the community in a very reactive and individualistic fashion and wider objectives concerned with community development have had to be set aside. Equally one can see how attempts to develop new forms of local accountabiliy within local government may divert energy and resources away from the more routine, but no less important, task of providing an efficient and responsive service.

18

This tension between a consumerist approach (emphasising service responsiveness) and a collectivist approach (emphasising service democracy) was highlighted in the introduction to this book. There we argued that the two aims can and should be linked and, whilst there are different emphases, even different ideologies, at work it would be most unfortunate if those concerned with public service reform found themselves being divided into two uncommunicative camps: the consumerists and the collectivists. Having said that, whilst there are no neat boundaries there are important differences and to expand on this point we now examine more closely what we mean by a consumerist approach in local government.[22]

The consumerist approach

Drawing on a paper[23] we prepared for a major seminar at SAUS held in February 1986 on 'Getting closer to the consumer' we outline four main criticisms of public services as they are presently delivered:

(1)   Most public sector organisations 'don't know the areas they serve' - they have little 'local knowledge'. Key personnel tend not to live in the area served by the organisation and the organisation seems to be unaware of how the community sees them.   These features create what might be termed a 'cultural rift' between the producers and consumers of services.[24]

(2)   Local government (and the NHS) tend to be organised primarily in a way which serves producer requirements and not consumer requirements.   Consider departmental boundaries, opening hours, who has to 'fit in' with whom in face-to-face encounters, etc.

(3)   Public sector organisations don't listen!   Typically they consider that front-line staff and service users have nothing to say of any importance regarding the manner in which services are provided. Organisational cultures are 'top down', often dominated by the doctrine of professional infallibility and, not surprisingly, encounter repeated problems in terms of the motivation and morale of lower level staff.

(4)   Public sector organisations encourage low expectations. As a consequence the actual need for all kinds of public service is often underrated.

19

Following on from the above, we may conclude that there is often a considerable gulf between provider organisations and their users. The opinion survey work which has been done on general public perceptions of public services supports this view. For example, when people are asked for their general views about, say, 'the council' their reactions tend to be negative. What is more encouraging is that when people are asked about the value they place on specific services their responses tend to be more positive. To build on the positive feelings some people may have and to develop new ways of 'bridging the gulf' we now outline three strategies which assume that existing forms of organisation and management largely remain:

(1)   Listening to the consumer.

(2)   Becoming more accessible to the consumer.

(3)   Speaking to the consumer.

These strategies cover the main elements of what might be described as a consumerist approach.[25]   A theme that cross cuts all three strategies is the desire to focus more attention on the quality as distinct from the quantity of service.[26]

(1)   Listening to the consumer   Public sector organisations respond to both 'need' and 'demand'. Without going into a sophisticated discussion of the nature of need we can think of demand as being need that has been given a voice.[27]   A key problem for public sector organisations is that the inarticulate do not get heard - their needs are often not translated into demands.   Moreover, the problem is not just one of finding out about needs which have been ignored. It is equally important for organisations to generate consumer feedback relating to their experience of the services which are already provided.   There are a variety of ways of 'listening to the consumer'. It may be helpful to distinguish approaches involving groups from approaches focused on individuals as follows.

Involving users and community groups   The extent to which need/feedback can be voiced is enhanced if efforts are made to encourage the articulation of views and if mechanisms are developed for channelling these views into the organisation. Public sector organisations can assist by adopting community development and/or advocacy approaches to their work (community health, community leisure, etc). A variety of experiments are taking place regarding the creation of new kinds of forum through which need/feedback can be expressed - neighbourhood committees, user group advisory and consultative bodies, co-options on to council committees, joint planning groups, patient participation groups etc.

Market research on individuals No matter how well organised users are some needs will 'slip through the net' - and this may be particularly true for the most disadvantaged groups. Moreover, public sector organisations should be engaged not just in listening but also in actively seeking views. The public sector could be more active in adopting techniques common in market research. Amongst these may be included:

-   use of opinion research questionnaires relating to specific service areas (eg Camden's research on the evaluation of its services for under-fives by service users) or the organisation as a whole (eg how do people see 'the council'?);[28]

-   the creation of 'customer circles' (eg the 'Gateway' project of Nottingham leisure services department);

-   the development of speedy and accessible complaints registering procedures (eg customer freephones).

(2) Becoming more accessible to the consumer Accessibility is both a physical and a social issue. It is a question which relates both to the design and location of buildings and to the manner and attitudes of staff who work in or from them.

Physical accessibility Crucial experiments (usually under the banner of 'decentralisation') are taking place here in the development of local offices which can provide a range of services ('one stop shopping'). New information technology has a very important potential role here - a number of neighbourhood offices within local government have fairly sophisticated, decentralised information systems so that local users can see where, for example, they are on a housing waiting list by just tapping in information to a computer on the local office reception counter. In this way services and information can literally be brought closer to the consumer. There are implications here for office location and office design and we have referred to these elsewhere.[29]

21

Social accessibility Barriers between consumers and staff are not just of a physical form. Professional training often equips staff with a set of attitudes which distances them from service users. There are a variety of training programmes around now which are designed to promote a greater customer sensitivity by professionals and non-professionals.[30] The ethnic composition of staff is also important: some service users have difficulty in speaking English and may feel more at ease if speaking to someone with the same ethnic background.

(3) <u>Speaking to the consumer</u> Relationships between service providing organisations and their consumers are, of course, two way. Strange as it may seem, most public sector organisations are poor at 'public speaking'. Whilst many organisations now have their own press and publicity officers, until quite recently few attempts were made to develop a more consciously proactive approach to marketing the organisation or its products. Most private sector organisations spend about 2% of their budget on product and company marketing - even at the height of its campaign against central government the GLC was spending less then 0.7%! A number of local authorities are now taking marketing seriously. Derbyshire County Council, for example, has recently executed an imaginative advertising campaign to improve awareness of the County's services (using posters on buses, television, radio and cinema commercials, advertisements in the local press, billboards and the council's own newspaper). A number of leisure services departments are probably also at the forefront of marketing services but a whole range of other opportunities exist, from campaigns to improve take-up of housing benefits through Islington's current use of billboards to advertise their new neighbourhood offices ('Been down your local yet?') to the Brighton Health Authority's initiative in providing information to patients and the public about health services.

Before closing this discussion of the consumerist approach we should note that attention in all three strategies is focused on methods of communication between the consumer and the organisation and vice versa. Two important sub-points should be noted. First, a neglected source of knowledge about consumer needs and concerns is the front-line worker. A range of methods is available for discovering and responding to the views of front-line workers of which the 'quality circle' method is but one - albeit one

22

that is increasing in popularity in both the public and the private sectors.[31] Second, we do not underestimate the enormously valuable contribution that voluntary organisations and community groups can make in articulating needs, pressurising public authorities, campaigning for change and taking direct action in providing services. These activities can be particularly valuable in advancing the concerns of disadvantaged and neglected groups.

Going beyond the consumerist approach

The main point we would wish to make about the consumerist approach is that, on the whole, it fails to address the issue of power. Good communication between providers and users of services is vital but is not enough, particularly when it is recognised that good communication can be a means whereby an organisation's control over the users of its services is enhanced.[32] There are two main sets of reasons why it is necessary to go beyond the consumerist approach in local government and empower the consumer (by using collectivist solutions).

The first stems from the need to recognise that many of these consumerist ideas have been imported from the private sector where, within limits, the consumer enjoys a degree of power by virtue of personal choice. If a retailer in the 'market place' is too expensive or sells a shoddy product it is possible (for most of us) to shop elsewhere. If a council tenant is receiving a poor service it is extremely difficult, if not impossible, to switch landlords. The contrast, then, is between the shopper who has some power (often a great deal) in the server-served relationship and the local authority service user who is virtually powerless. We would argue that it is this imbalance of power in the server-served relationship which accounts for many of the drawbacks with current forms of service provision by the welfare state. The consumerist approach fails to address the absence of choice within the public sector.

The second major limitation of the consumerist approach is that it has difficulty coping with the needs of groups of consumers. Unlike private companies local authorities have both 'individual' and 'collective' consumers. We can note here the existence of a respected theoretical approach to the study of urban politics and urban structure centred on the notion of 'collective consumption'.[33] In this literature study focuses on 'the organisation of the means of collective consumption at the basis of the daily life of all social groups: housing, education, health culture, commerce, transport, etc'.[34] For our purposes, which in this context are rather more narrow, we would want to highlight the fact that many local authority services are provided to groups of consumers and that there are therefore clear limits to an individual approach. Clean air, roads, environmental quality, footpaths, street lighting, and schooling are just some of the services that are both provided and consumed on a collective basis.

Perhaps a more specific example will illustrate our point. A local authority housing department certainly needs to be able to develop ways of responding swiftly and sensitively to the needs of individual tenants, but the department will also need to develop new ways of relating to the collective tenant. Many local authority decisions (eg concerning local environmental improvements or play facilities or meeting room facilities or lighting systems for external areas on an estate) seek to address collective problems or needs that tenants may have. There are likely to be conflicts of view within the community on how best to tackle these issues and, in a healthy democracy, these views need to be given expression and need to be heard. More than that, people need to be able to influence decisions if they are not to become alienated and distrustful.

So far we have pointed to the limitations of the consumerist approach even within a frame of reference concerned mainly with service responsiveness. However, if the frame is broadened to embrace wider objectives related to strengthening local democracy (as a contribution to sustaining democracy as a whole) and diffusing power and responsibility within society then the limitations of a consumerist approach become ever more visible. Hence the attraction of what we have called collectivist solutions. The whole of Chapter 4 is devoted to an exploration of these approaches which are designed not only to improve service responsiveness, but also to democratise public services. At this point, however, we can note that collectivist approaches (in contrast to consumerist approaches) do not assume that existing forms of organisation and management largely remain. On the contrary if a local authority is genuinely to open itself to different perspectives, if it is to draw upon the wealth of experience and ability present within the community, and if it is to respond swiftly and effectively to the issues identified, it will have to make changes to itself which go well beyond adding new techniques and strategies to an essentially unresponsive core. We are talking of the need to develop a new kind of organisational culture which is capable of being more open, democratic and self-critical - an organisational culture which is anxious to learn and eager to appraise its own performance. Such an organisational culture is very different from the form of service provision we have labelled bureaucratic paternalism.

Notes and References

1. **Dearlove, J. and Saunders, P.** (1984) <u>Introduction to British politics</u>, Cambridge: Polity Press, pp 1-3.

2. **Hambleton, R. and Hoggett, P.** eds (1984) <u>The politics of decentralisation: theory and practice of a radical local government initiative</u>, Working Paper 46, School for Advanced Urban Studies, University of Bristol.

3. **Widdicombe Report** (1986) <u>The conduct of local authority business</u>, Cmnd 9797, June, p 15 and pp 58-67.

4. **Ibid,** p 54.

5. **Ibid,** p 15.

6. **Gyford, J.** (1985) <u>The politics of local socialism</u>, London: George Allen and Unwin, p 43.

7. **Boddy, M. and Fudge, C.** (1984) <u>Local socialism?</u>, London: Macmillan.

8. We would point to critiques of the theoretical underpinnings of radical right arguments. See, for example, **Newton, K. and Karran, T.J.** (1985) <u>The politics of local expenditure</u>, London: Macmillan, pp 20-35. For a more wide ranging attack on modern market economics see **Bodington, S., George, M. and Michaelson, J.** (1986) <u>Developing the socially useful economy</u>, London: Macmillan.

9. **Ascher, K.** (1987) <u>The politics of privatisation</u>, London: Macmillan.

10. **Leach, S. and Stewart, J.** (1986) 'The hung county councils', <u>New Society</u>, 4 April, pp 7-9.

11. **Layfield Report** (1976) <u>Report of the Committee of Enquiry into Local Government Finance</u>, Cmnd 6453, May.

12. **H.M. Government** (1977) Local government finance, Green Paper, Cmnd 6813, May.

13. **Newton and Karran** op cit, Chapter 8.

14. **Jones, G. and Stewart, J.D.** (1983) The case for local government, London: George Allen and Unwin.

15. **Cochrane, A.** (1985) 'The attack on local government: what it is and what it isn't', Critical Social Policy, January, pp 44-62.

16. **Bramley, G.** (1985) 'Incrementalism run amok? Local government finance in Britain', Public Administration, Spring, pp 100-107.

17. **Hambleton, R.** (1986) Rethinking policy planning. A study of planning systems linking central and local government, School for Advanced Urban Studies, University of Bristol.

18. **Hoggett, P. and Hambleton, R.** (1986) Emerging patterns of relationship between local authorities and their communities, Study Paper No 1. The future role and organisation of local government, Institute of Local Government Studies, University of Birmingham, January.

19. **Blunkett, D.** (1985) 'Ratecap resistance', Marxism Today, March, p 9.

20. **Peters, T.J. and Waterman, R.H.** (1982) In search of excellence. Lessons from America's best-run companies, New York: Harper and Row.

21. **Ascher,** op cit, Chapter 1.

22. The words 'consumer' and 'customer' both have a private sector ring. The traditional vocabulary of the public sector uses terms like 'client', 'recipient' and 'patient'. All of these tend to assign a rather passive role to the member of the public. Perhaps service 'user' is a better word. For the purposes of this discussion we will stick with 'consumer'.

23. This is reproduced as an Annex in op cit **Hoggett and Hambleton** (1986).

24. Interestingly researchers who have studied American decentralisation have suggested that if you go back 50 years or more this cultural rift was non-existent. Historically there was a kind of social symmetry in service delivery with servers and served sharing the same neighbourhood and living conditions. See **Yin, R.K. and Yates, D.** (1975) Street-level governments, Mass: Lexington Books, Chapter 1. It is possible, even likely, that this was also the case in British local government in the early part of this century.

25. We have benefited from exchanges with John Stewart and Michael Clarke in developing these ideas. Their paper on the 'public service orientation' makes some important general points about public service as a key value and about the management consequences of adopting such an approach. See **Clarke, M. and Stewart, J.** (1985) Local government and the public service orientation: or does a public service provide for the public?, Local Government Training Board, August.

26. This need to concentrate more on quality and the personal experience of service provision was stressed in our last collection of papers. See **Hoggett, P.** (1984) 'Decentralisation, labourism and the professionalised welfare state apparatus' in **Hambleton and Hoggett** op cit, Chapter 2.

27. For a deeper discussion see **Bradshaw, J.** (1972) 'The concept of social need', New Society, 30 March, pp 640-643.

28. Opinion research is not new to local government. For example, planning departments have, ever since the 1968 Town and Country Planning Act, been concerned to discover community views as part of the process of public participation in land use planning. Some councils instituted annual public opinion surveys over ten years ago. See, for example, **Vamplew, C. and Gallant, V.** (1983) 'The Cleveland case', Local Government Policy Making, November, pp 39-42. However, experiments with opinion research are growing in local government with professional market research firms becoming increasingly involved. See, for example, **MORI** (1986) 1986 residents' attitudes survey for the London Borough of Richmond upon Thames, March. In addition, the National Consumer Council has, in recent years, started to develop a national level interest in local government. See, for example, **Potter, J.** (1983) 'Consumers' views of local government services: the national picture', Local

Government Policy Making, November pp 35-38 and **Potter, J.** (1986) Measuring up, National Consumer Council (this attempts to develop ways of assessing the performance of council services from the point of view of the users of the services).

29. **Hambleton and Hoggett** (1984) op cit, pp 9-10.

30. For example, the School for Advanced Urban Studies runs a number of courses along these lines such as 'Face to face: dealing with the public' and 'The approachable professional'.

31. **Hutchins, D.** (1985) Quality circles handbook, London: Pitman.

32. Arguably still the best warning note about this danger is the classic: **Packard, V.** (1957) The hidden persuaders, published by Penguin in 1960.

33. **Castells, M.** (1978) City, class and power, Macmillan, London, Chapter 2; **Dunleavy, P.** (1980) Urban political analysis, London: Macmillan, Chapter 2.

34. **Castells,** ibid, p 3.

2

CENTRAL/LOCAL CONFLICTS: THE VIEW FROM ISLINGTON

Margaret Hodge

Introduction

I think we have to start by asking ourselves the question 'Why change local government?' and I think the answer is that local government is in crisis, and we must all recognise that. Its continued existence as an independent, innovative, and separate tier of government is under threat. For those of us who do believe in local government I think we have a massive task in moving the monolith to restore confidence in local government. We must reclaim the legitimacy that such an institution had in the past if we wish to carry it forward into the 21st century.

First, let us look at the symptoms of this malaise of local government and be absolutely honest about it. People don't like local government. They may like some of the services that it provides but their overall image of local government is a poor one. We are seen as anonymous, we are seen as big, we are seen as bureaucratic, inefficient, wasteful. We in Islington as a council may be trying to ban anti Irish jokes but we would have had even less success if we tried to ban anti local government jokes. Councils are always blamed if things go wrong and the council has become a scapegoat for many of the ills that people experience in these present times. Another indication of our malaise is the depressingly low turnout at local government elections. Knowledge of the services that the council provides is also very low. The most recent survey that Islington conducted, just before the summer of 1985, discovered that the majority of respondents thought that social services were actually provided by the GLC. There is an increasing difficulty in attracting and keeping good councillors. This is partly because councillors are not paid, and I am a great advocate of paying local councillors for the very large organisations that they actually help run. Partly this must also be due to the government's financial and political constraints imposed

29

upon local government in the 80s so that being a councillor is now very much a form of damage limitation rather than the more creative and innovative world that it was perhaps in the 1970s. Finally, people undoubtedly vote in local elections on the basis of national issues and that is a real weakness for us in local government.

As a consequence of these weaknesses it has been very easy for central government to attack us. Besides those attacks bound up with rate capping and the dissolution of the metropolitan counties we are also having to contend at the moment with the strategy of sniping at small elements of local government practice that perhaps it doesn't agree with, using the vehicle of the Widdicombe Enquiry. What we wanted through Widdicombe was a real review of local government, one which would actually strengthen local democracy rather than a piecemeal attack on such local practices as the corpus, our ability to finance local voluntary organisations and local economic initiatives, our ability to co-opt representatives of community groups on to council committees, and so on. What now seems to be on the agenda is a further round of central government attacks including the Waldegrave/Baker Review which looks like calling for the removal of education services from local government.

If we are going to survive we must change. I am now going to look at three areas - campaigning for local government, decentralisation, equal opportunities - where we can change in such a way as to restore legitimacy and public confidence in local government.

Campaigning for local government

Where local authorities have attempted to campaign for local government they have achieved considerable success. There can be no doubt that in certain areas, perhaps such as London, a turnround in consciousness has been achieved whereby issues concerning local democracy can no longer be ignored by any future central government. That is important because cuts in local expenditure were first mooted under the last Labour administration, and indeed an embryonic form of rate capping legislation was on Peter Shore's desk whilst he was the Home Secretary in the late 70s. Moreover the present government has found that its rate capping legislation is far more difficult to implement than to actually formulate. Everyone assumed that in the second year of rate capping the legislation would be extended to at least 30 or so authorities;

instead we still have the original 12 authorities on the hit list. The campaign for local government has also succeeded in changing people's understanding of exactly who is responsible for rate increases. The average person in the street no longer believes that rate increases are due to the profligacy of local government; they are much more likely to believe that such increases are due to the withdrawal of grants from central government to local government.

We have also built up a greater awareness of the services that local government does provide. Our own market research in Islington now suggests that people realise that we do more than just empty the dustbins inefficiently. This has involved not just leafleting, billboards and other forms of advertising, it has also involved putting notices up in all council owned properties so that the people realise that such facilities (libraries, swimming pools, laundrettes, and so on) are actually provided by the local council.

No clearer indication of our success could be given than the fact that virtually no local authorities in the front line of rate capping have actually had to make cuts. In Islington we have just done an analysis of what has happened to our own spending over the last three years and we have found that it has actually increased by 44%. We have increased our capital spending, despite the massive cuts in capital allocations, by 134% since 1982. We have increased our staff by 20% and our grants to the voluntary sector by 150% in the same period. I actually do not believe that central government can contain and control local authority spending. That for me is the lesson of rate capping. Our success has been partially achieved by the fact that local government has become big business, and it is paradoxically many of Thatcher's friends in the City that have enabled local authorities to find the funds to defy the expenditure level set by rate capping.

We shouldn't be frightened of spending on campaigning. Any commercial organisation spends about 2% of its turnover on campaigning while the GLC only spends 1% of its turnover on campaigning, and the London Borough of Islington has been receiving flack for spending 0.2 of 1% of its turnover on campaigning issues.

So we have to campaign for local government, but campaigning for local government is not enough. We have actually got to improve the public services that we provide. We have got to restore belief in the efficacy of collective, community provision. We must challenge the Tory values of greed and self-interest with our own values of care and compassion and we have to demonstrate that care and compassion exist in the quality of the services that we provide. Ironically it was because of our perception of the limits to growth in 1982 that we as a new council became interested in looking at the quality of service provided rather than just its quantity, thus we became involved with decentralisation. By the May 1986 local government elections we will have achieved a comprehensive decentralisation of many of our services into 24 neighbourhood offices. [This talk was given in September 1985].

Decentralisation

Why did we go for decentralisation? Our motives were highly pragmatic, concerned with the efficiency and coordination of the service that we provide. To give an example, we discovered that over 50% of all enquiries that came into our area social services offices also had a housing component and had eventually to be redirected to the housing department. We also found that we have now become a huge municipal landlord, with over 40,000 properties, and our ability to control voids and order and effect repairs in an efficient manner was becoming increasingly inhibited by the enormous scale of our operation. We also undertook decentralisation to overcome the anonymity of services, to change them in a more sensitive and personalised direction. For example, most members of the public who call into one of our offices on the 'phone have no idea who it is they have talked to, they are received by a voice but without a name. It is these kinds of practices that decentralisation seeks to address, practices that alienate the consumer and provide very poor job satisfaction to the producers of the services themselves. Finally there are ideological reasons for undertaking decentralisation. In the context of Islington these are important but secondary. They concern the value of participation by the consumers of services in the planning and decision-making process, they concern issues of local control over services and facilities. And in this light we have moved towards the creation of local neighbourhood forums alongside the neighbourhood offices and have taken a first step towards the development of local budgets.

Our approach to decentralisation has been comprehensive. We have decentralised all of our housing services, all of our social services (residential, day care and field services), our environmental health services, our routine maintenance and repairs services, street sweeping, welfare rights, and so on. All of these

32

workers are in the same neighbourhood office, working alongside each other, from different professional backgrounds, manual and white collar. I want to look at some of the lessons we have learned so far. First of all people like it, it is popular. The market research we did before summer 1985, when only four offices were open, indicated the enormous popularity of this new initiative. It is popular with the little old lady who no longer feels she has to walk miles to get to a local council office, and it is popular with tenants' leaders who feel they are beginning to have some control over the nature of the housing services that they receive. By adopting a pragmatic approach, which puts questions of efficiency and effectiveness first and issues of power and control second, we have been actually able to implement a radical programme where other local authorities such as Hackney, which had adopted a more ideological approach, have become bogged down in all sorts of difficulties. It has been expensive, we reckon it has now cost us in the region of £5m and there will be very few long-term savings as we are already finding that the increased efficiency of the services being provided has led to greatly increased demand. Thus, 90% of our day to day repairs are now completed within two weeks. This hasn't enabled us to save any money because demand has increased so enormously.

There have been difficulties that we have encountered in decentralisation. The greatest resistance from our trade unions actually came from social services teams who were already partially decentralised. I think this is partly to do with their professionalism, and their tendency to see themselves as slightly superior to staff in housing, I think it is also to do with the fact that even the most radical local government officers are afraid of change. Professionalism has also proved a problem when we have tried to redetermine lines of accountability for staff at neighbourhood level. For example, who do your neighbourhood social workers report to? Are they accountable to the social services structure, or to the new neighbourhood office structure? In Islington we have tended to fudge that issue at the present moment and the result has been the form of 'dual accountability'. If we are really to pursue a decentralised approach in the future, accountability must be located at the neighbourhood level. There have also been problems for members: because we didn't decentralise into ward boundaries many ward councillors are actually meant to liaise with two or three neighbourhood offices and neighbourhood forums. It really is extremely difficult for local councillors to be able to respond to the interests that the initiative has awakened. Moreover, members are resistant to giving up

33

political control. In some instances this resistance may be justified (eg homeless policies), however members have also been resistant to giving up their power to decide in areas without such political sensitivity. One of the interesting things that is beginning to emerge from decentralisation is that it has started to force the centre to set performance standards. For example, in an area such as 'children at risk' it is imperative to set proper performance standards for the conduct of social service workers in neighbourhood offices - however, we are finding that this practice is now generalising to other areas where the importance of performance standards had previously been overlooked.

We cannot over-estimate the importance of political commitment to decentralisation. In Islington we have been very fortunate to have had one councillor who has devoted himself almost single mindedly to decentralisation over the last three years. We have also had one very talented chief officer who has given us a commitment to see the initiative through. I should also stress the importance of the commitment shown consistently by both labour groups and by the local parties to see decentralisation as our top priority. Another development which I think decentralisation has started to lead to in Islington is the scrapping of division between manual and mental labour, and the initiative has also enabled us (through the introduction of new posts and the re-jigging of old structures) to bring into the workforce a large number of women and ethnic minority workers into positions of power and authority which they previously didn't enjoy.

Equal opportunities

Turning now to equal opportunities, the third area of major change within Islington, I can say that equal opportunities has been both exciting but difficult. To give an example, Williams & Glyn's bank are moving major parts of their Head Office into our borough. I had an interview with them recently in which I asked them what they were going to do for local employment and particularly the employment of local blacks. Their reply, predictably enough, was that they are only interested in employing the best staff available! We have pushed through some important innovations with the local authority concerning, for example, maternity leave which I think will provide a major means for overcoming discrimination against women in employment within our own local authority. What have been the constraints? Well, first of all opposition from trade unions. We had opposition from NALGO to conducting a 'headcount' which would have enabled us to have seen where women and ethnic minorities were presently employed within the local authority. NALGO's opposition was based on the fact that we had not developed any policy for gays and lesbians; they wanted us to proceed on an across the board basis whereas we argued that our policy for gays and lesbians was far less developed and that the discrimination that they experienced was of a quite different nature to that experienced by women and ethnic minorities. We then encountered opposition from the General and Municipal Workers Union to the 'headcount', basically because of racism. As a result although we have now conducted a headcount within our white collar staff we have still not been able to accomplish one for our manual workers. Opposition from the community has also been a constraint, and that was absolutely clear on the gay and lesbian issue which has undoubtedly cost us votes, particularly in the south of the borough. Will the success of our decentralisation outweigh the electoral costs of our gay and lesbian strategy?

Other problems we have encountered with regard to equal opportunities policies concern training and recruitment practices. Reviewing a couple of years' work we conclude that advertising posts in ethnic minority press has absolutely zero impact. We all do it, and we have to do it, but it is an expensive symbolic gesture. It is also difficult to overcome middle management prejudices and convince them that those who can best do a job are not necessarily those with the best formal qualifications and formal experience for doing that job. It is particularly difficult nowadays because of the great mass of graduates competing for quite mundane clerical jobs within local authorities such as Islington.

A major difficulty however is in dealing with racism within the local authority organisation itself. We have just had our first case of bringing charges of racial harassment against some members of our own staff. We discovered, in a small rent accounting section within our housing department, quite widespread and nasty racism. This continued for a long while with management basically doing nothing until a new black staff member within that section decided to take on her racist superiors. This is where we encountered our difficulties. All our disciplinary procedures are not designed to cope with sexual or racial harassment. In such cases it is very often not so much that A thumps B, it is more a question of what A says to B and what the manner of A is towards B. The actual procedures themselves are simply not geared to dealing with racial harassment. In the end we found against two of those responsible, the third was the section head who just didn't know how to cope with the problems that faced her and had no support from her own senior management. We reprimanded her, which was all we were able to do on the basis of the flimsy evidence that we had against her, but in doing so we found that we unleashed something we didn't know how to handle. Two things happened. First of all the latent racists suddently felt that their racism had been legitimised by this awful looney left wing council persecuting staff simply because of the views that they held about blacks, but on the other side there were a whole group of people within the housing department who felt that we hadn't gone far enough. The staff and the trade unions became split down the middle. The resulting conflict has been quite nasty and has been very difficult to resolve. These then are some of the difficulties in really trying to implement an equal opportunities policy. Undoubtedly bad management has played its role in allowing a difficult situation to escalate into an impossible one. Clearly however there is more to it than this; we have unleashed an awful lot of latent racism within our own organisation and we aren't sure how best to handle it. We are seeking to find the right answers, we are experimenting, and we are seeking to see how we can use existing procedures in a more effective fashion and how we can then build towards a real multi-racial workforce.

So, local government is in a perilous state but I think the fight to preserve it can be successful. We can see off central government in its attempts to shackle the freedom that we have at the local level, we can change the nature of services so that they become something that people want to fight for, and I believe we can build participation by the community in those services into the future of local government which would render any future attempts to destroy local government impossible. I want to stay in local government and I am determined to make it work.

[This chapter is based upon the transcript of a talk Margaret Hodge gave at a seminar at SAUS on 16 September 1985.]

3

POLITICAL PARTIES, COMMUNITY ACTION AND THE REFORM OF MUNICIPAL GOVERNMENT IN EUROPE

Paul Hoggett

As we mention again in Chapter 12 there is a grave danger of becoming very parochial when examining decentralisation. It injures our national pride somewhat to realise that radical forms of decentralisation have been pursued far further in Sweden and Italy than in the UK or that tenant self-organisation is far, far stronger in most Scandinavian countries than here. A realisation that 'we are not alone' in pursuing such strategics but, indeed, may be lagging behind some of our European contemporaries should encourage confidence that decentralisation is not a 'passing fad' but perhaps a sign that the reform of the welfare state is on the agenda of all European social democracies. However recent European experience also discloses the existence of some real dilemmas, in particular the complex dialectic at work in the relationship between the local state, political parties and community action. The purpose of this chapter, then, is twofold: to document recent European developments - community struggles, decentralisation initiatives, etc; to explore the ambiguous relationship between progressive political parties, reforming strategies and the self-organised action of communities.

Alternative models of service provision: housing in Scandinavia

The attitudes of local political activists and state workers often constitute a highly effective barrier to the reform of public service organisations. One of the strongest prejudices relates to the ability of people outside the state and political parties to play any effective role in public service provision. For example, by listening to many councillors and officers one would conclude that tenants are congenitally incapable of playing a strong yet responsible role in the planning and delivery of public housing services.

It is interesting therefore to contrast such attitudes with the experience of certain European countries, particularly the Scandinavian nations,[1] where entirely different and more tenant-based models of public sector housing exist. In Sweden, where the publicly rented sector is proportionately larger than in the UK, a 'negotiating model' has emerged as the dominant form. The model assumes a basic conflict of interest between tenants and management (in Sweden public sector housing is not directly provided by municipal authorities but by municipal 'public utility housing companies' - political control of the municipality is reflected in the shareholding of the company) and thus both sides build up their organisational strength to meet each other across the negotiating table. Without doubt the 'tenants' levy' has played a key role in facilitating the emergence of a well organised and resourced tenants' movement. Through the levy a portion of all rent paid is allocated to the tenants' organisations - the result is a remarkably strong movement at both national and local level, with far more full time organisers than in the whole of the UK and with its own resource centres for training and administration, etc. Given this strength real bargaining can and does take place over all housing issues - from determining rent levels to the planning of maintenance strategies - in much the same way that bargaining takes place between employers and trade unions in Britain.

A 'self-management model' also exists in Sweden but is much stronger in Norway and particularly Denmark where housing co-operatives constitute the main elements of the public sector (a sector comprising about 17% of total housing stock). In West Germany[2] the housing co-operative movement is also strong, accounting for a stock of nearly one million dwellings. In Denmark the typical housing co-op comprises a public utility company whose board consists of elected tenant representatives. This elected board then hires and controls its own housing management and maintenance staff. A vigorous tenants' movement exists in Denmark; many associations are not just concerned with housing issues but are also involved in planning or providing cultural, social care and health services.

Struggles around housing in other European nations

Whereas in Scandinavian countries a tenant-based model of public housing finds its roots in the history of housing based struggles in the earlier part of the 20th century, in other European countries tenants' movements are still struggling to establish a comparably powerful role. In France, for example, the major expansion of public sector housing took place in the 1960s and early 1970s and assumed the form of the 'grands ensembles'. These large, low cost, high rise estates on the outer fringe of the main French cities were the site for major forms of tenants' action throughout the 1960s.[3] Tenants' action was very much focused upon 'bread and butter issues', mainly issues concerning rent levels, safety, housing conditions and repairs, and so on. Discontent with these housing estates mounted to such a pitch that in 1973 the last 'grands ensembles' were built. Since the early 1970s basic forms of tenant organisation seem to have subsided in France and if anything it is the more middle class tenants who have been the most active throughout the 1970s, particularly around environmental concerns and grassroots democracy. Castells suggests two reasons for the decline of more working class based tenants' organisations in France. Firstly, their very success in the 1960s led to improvements in existing public housing estates. Not only did the general level of design and construction improve, but within existing estates small neighbourhood estate management units were set up to respond quickly to tenant problems and complaints. Secondly, it seems that in many areas the mobilisation of tenants in the large housing estates was quickly followed by socialist or communist victories at the local municipal level. By taking on board many of the tenants' problems and complaints these municipalities paradoxically undermined the combativity of the tenants' organisations themselves. As a result those tenants' associations with a narrow 'rent and conditions' focus such as the communist led CNL have lost ground throughout the 1970s whereas the other largest nationwide organisation of tenants, the CSCV, has received new life by expanding its realm of initiatives and activities to demands going beyond housing to all issues concerned with the urban environment.

Clearly attempts to reform the management of the 'grands ensembles' had limited success. By the early 1980s the social and physical fabric of many of the high-rise estates the 1960s had deteriorated to such an extent that sporadic and unco-ordinated violence had become routine. In 1981 full scale riots broke out at Les Minguettes in Lyons; two years later further riots occurred on estates in Paris and Lyons. As a result a national initiative was launched combining major estate rehabilitation with localised management schemes in a number of priority areas.[4]

The experience of tenants' self organisation in Spain appears to correspond with the experience in France in many respects. The mobilisation of tenants in the publicly rented housing sector was one of four prongs of what became known as the 'Citizens' Movement'. As in France, public sector housing had been built very rapidly and at very low cost throughout the 1960s and had led to chronic conditions in many large public sector outer city estates. The tenants organised through block committees which in turn were represented on neighbourhood associations. These neighbourhood associations formed the building blocks of the Citizens' Movement in Madrid, Barcelona, etc. Here then tenants' struggles became part of a wider movement concerned with conditions of urban living in Spain in the 1970s leading eventually to institutional reform and the setting up of democratic institutions of local government. Paradoxically it appears that it was precisely the success of communist and socialist parties in these local government institutions which led to the demobilisation of the Citizens' Movement in most of the main Spanish cities and in turn to the collapse of tenants' associations in many areas.[5]

Chronic housing shortages, especially for young single people, have also led to the growth of large scale squatting particularly in The Netherlands and West Germany. Whilst many tenants' movements appear to have been undermined through too much contact with sympathetic political parties, the experience of recent squatters' struggles appears to suggest that total autonomy also leads to eventual defeat. There can be no doubt that the rapid growth of squatting in The Netherlands led to a major confrontation between the squatters, mostly Dutch youths, on the one hand and the state, and particularly the local municipal state, on the other hand. Throughout the period 1980-1982 an escalating series of eviction battles took place between police and squatters in Amsterdam culminating in a three day state of emergency declared in October 1982 in the city.[6] As squatters reverted to increasingly violent tactics they tended to lose a lot of the public sympathy that they first had, and especially the solidarity of the neighbourhood action groups and tenants' associations. It is difficult to tell exactly who the squatters were, though the evidence available suggests they were mostly white Dutch youths ('foreigners' were less likely to obtain an allocation via squatters' bureaux than by municipal housing authorities).[7]

The squatting movement was also strong during the same period in West Berlin. Here however squatters appeared to give much more emphasis to the self improvement and maintenance of the poor quality buildings that they were squatting in; it became known as 'rehab squatting'.[8] The familiar struggle developed between squatters and police, and evictions culminated in riots in 1980,

40

which served to focus public attention on housing as an issue particularly for youth and other marginalised groups in the city. Most of the squatting had taken place in Kreuzberg, an area in Berlin of high immigrant population. In the ensuing years an attempt was made to set up an alternative urban renewal agent called Trager. This was established in 1982 to represent squatters' interests within the local municipal state and was supported by a self help organisation called Netzwerk, which had a long established tradition as an alternative community trust.

What has been striking about the squatting movement in Amsterdam, Berlin and elsewhere is its sectionalism:

> .... the characteristic of these recent social movements is that they do not let themselves be pressed into the comprehensive policy simulated by political parties or by theoreticians.[9]

In other words, the sectionalism of such developments, their refusal to be incorporated into local politics, their refusal to make alliances with other like minded community groups or political organisations, all such signs of sectionalism can be interpreted both as a defence against incorporation and legalisation and as a positive assertion of their particular needs and their particular problems. Thus the inability of the squatting movement to take 'a wider view' is perhaps an 'unwillingness' based on an understanding that 'such a wider view' if attained may be at the expense of the militancy of the movement itself.

Other forms of 'direct action' in Europe

The self organisation of tenants or squatters can be usefully conceived of as a form of 'direct' or 'participative' democracy in contrast to 'representative' democracy - the self organisation of citizens through political parties. Such forms of direct democracy are worth examining for a number of reasons. First of all it seems that they have often emerged either as responses to the absence of forms of representative democracy (as was the case in Spain) or as a response to the inadequacies of such forms of representative democracy (as was more the case in France and Italy). Secondly, we have already noted the complex interplay and tension between these two forms of democratic organisation. However the distinctive feature of parliamentary democracies is their ability to largely absorb the energies of political parties within the channels of the representative state. At local levels this tension between representative and direct democracy thus tends to become displaced into a tension between the local representative state (ie municipal governments within which progressive parties become 'nested') and self organised communities (ethnic minorities, user groups, neighbourhoods, etc).

Undoubtedly the first major flowering of forms of direct democracy took place in the late 1960s and early 1970s. This development corresponded to the political crisis which affected a whole number of European states during those years. Although one thinks of the events in France in 1968 in this context, undoubtedly the most radical and widespread forms of direct action took place in Italy in the early 1970s. Most Italian cities witnessed extended forms of social conflict[10] around issues such as the occupation of vacant houses and rent strikes, struggles for better mass transit, 'self reduction' of telephone, electricity and other utility bills, and so on. These forms of conflict were in no way middle class but involved young people, senior citizens, immigrant families and blue collar workers. Moreover the trade unions were deeply involved in this process of change and often directly supported the struggles and the grass root organisations which were behind them.

In both France[11] and Italy this phase, during which forms of direct democracy flowered, was followed by a period in which the political climate at local level altered dramatically. For the first time working class political parties, both socialist and communist, gained control of the administration of the largest cities. For example, whereas in 1975 the Italian Communist Party only had control of one Italian city (Bologna), after 1976 the same party either governed or participated in the government of eight of the ten largest Italian cities. One can see how, for different reasons, working class parties had been excluded from the political state in both Italian and French societies. The strategy of conquering the margins of the state (ie the administration of the towns and cities) was therefore a more or less conscious initiative developed by working class parties in these two countries. Thus it is possible to understand how the pressures to decentralise both the French and Italian states were focused largely around the efforts of the Socialist and Communist Parties. In Italy the Communist Party was both the pioneer of decentralisation in Bologna and the strongest political force behind the Italian decentralisation laws of 1976.[12] Similarly in France the Socialist Party pioneered forms of decentralisation in cities such as Grenoble and was responsible for the major decentralisation laws passed under the Mitterrand government in 1980.[13]

Thus in each of these countries the flowering of direct democracy led to the reform of representative democracy. However, if the Italian experience is anything to go by, the very success of the reform of representative democracy has led to the decline in forms of direct democracy. The radical mobilisation of the early 1970s is now definitely a thing of the past. Many of the community activists of the early 1970s have now been totally absorbed into the new forms of neighbourhood government in Italian cities, either as officers or as local councillors. A number of writers have pointed to the reluctance of political parties to accept forms of political pluralism. Thus whilst the growth and development of both the Italian and Spanish Communist Parties in the 1970s owed much to the flowering of direct democracy at this time it is also clear that once these parties captured forms of local political power they sought to absorb and encompass all forms of political protest and direct action within the party machinery and, by implication, into the local representative state. A similar desire to monopolise all forms of political protest can be seen at work within the British Labour Party,[14] the French Socialist Party and the German Social Democratic Party. How one maintains the strategy of reforming the state whilst at the same time acknowledging and encouraging forms of protest outside of the state remains an essential dilemma for leftist political parties in Europe.

Decentralisation of municipal government in Europe

Before surveying recent developments it is necessary to understand that the decentralist current which has flowed across Europe during the last decade differs from the British experience in a number of important respects. Firstly, the primary thrust within European developments has focused upon the democratisation of municipal government rather than its localisation. In other words emphasis has been given to developing more devolved political forms of decision making (eg area, neighbourhood committees etc) rather than to experimenting with localised forms of administration and service delivery (eg neighbourhood office structures). Secondly, this decentralist trend has proceeded from widely differing starting points according to degree of existing centralisation in different European nations.[15] In some, for example France and Spain, a highly centralised state is only now in the process of decentralising to truly municipal levels. In other countries, such as Italy, a highly centralised state is decentralising in a massive leap down from central to regional, municipal, and even neighbourhood levels. In several north European countries decentralised forms of municipal administration were already in existence. In these nations efforts to pursue further decentralisation to sub-municipal levels can be perceived, particularly in Sweden, The Netherlands and Britain.

Political decentralisation in France obtained its impetus from legislation passed by the Mitterrand government in March 1982. Most commentators seem to agree that the legislation itself constitutes an 'ambiguous mixture'.[16] Prior to the passing of this legislation government in France was exercised at three levels: at the level of the region, at the level of 'departement' and at the level of the commune. The region (without formal constitutional status) consisted of political representatives elected indirectly from the departemental and communal councils. However, undoubtedly the most powerful layer of government was the 'departement' controlled by a central government official called the Prefect. Regions lacked their own executive powers, as did most communes, only the largest cities having any employee resources of their own. The new legislation provides for direct elections of representatives at all three levels of government. Furthermore, regions acquired their own executive and the powers of the Prefect to control activities at the commune level were severely undermined. The aim of the legislation was to establish a clear role for each level of government. The commune was to be responsible for the exercise of urban and local planning and for local infrastructures (technical services, etc); the departement was to be responsible for redistributive services, social benefits and the reallocation of resources among communes; and the region was to be responsible for planning, development and economic intervention. Both housing and educational services appear to have escaped from the trend towards decentralisation. However, perhaps one of the strengths of the decentralisation initiative in France is its concern to decentralise economic and infrastructural decision making alongside 'redistributive' aspects of welfare. Even the radical advocates of decentralisation acknowledged the danger of establishing a form of dual state where decentralisation merely involved giving the power to cope with the consequences of economic decision-making which remained centralised. Under the new legislation regions, departements and communes have been given direct freedom to undertake their own economic initiatives, although in reality, at the moment, these powers are fairly limited and there are major questions surrounding the decentralisation of the resource bases.

Clearly only a very early evaluation of the decentralisation initiative in France can be made.[17] Some limitations to the initiative however appear to be clear. With the exception of the three largest cities - Paris, Marseilles and Lyons - no attempt has been made to develop sub-municipal forms of political decision making and no attempt has been made to involve members of the public or community groups in forms of local government. In other words the reforms have only concerned the existing system of representative political democracy.

In one sense it appears that France, long a centralised state, is only now moving towards a pattern of local government which has been long established in countries like Britain and The Netherlands, although with 36,000 communes and around half a million 'elus', the tradition of local democracy is as strong as in these two countries. During the last four years attempts have been made in The Netherlands to develop sub-municipal administrative structures alongside sub-municipal political structures. However, in The Netherlands this approach is limited by the fact that the bulk of welfare services are provided by large voluntary organisations outside the system of local government entirely. In both Britain and The Netherlands the movement towards sub-municipal forms of decentralisation has been undertaken by the municipalities themselves, and is not the outcome of national legislation initiatives. In many respects the establishment of district committees in Amsterdam[18] resembles closely the establishment of area committees in Birmingham. In each case the sub-municipal units relate to quite sizeable localities whose populations vary between 40,000 and 80,000. In neither case are the sub-municipal committees directly elected but they do reflect the strength of the political parties in that locality. This contrasts to the very different system in Oslo, where political control of sub-municipal area committees simply reflects the strength of political parties at the overall municipal level.[19] The sub-municipal areas in Oslo are much smaller in size than in either Birmingham or Amsterdam and correspond more closely to the neighbourhood structures which exist in Islington. In both Islington and Oslo considerable efforts have been made to set up neighbourhood office structures alongside the strong neighbourhood political structures. In the case of Oslo, all social work and primary health care services have been relocated to new neighbourhood bases. In each neighbourhood a chief administrator co-ordinates three professional teams each with its own professional leadership - a head of medical services, head of social services and head of nursing services - again this is very analogous to the way in which Islington's neighbourhood offices are co-ordinated. What makes the Oslo model particularly interesting however is that the corresponding sub-municipal political committee has complete employer and budgetary powers and responsibilities for the functioning of that neighbourhood and its staff. These neighbourhood budgets, which to begin with were tied to previously existing expenditure patterns recalculated on a geographical rather than a functional basis, assume the form of block grants allocated by the full Oslo City Council to the neighbourhoods.

In both Birmingham and Amsterdam thought is now being given to how to involve citizens directly at the local level other than through their local political representatives, and both cities have adopted the system of devoting the first half hour of their monthly public meetings to issues raised by members of the public. Clearly this gives some room for greater citizen participation in local levels of government but community groups cannot put their own nominees on to the local committees nor are the local committees directly elected by the people in that area.

Decentralisation appears to have progressed most rapidly in Italy and Sweden. In the late 1950s a few Italian municipalities (eg Bologna) experimented with their own forms of decentralisation in a manner analogous to many Dutch and British cities at the present moment. In the mid 1970s many other cities began to undertake such forms of experimentation. The 1976 law on the institutionalisation of neighbourhood government can therefore be seen as an attempt to formalise practices which were already widely in existence rather than as an attempt to develop something new. The law at first represented:

.... the only example of an institutionalised nationwide example of urban decentralisation that is not ad hoc, temporary, or simply based on local voluntarism.

As is the case with France the recency of the legislation makes evaluation difficult, while the legislation itself was a mixture of prescription and permission. The permissive element of the legislation has meant that different Italian cities have embarked upon decentralisation with differing degrees of commitment and vigour. Surveying the scene, Nanetti[20] concludes that where the left has controlled Italian cities decentralisation has been pushed furthest. Only in leftist controlled cities such as Milan and Bologna do neighbourhood councils meet on a monthly basis where they are given responsibility for the making of major decisions. It also seems that in the more leftist areas neighbourhood councils enjoy decision making powers over large areas of social service, housing and development whereas in the more conservative southern Italian cities their areas of responsibility appear to be more limited. The neighbourhood councils are directly elected. The neighbourhood councillors in turn elect a president. The president appears to be the real and only executive power at neighbourhood level. Besides the president and the neighbourhood council, neighbourhoods are also able to hold regular neighbourhood assemblies which constitute a forum for direct forms of citizen participation. Unlike full council meetings the neighbourhood assemblies are open meetings with an open agenda in which individuals, groups and parties are able to participate. The final element of the local structure is the citizens' commission. A citizens' commission is essentially a joint working group of officers, councillors and lay people whose brief is to work up specific projects and proposals for submission to full council.

Crucial to the power of neighbourhood structures is financial devolution. In Italy the 1976 legislation makes reference to local operating budgets but the way in which these budgets are constructed seems very much open to discretion at municipal level. Some municipalities appear to provide a token budget for the neighbourhood council to conduct its business, advertise meetings etc, whereas other municipalities seem to be moving towards fully devolved neighbourhood budgets so that neighbourhoods have financial powers to appoint staff, to develop their own capital projects and so on. Again there are wide variations here, but it appears to be the more leftist inclined municipalities which are experimenting most radically with forms of devolved financial control. Whilst the experiments in decentralisation in Italy probably go furthest (both in terms of devolving political power within representative democratic institutions and in terms of involving the public and community groups in these neighbourhood representative institutions) developments in Sweden are also worth considering because here too national legislation has been constructed to facilitate sub-municipal forms of decentralisation.

Conclusion

The legislation in question, the 'Local Bodies Act' of 1980, enabled municipal councils to develop new forms of local political decision-making. The idea has been to establish a fully-fledged two tier system at the municipal level which excludes councillors from one tier also functioning at the other. As was the case in Italy the legislation is permissive rather than prescriptive and as a result some towns and cities have done little whereas others have experimented radically.[21]

The city of Orebro (population 120,000) has probably taken things further than elsewhere. It has established 15 sub-municipal councils (covering areas from 2 to 10,000 in population) which have taken over the powers of the previous central service committees. In the British context this is equivalent to transferring the executive powers of social services, personnel, housing and other committees to the sub-municipal area committee. Executive powers are therefore exercised by a single central policy making and budget setting committee (equivalent to a 'policy and resources' or 'finance and general purposes' committee) and 15 area committees. The area committees are indirectly elected (so if, say, the Social Democrats control the city council they also control all 15 area committees) but city councillors cannot also be councillors on area committees (candidates for these places are elected by local branches of the political parties).

The effects of the legislation are clearly hard to ascertain at the present moment. Nevertheless in a city such as Orebro certain trends are already clear. First of all specialist committees and departments have become subordinate to locality requirements - they retain a residual advisory and monitoring function but no powers to stop or direct outside their delegated legal responsibilities in education or social services. Secondly the number of political representatives engaged in governing the city has greatly increased thereby correcting the balance of power between professional officers and political actors. Thirdly the powers and role of local party benches has greatly increased - they are now directly involved in political decision-making and not, as before, only indirectly through influence exerted on the party group on full council.

The dilemma highlighted by all the forms of community action is that of the tension between greater involvement and so greater influence, control and power over local urban services on the one hand and the threat of incorporation into the formal state system which greater involvement brings on the other. Variation in the structure of community action between different countries does not conceal the common strands linking them. Thus whether such action is sectional, issue oriented and specific to particular local struggles or whether it is more broadly based around the multiple interests of groups or neighbourhoods; whether action is outside the formal political system or channelled through it, the strength or the weakness of community movements is strongly determined by the role taken by the local state. Given the extent of fiscal crisis it is not surprising that there is evidence of withdrawal of the state from local urban service provision. In some instances this is reflected in the provision of a wider role for the private sector and the development of a market allocation process for urban services. In other instances decentralisation of administrative structures and/or the encouragement of voluntary action offers greater room for community involvement but does not offer the necessary resources or support for such involvement.

Thus decentralisation alone is not sufficient to provide all sections of the community with access to political power. We have previously noted the 'sectionalism' of many community movements (squatters, etc). It has been argued that part of their strength lies in this sectionalism; many of these movements have proved highly resistant to incorporation within government no matter how sensitively organised at the local and neighbourhood level. Again, in Italy, there is ample evidence to suggest that the shift towards decentralisation and community involvement in neighbourhood councils has had a fragmenting effect upon many community movements in Italian society.[22] Whilst the vast bulk have moved towards participation within the new structures some (particularly youth movements) have remained outside the new framework of localised democracies. One can point to a similar phenomenon in Britain with the black community. It seems that certain social groups, very often those with the most pressing needs, do not easily participate within institutions of representative democracy no matter how locally based. They remain outside the parliamentary state and the political party system. Very often their own forms of self-organisation are quite rudimentary and they are likely to make their needs felt in direct, unmediated, and sometimes violent forms.

Notes and References

1. **Cronberg, T.** (1985) Tenants' involvement in the management of social housing in the Nordic countries, paper presented to OECD/Sweden seminar on Community Involvement in Urban Service Provision.

2. **Grosstians, H.** (1985) Tenant participation in the Federal Republic of Germany, paper presented to OECD/Sweden seminar on Community Involvement in Urban Service Provision.

3.   **Castells, M.** (1983) The city and the grassroots, Edward Arnold.

4.   **Tuppen, J.N.** and **Mingret P.** (1986) Suburban malaise in French cities: the quest for a solution, Town Planning Review, 57, 2.

5.   **Castells** (1983) op cit.

6.   **Draaisma, J.** and **Van Hoogstraten, P.** (1983) 'The squatter movement in Amsterdam', International Journal of Urban and Regional Research, Vol 7, No 3.

7.   **Priemus, H.** (1983) 'Squatters in Amsterdam', International Journal of Urban and Regional Research, Vol 7, No 3.

8.   **Katz, S.** and **Meyer, M.** (1985) 'Gimme shelter: self-help housing struggles within and against the state', International Journal of Urban and Regional Research, Vol 9, No 1.

9.   **Draaisma** and **Van Hoogstraten** (1983) op cit.

10. **Pickvance, C.** (1985) 'The rise and fall of urban movements and the role of comparative analysis', Society and Space, Vol 3; **Evers, A.** (1981) 'Social movements and political power: a survey of a theoretical and political controversy', Comparative Urban Research, 8.2; **Ceccarelli, P.** (1982) 'Politics, parties and urban movements', in Fainstein, N. and Fainstein, S. (eds) Urban policy under capitalism, Sage.

11. **Gendrot, S.** (1982) 'Governmental responses to popular movements: France and the USA', in Fainstein and Fainstein (eds) ibid.

12. **Nanetti, R.** (1985) 'Neighbourhood institutions and policy outputs: the Italian case', International Journal of Urban and Regional Research, 9.1.

13. **Keating, M.** (1983) 'Decentralisation in Mitterrand's France', Public Administration, 61.1.

14. See Chapter 10 in this volume.

15. **Kjellberg, O.** (1979) 'A comparative view of municipal decentralisation: neighbourhood democracy in Oslo and Bologna', in Sharpe, J. (ed) Decentralist trends in Western democracies, London: Sage.

16. **Lojkine, J.** (1984) 'French experiments in socialist and communist municipalities', in Szelenyi (ed) Cities in recession, London: Sage; **Schabert, T.** (1985) 'New urban policy in France', Urban Law and Policy, 7.1; **Keating, M.** (1983) op cit.

17. **Garrish, S.** (1986) Centralisation and decentralisation in England and France, Occasional Paper 27, School for Advanced Urban Studies.

18. **Brouwes, J.** (1985) Municipal decentralisation in Amsterdam, paper presented to OECD/Sweden seminar on Community Involvement in Urban Service Provision.

19. **Hallen, H. and Rose, L.** (1985) Decentralisation in health care and social services in Oslo municipality, paper presented to OECD/Sweden seminar on Community Involvement in Urban Service Provision.

20. **Nanetti** (1985) op cit.

21. **Amna, E.** (1985) Increased participation and effectiveness through decentralisation and integration: three Swedish municipalities' experiments with sub-municipal councils, unpublished paper prepared for Urban Affairs Project Group on Urban Service Provision.

22. **Ceccarelli** (1982) op cit.

51

PART 2
A REVIEW OF CURRENT DEVELOPMENTS

4

THE DEMOCRATISATION OF PUBLIC SERVICES

Robin Hambleton and Paul Hoggett

Introduction

In Chapter 2 we made what we regard as a crucial distinction between decentralising and democratising public services. We contrasted a consumerist approach to public sector reform (which emphasises service responsiveness) with a collectivist approach (which emphasises service democracy). The former approach tends to view local government as a management system - the latter emphasises the political nature of local government. In practice local government faces political and managerial challenges and paths to reform can draw on both consumerist and collectivist ideas. Having discussed the consumerist approach in Chapter 2 in this chapter we concentrate on the collectivist approach.

When we look at developments over the past five years, we cannot but conclude that most progress has been made by local authorities in the reform of local government considered only as a productive and administrative system. Neighbourhood and district offices appear to be springing up everywhere, flatter forms of organisational structure are slowly emerging, steps have been taken to devolve personnel and budgetary powers to front-line level and more participative forms of management are being tried out. Further, many of these developments have taken place across service delivery boundaries as well as within traditional service departments. However when we look for attempts to reform the political nature of local government, by the extension of representative democracy to neighbourhood level, or by the development of new local forms of direct democracy, then it has to be admitted that progress and experimentation have been far more patchy. However, despite this patchiness, whereas the more consumerist experiments have tended to develop a few standardised models (eg the neighbourhood office) attempts to democratise local government have led to a baffling variety of different forms and structures. To try and bring some coherence to our description and analyses of some of these developments it would be useful to try and group some of these experiments within some more general categories.

Different approaches to democratisation

The first distinction we can make is between attempts to extend <u>representative</u> democracy on the one hand, and attempts to encourage the growth of <u>direct</u> or participatory democracy on the other. The distinction between representative and direct democracy is an important one. Whereas our system of representative democracy hinges upon the activities of the major political parties at national and local level, direct democracy refers to non-party forms of self organisation. Direct democracy therefore hinges upon the activity of organisations such as tenants' associations, community action groups, voluntary organisations, sports and leisure clubs and societies, self-help organisations, and so on. Many, but not all, of these organisations enjoy a representative role by either seeking to express the needs of particular 'communities of interest' (eg an ethnic minority group, old age pensioners, the handicapped) or by expressing the needs of particular geographical communities (eg residents' associations, redevelopment action groups, environmental groups). Within any local authority area we would expect to find a variety of groups representing both interests and areas. Whilst in some instances it would be correct to say that the development of direct forms of democracy reflects the failure of the political party systems (eg it may be because blacks are denied access to power through the existing competitive party political system that they organise on their own) it would be wrong to see direct democracy as a sub-form of representative democracy. Through forms of direct democracy the link between community needs and political action is much more immediate. Tenants' associations, ethnic minority groups, etc resemble trade unions more closely than they do political parties in the sense that their concerns are more specific and sectional than the political parties which have wider, often ideological, objectives.

The relationship between representative democracy and direct democracy has always been one fraught with tension. Many recent European examples can be given where these two forms of democracy have clashed head on.[1] In such instances the political party system has nearly always emerged victorious. What is at stake here is the willingness of the main political parties to tolerate strong, alternative, organised bases of power within the community - bases which do not recognise the monopoly political parties claim to have over the representation of the people. This is a crucial issue and one which we will return to later.

We have suggested that the extension of representative and participatory forms of democracy are examples of a collectivist approach to the reform of public services - collectivist in that they focus primarily upon 'collectivities' and their representation or mobilisation. In a limited way however consumerist reforms of the public service can directly contribute to the process of democratisation by bringing the individual, as opposed to the collective consumer, more fully into the organisational decision-making process. This is important for it is clear that the majority of individuals in receipt of public services never become organised or participate in local representative forms of democracy - the majority don't even vote in local government elections let alone attend public meetings. If 'private sector' techniques, particularly those involved in marketing and market research, can address this lacuna then one should not shun them simply because of their assumed 'individualism'.

Whilst aware of the dangers of drawing arbitrary boundaries it is nevertheless possible to identify four possible approaches to the democratisation of public services.

Figure 2: Democratisation of public services

Extend representative democracy	Extend direct democracy	Extend 'consumer' democracy
(constituency, ward or parish based committees of elected representatives)	(community development; funding of non-statutory groups; user group participation)	(consumer rights; consumer advocacy; market research and opinion surveys; 'non-user' groups)

Infuse representative with direct democracy

(local committees comprising elected representatives, community groups and under represented groups; co-optation)

The point has now been reached where we can consider some of the practical experiments which have been undertaken in the pursuit of the further democratisation of local government. In line with the distinctions we have already made, we will first consider those attempts which are focused primarily upon extending the existing system of representative democracy.

Initiatives to extend representative democracy

In this section we will discuss three examples:

- Priority Area Teams in Newcastle

- Area committees in Birmingham

- Urban parish councils.

There are other examples of innovation of this kind some of which are referred to in our previous collection of papers on decentralisation in local government.[2] These three examples do, however, provide an interesting cross section - the first two represent attempts to make the existing council system more localised, the third seeks to introduce a third tier into local government as an alternative to reforming the existing municipal tier. Whilst our comments on all three initiatives are critical we believe they point towards avenues of change which deserve further exploration.

<u>Priority Area Teams (PATs) in Newcastle</u> Newcastle's system of PATs is one of the longest standing examples of sub-municipal forms of political decision-making. Starting in 1976, 12 (later increased to 14) ward based PATs have been created covering the more deprived part of the city. The average population of each ward is 10,000. Interestingly enough, whilst the PATs have provided an opportunity for councillors to become more involved politically at ward level, their primary aim has been to redistribute resources to 'stress' areas rather than to extend democracy to more local levels. Each team has an annual budget of around £40,000 to spend on projects which will benefit people living in its ward. Each PAT has five key members - the three ward councillors, one county councillor and the seconded officer (the team leader). Most teams meet on a monthly basis, very often at different locations within the ward. Meetings are open to the public and are fairly well advertised. They have clearly played a useful role in allocating small moneys to local schemes. A city council review of the PAT scheme in 1981 found that recommendations to PATs for spending appeared to be evenly divided between three sources - local voluntary organisations, PAT members themselves and main service departments such as education, social services etc. Teams can spend sums of £500 or less on their own authority. Sums greater than this have to be approved by the Priority Area Team sub committee (a sub committee of the policy and resources committee). Evidence suggests that approval for such spending is seldom withheld. Very few local authorities have managed to devolve specific spending powers in this way.

In reality the experience of PATs varies enormously from ward to ward. This variation appears to be due to a number of factors but the attitude of local councillors appears to be a key factor. In some wards the PATs are very active, meetings are well attended by the public, close liaison with voluntary organisations is maintained, PATs produce regular and lively newsletters and often find themselves involved in local campaigns and projects. Whilst this is true for some wards, such as Byker, evidence suggests that these are in a minority. Many PATs still hold the majority of their meetings within the civic centre rather than within the locality.

Other teams that do hold their meetings locally put little effort into conducting meetings in a way which is accessible and informative for the public. Evidence suggests that the majority of councillors regard their role on main committees as being far more important than their role within PATs (interestingly enough many chairs of PATs are also chairs of main committees!) Some of the most interesting evidence submitted to the city council's review of PATs in 1981 was provided by the city's voluntary organisations through the medium of the Inner Cities Forum. Their evidence suggests:

> The lack of involvement which the vast majority of neighbourhood groups have in Priority Area Teams, other than what might be described as a realistic 'take the money and run' attitude.[3]

The Inner Cities Forum felt that 'the community' was almost entirely uninvolved in team discussions and decisions. It was felt that the PATs often deliberately excluded the community from participating in decisions. Perhaps even more importantly it was felt that where councillors did encourage local involvement the very structure of PAT meetings prevented this involvement from happening. In a way which, as we shall see, resonates strongly with the experience of Birmingham, the Inner Cities Forum argued:

> The fact that team meetings are structured in a manner of council committees, ie with lengthy agendas, formal reports, and more than half the time given over to applications for grants, militates against discussion in depth of issues affecting the area, even if councillors wished to present these in an open way.[4]

The other main problem facing the PATs in Newcastle is their effective marginalisation by the main committees and main departments. Like many other big cities, departmental structures are very strong. All of the major service departments nominate a representative to the local PAT. In practice, however, it seems that these representatives have little influence over departmental priorities and spending, and their presence on the PATs appears to be largely ritualistic. There appears to be a fairly widespread acknowledgement of the inability of the PATs to 'bend' main spending programmes but a lack of will at the top to do anything about it. The team leaders work within the Chief Executive's department, but even within this department their function appears to be given a very low priority. The result is that, not only do teams have little impact on the priorities and spending of main departments, but very often they allocate their own budget to items which should be the responsibility of the main service department. The weakness of the PATs is perhaps best illustrated by their own inability to increase the amount of officer support they receive. Up until the 1981 review each PAT was supported by a single officer whose time was split 50/50 between professional/departmental responsibilities and PAT responsibilities. Efforts were made to make PAT leaders full-time and, whilst this was eventually achieved, it was done so at some cost - most of the full-time officers are responsible for two PATs. Thus, with the exception of one or two wards where special provision has been made, the overall level of staff support to PATs has not increased since 1976 and, as a result, officers have had little time to engage in outreach and community development forms of activity - much of their work is purely administrative. Thus, despite a fairly widespread acknowledgement that the 'community' has not been sufficiently involved in the work of most PATs, no additional resources have been released to try and enhance levels of participation.

Interestingly enough, the Inner Cities Forum suggested that PATs would remain powerless as long as they existed alongside a network of large centralised and powerful service departments. They argue that the political decision-making structure within each of the main service departments should be decentralised towards area level. It will be interesting to see whether the decentralisation of the main service departments in Newcastle (which has now begun in the housing department) will save the PATs from their political marginalisation. In summary, we may conclude that the creation of the Priority Area Team system in 1976 was a bold innovation which opened up new opportunities for changing the relationship between the local authority and people living in selected inner city wards. In practice, whilst some spending powers have been devolved to ward level, the impact on the town hall-public relationship has not been very significant.

Area committees in Birmingham There are many parallels between the area committee system in Birmingham and the PAT system in Newcastle. Indeed, before Birmingham's area committee initiative was established, councillors and officers in Birmingham met with Peter Kendrick, the lead officer for PATs in Newcastle. The area committee system in Birmingham was only established in 1984 so it is still early days. Nevertheless, on the basis of research we conducted in 1984/85, it is possible to provide an initial evaluation.[5]

The Birmingham City Labour Party manifesto of May 1984 stated:

> The Council needs to respond to the criticism that it is too remote and insufficiently accountable for its actions. Labour's objective is to involve local communities on a permanent basis in decisions that affect their lives. Upon taking control, we will move immediately to devolve decision making functions to area committees.

In the event the City Labour Party chose to set up 12 area sub committees corresponding to the 12 parliamentary constituencies which exist within the city boundaries. The areas covered by each committee are large. The average population is 90,000 - nine times the size of the areas served by the Newcastle Priority Area Teams. Considerable debate took place within the City Labour Party concerning the appropriate size of the devolved decision-making units. It appears that the 12 areas were chosen because they provided units large enough to take strategic decisions, they could be regarded as a transitional step towards more local committees, and they tied in well with the existing organisational structure of the Labour Party.

Each area committee covers three or four wards. Membership therefore consists of nine or 12 city councillors, three or four county councillors, and the local MP. In practice, of course, this means that opposition councillors constitute the effective majority on some area committees, such as Sutton Coldfield, Edgbaston and so on. An opposing model was entertained whereby the political majority on each area committee would reflect the overall political majority on the city council. This model, which is being pursued by some European cities such as Oslo, was eventually rejected by those councillors who emphasised the importance of local democracy irrespective of local party control.

The May 1984 manifesto clearly suggested that local community representatives would be given places on the area sub committees as well as local councillors. This manifesto commitment appears to have been dropped. Indeed, the City Solicitor appears to have given the Labour Group erroneous advice in 1984 when suggesting that area committees had no powers to co-opt members on to themselves. Section 102 of the Local Government Act of 1972 quite clearly provides considerable scope for a co-optation on to local authority committees and sub committees. The council can easily co-opt non councillors on to area sub committees and give them voting rights if it wants to. Our own research in Birmingham suggested that many councillors and officers displayed considerable antipathy and wariness towards the city's community organisations. In this sense it is not surprising to find that the city councillors sought to devolve some aspects of political decision-making whilst being careful to bypass existing forms of community organisation.

The powers and responsibilities of the area sub committees are a strange hotchpotch. At first it was decided that the area sub committees would concentrate on monitoring the performance of council services and advise on gaps in provision or duplication. However, it was then decided that important duties could be delegated but the responsibility for deciding which powers could be delegated and which could not was given to the main committees themselves. Thus, each main committee considered what it would delegate in isolation. There appears to have been no effort to define the role of area committees in the round, still less has there been a serious attempt to develop a distinctive philosophy for the area committees. As a result some functions are remarkably broad and general, for example to make recommendations on 'any matters' to the main service committees. On the other hand some functions are extremely specific, for example 'to provide litter bins'.

Within the first year of their functioning, many councillors were already becoming concerned that the new area sub committees were 'turning into talking shops'. However, those Labour councillors arguing for real powers at the area committee level had to contend with the argument that in five of the 12 areas this would involve giving the real powers to the minority group. This strikes us as a superficial argument. There would have to be an extraordinary amount of delegation before significant power had been 'given away' and, so far as budgets are concerned, these would presumably have been need based so that poorer areas would stand to gain most. If Birmingham's area sub committees are to have much impact, their powers and responsibilities certainly do need strengthening.

The area sub committees meet on a monthly basis in each constituency throughout the city. The 12 committees are supported by six committee clerks and six clerk typists based within the department of administration. Many of the area sub committees change their venue each month so that each of the three or four wards within the constituencies are visited in turn. The vast majority of area sub committees hold their meetings at seven in the evening though some, such as Hall Green, hold meetings in the afternoon as well. All area sub committees allocate half an hour of their time to the public to raise any matter of concern provided that it is of a non personal nature.

Again, as with Newcastle, considerable variations can already be found in terms of the effectiveness and functioning of the area sub committees in Birmingham. Some are well attended with up to 40 or 50 members of the public regularly present. Some are run in an open, friendly and informal manner with public participation in the business of the meeting invited throughout and not just during the half an hour devoted specifically for that matter. However, these successes would appear to be the exception rather than the rule.

The major failing of the area sub committee meetings in Birmingham is reflected in their inability to appreciate the need to develop a new style and form of working which will encourage local participation. Agenda papers typically look very much like service committee papers. They often have approaching 20 items, sometimes more. Some of these items, for example outstanding minutes, would have several sub items. Typically they contain over 100 pages of paper. Even if you have a full set of papers (and many members of the public at the meetings do not) it is difficult to follow the order of business during the meeting unless you are familiar with local government procedures. There are frequent references to past meetings, future agenda items, reports of other committees, and councillors and officers alike often lapse into forms of indecipherable shorthand and jargon. When this happened at one meeting we heard a resident complain to a friend: "It's just like being at a council meeting but it's happening in public". Finally, on the whole, the meetings last far too long. Very often they run for three hours or more and whilst this may not be a deterrent to councillors it is clearly much too long for the average member of the public. By 9.45 at one area sub committee meeting in Ladywood just two members of the public remained in attendance.

Little thought has been given to agenda construction. If the idea of the area sub committee is to promote local forms of democracy then the agenda should be designed with the explicit purpose of enhancing public involvement and participation. Giving the public the half hour for their say is a valuable and important innovation, but it does not go far enough - the whole agenda needs to be structured to stimulate the involvement of local people. It is, of course, more than just the structure of the agenda which needs to be examined. The atmosphere within the meeting room is equally important. Whilst at some area sub committees the atmosphere is good, at others care and attention has not been given to simple things such as the arrangement of chairs. Thus a kind of 'them and us' situation is quickly set up with a phalanx of councillors sitting behind five tables at the front of the meeting with the public seated very much as an audience would be at a political meeting.

Still less thought appears to have been given to advertising of area sub committee meetings. The display material is classically local government in style, the distribution of the material appears to be haphazard and the support received from the committee clerk varies enormously. Whilst some have taken to their new role enthusiastically others have quite clearly been unable to move beyond the traditional role of local government administrators. Even the enthusiastic officers have little time or experience to bring a community development angle to their work. Sadly, whilst a wealth of community development experience exists within the voluntary sector and within certain council departments, few efforts seem to have been made to tap into this experience when establishing the area sub committee system.[6]

Another issue which has emerged within the area sub committee initiative is often referred to in terms of 'playing to the gallery.'. Only rarely did we hear councillors openly oppose demands coming from members of the public present at the committee meeting. Very often councillors would support local bids for resources or complaints although they knew that the requests were hopelessly unrealistic. It was easy for them at a subsequent date to then blame the main service committees for a lack of responsiveness, even though these councillors were often members of the service committees that they were attacking. Behaviour of this kind involving 'dumping issues onto service committees' rather than attempting to resolve them is built into a system where area sub committees lack any real powers of their own.

In summary, we may conclude that the creation of the area sub committee system in 1984 represented a remarkable step forward for a highly centralised and highly departmentalised local authority like Birmingham. New opportunities for dialogue with the public have been opened up. However, our assessment of the early stages is that the initiative has not gone far enough - the areas are too big, the committees lack power and insufficient attention has been given to public involvement.

One example of a local authority which is trying to devolve power (in this case to mini town halls) is Liberal-controlled Tower Hamlets. Within months of taking control in May 1986 a radical strategy of devolving power to seven neighbourhood committees was embarked upon by the Liberal Group. Whilst obviously at too earlier a stage for any evaluation it is interesting to note that the Tower Hamlets initiative is, like Labour-controlled Basildon, dismantling its functionally-based service committees (all traditional council committees with the exception of policy and resources, social services, a housing sub committee and decentralisation committee have been abolished). It also seems clear that the neighbourhood committees are to have real budgets as mainline departmental budgeting is replaced by area based budgeting. How local 'block grants' will be allocated to the seven neighbourhoods is not yet clear, nor is it clear how centrally-based performance standards are to be maintained (indeed this may not be seen as politically desirable).

Urban parish councils   Some cities, including Birmingham, are considering the possibility of establishing urban parish councils. English parish councils, which have a long history stemming from ecclesiastical roots, number 10,200 and cover most of the shire counties. Wales and Scotland have similar grassroots organisations called community councils. Due to the accidents of history, rather than any particular logic, there are comparatively few parish councils in cities - indeed legislation prohibits the creation of such councils in London. The Redcliffe-Maud Commission on Local Government in England (1966-69) recommended the creation of very 'local councils'. These would be elected, would have the duty of representing local opinion and would, possibly, have powers to provide some local services. In the event the Local Government Act 1972 did not provide for a comprehensive tier of such councils. However parish (or town) councils were formed from existing parishes.[7]

Urban parish councils are statutory bodies with their own power to precept upon the rates. They are the urban form of parish councils which remain a strong feature of local government in the more rural areas. Parish councils have no mandatory responsibilities, rather all of their powers are permissive. In reality only a minority precept a rate at all, the average being little more than a penny in the pound. Members of parish councils are directly elected by voters from the electoral register. The boundaries of a parish council are established by negotiation between the applicants and the Boundary Commission. The city council in Birmingham is hoping to establish 90 odd parish councils corresponding to the boundaries of the present electoral wards. We understand that some other urban authorities are toying with the idea. Meanwhile the Social Democratic Party is giving active consideration to the idea of introducing a comprehensive tier of very local 'community councils'.[8]

Research and evaluation of the role and worth of parish councils is largely absent at the present moment.[9] The evidence available suggests that by and large the competitive party system breaks down at the parish level, representatives on parish councils commonly being 'independents' rather than affiliates to any of the main political parties. Interestingly enough this is not the experience overseas. In both Sweden[10] and Italy[11] neighbourhood committees are directly elected by the local electorate and yet representatives of the main political parties dominate the lists of neighbourhood representatives returned. Perhaps one of the key features of the parish council is that it corresponds to a statutory body with independent powers to finance itself. This could guarantee its autonomy from the larger municipal councils within which it is contained. The contrary view is that yet another council will confuse people or dilute their loyalties to existing authorities. We would agree with Byrne:

> If they are to be a genuine and effective vehicle for the expression of community or grassroots feeling, they must not become or _appear_ to become too formal, bureaucratic or cliquish.[12]

Finally, we should note that this discussion has focused on statutory 'local councils'. There are approximately 240 non-statutory neighbourhood councils in English urban areas (compared to 150 in 1975). Our personal experience with neighbourhood councils in Stockport and Lambeth in the 1970s leads us to believe that non-statutory arrangements of this kind are comparatively weak. Indeed we are not convinced that a comprehensive coverage of statutory 'local councils' would make a big difference to urban government in England _if_ they were restricted to the current 'parish form'. Nevertheless, the urban parish council is an option which deserves further exploration. Having considered three initiatives designed to extend representative democracy, in the next section we discuss forms of direct democracy.

Extending direct democracy

Is life permitted outside the local state? This question is prompted
by our observation of the continued presence of an almost reflex
assumption that if 'public needs' are to be met then the state
should provide, and if needs are to be represented adequately this
must be done through the existing competitive party political
system at local and national level. Clearly 'Thatcherism', through
its strategy of privatisation, presents one form of challenge to
these assumptions. As we have already noted in the discussion of
privatisation in Chapter 1, Thatcherism challenges these
assumptions by seeking to replace collective mechanisms by
market mechanisms. The challenge also makes rather empty
exhortations towards greater voluntary effort. However, during
the last five years a second challenge has been mounted to the
'statist' assumptions of the main political parties. This second
challenge remains committed to a collectivist approach that is
libertarian rather than statist in its character. Not only does it
refuse the equation frequently drawn between collective provision
and state provision, it also seeks to challenge the idea that the
local representative state (ie local government) is the only
effective form of political representation at the local level. This
new approach to the politics of service provision at local level has
found expression in three related forms of local strategy:

(1)   resourcing non-statutory organisations,

(2)   community development approaches,

(3)   involvement of user groups.

(1)   Resourcing non-statutory organisations

One strategy which has emerged, perhaps best illustrated by the
work of the GLC, seeks to use local government resources to
support non-statutory organisations. This strategy has marked a
fundamental break with a notion that the local state should always
be the vehicle through which local needs are met. It is also a
challenge to the Thatcherite idea that the voluntary sector can be
built up simply by exhorting it to do so - non-statutory initiatives
certainly do draw heavily upon voluntary effort but they also need
sound and stable financing. In this context it is also worth
mentioning the way in which certain London boroughs (particularly
Hackney, Islington and Lambeth) have been able to use the Inner
City Partnership scheme to facilitate the development of a strong,
alternative and non-statutory voice within their own areas.

By and large local authorities have been hesitant in using their own finances to support non-statutory organisations. The idea that departmental budgets should be frozen or even cut in order for resources to be shifted out of the state seems incredible to management and unions alike. As a consequence a largely white, male and middle-class stratum of public sector professionals continue to administer to the needs of a clientele who possess few, if any, of those demographic characteristics themselves. Whilst many of us are now aware that 'public ownership' does not necessarily mean 'state ownership', a similar realisation that 'public provision' does not necessarily mean 'state provision' seems much slower in dawning.

(2)   Community development approaches

A second strategy which has emerged hinges around the concept of community development. What differentiates this from the community development activities of the 1970s is the way in which attempts are now being made to bring such a perspective into the mainstream day-to-day practice of local government. Some local authorities have tried to achieve this by creating new, centrally located community development 'mini-departments' and corresponding political committees. In Hackney[13] where perhaps these efforts have been taken furthest, political commitment has found expression in the creation of a Community Development Committee (a full council committee). Hackney has also established its own Community Development Unit within the chief executive's department, though the staffing of this unit to its full complement has not been achieved without some difficulty. Clearly in some respects Hackney's is a traditional solution to a new problem - ie set up a new central department to deal with it. The main danger with such a strategy is that it tends to collude with other departments' evasion of their own responsibilities for adopting a community development approach.

A converse strategy is to place community development workers in all the main service delivery departments. In many local authorities this has already occurred but not as part of an overall strategy - thus one can find a youth and community team within the education department, tenant liaison officers within the housing department, community social workers within social services, and so on. The key problem with this approach lies in the way in which it tends to subordinate community development to departmental concerns - hence the development workers become part of the problem and not part of the solution. The work tends to become de-politicised and it fails to contribute to, or be informed by, any corporate local authority strategy. Moreover it tends to reproduce limited ways of tackling issues which in reality are not characterised by such neat professional boundaries - as Beresford and Croft[14] found, many of the needs of actual and potential users of the East Sussex social services department had nothing to do with 'social services' as narrowly defined at all.

How can such dilemmas be overcome? One strategy is to combine a central community development structure with outposted workers placed in other departments or geographical neighbourhoods. Both Brent and Birmingham, for example, have established area community work teams. Another strategy is to introduce community development workers to points within the local authority where departmental and professional boundaries are potentially at their weakest. Thus Islington has allocated roughly one half-time community worker to each of its multi-disciplinary neighbourhood offices.

More importantly, in the long run, a community development approach must become a central ingredient of all forms of professional practice. The problem is that this is virtually incompatible with professionalism as it is presently constituted, as it touches on the very nerve ending of professional power.[15] Nevertheless interesting self critical developments within various professional groups have emerged over the last few years. Beresford and Croft,[16] for example, analyse the strengths and weaknesses of the 'community social work' approach within the sphere of social services. Recent developments in 'community architecture'[17] have received even more public attention (partly due to the interest of a certain royal personage in such affairs). Within housing a pool of experience is also beginning to emerge based upon learning from priority estates projects and the community development work being undertaken by housing officers in Walsall and Lambeth and elsewhere.

The strength and depth of community forms of self organisation vary enormously from area to area and region to region. Clearly local government, if it had the will to do so, could play a major role in enabling such forms of self organisation to develop. For many years, it has to be said, local government has had precisely the opposite effect largely because of its 'we know best/leave it to us' attitude. If we are to talk of an enabling role for local government, this will necessarily entail a recognition that many community organisations have been quietly getting on with things for decades without local government even noticing them. This is particularly true in the sphere of recreation and leisure, where our own recent investigations revealed a staggering range and complexity of clubs and associations even within small district councils which are regarded as backwaters of community activity. The presumption is often made that only local government officers or politicians have experience of administration and organising things. Our own research suggested that even in a small district council such as Kingswood (with a population of 78,000) well over a thousand individuals were actively engaged on local committees of one form or another. Our research suggests that people do participate, do organise and do take on responsibilities so long as such organisations directly relate to their interests and so long as they feel they are exercising real control.[18]

(3)   Involvement of user groups

The third strategy emerging within local government, one tied closely to community development, relates to the creation, support and involvement of 'user groups'. Whilst one can see tenants' associations as a long standing form of user group more recently a whole variety of new user groups seeking some say over how council services are planned and delivered have appeared. This has happened particularly in the sphere of leisure and recreation - in cities like Leicester, Newcastle and Birmingham user group involvement in the running of major facilities is now quite common. Other forms of user groups are also starting to emerge - for the parents of children in day nurseries and facilities for the under-fives,[19] transport users' groups, parks users' groups, and so on.

Many of these groups, for example tenants' associations, emerged spontaneously in response to felt problems or complaints. However, many groups have been helped to form by the activities of local government officers. A good example illustrating this phenomenon occurred recently in Birmingham. With the collapse of the manufacturing sector in Birmingham many large companies have either been closing down or have been selling off their facilities. Very often the first facilities to go consist of playing fields, company sports pavilions, etc. In Birmingham the city council recreation department was able to buy up the sports and playing field facilities of Lucas at a bargain price, but were nevertheless faced with the problem of finding revenue for funding staff to manage the facilities they had acquired. In line with their emerging philosophy of community participation and public control, the recreation department called a public meeting to which all potential users of the new facilities were invited. As a result, a steering committee consisting of casual users, organised clubs and representatives of statutory agencies was constructed which now administers and runs what is a fairly major but newly acquired set of facilities. This then is an example of user control and management of local authority capital resources. It is analogous in the housing sphere to the creation of tenant management co-operatives where the housing stock remains the property of the local authority, but the powers and responsibilities for the management, maintenance and repair of the properties is handed over to a properly constituted tenant management co-operative. Although this model of housing provision may seem unfamiliar to us, in some European countries such as Denmark it is in fact the main form of public sector housing provision.[20]

Clearly we need to think of a continuum in terms of user management committees. At one extreme the management committee (as with tenant management co-ops) is composed entirely of users; at another point on the continuum one encounters a variety of joint management committees on which both state officials and local users find representation; at the other extreme one encounters what should probably be called consultative bodies rather than joint management bodies. Of course the grey area lies in the middle. We have attended joint management committees governing community schools and community centres in which local authority staff have been in a very small minority yet nevertheless their power has been so great that such committees were in effect consultative bodies rather than joint management bodies. In other words, the numerical composition of a committee is a poor indicator of its character. Just as important are questions such as 'Who controls and devises the agenda?' 'Who chairs?', 'Who prepares reports and in what 'language' are these reports prepared?' and issues relating to the manner and style in which local authority councillors and staff conduct themselves. Clearly user groups are mostly established in relation to the management of particular facilities - sports centres, parks, residential establishments, libraries etc - they are less easy to establish where users are in common receipt of home-based services (eg refuse collection, social and health services and so on).

The following summary of a study recently carried out by Bolan[21] of a tenant self-management co-operative in Rochdale highlights some of the advantages, difficulties and dilemmas arising where control over important resources and decisions is properly delegated to the users of services themselves.

By 1981, tenant anger and discontent, on a classic difficult-to-let but pleasantly laid out 1930s estate, had risen sufficiently to provide the catalyst for community action. A tenants' association was formed claiming that it was capable of doing a far better job of managing the estate than the local authority.

This claim was taken seriously by the Borough Housing Manager and through his support community energies were harnessed to a radical initiative. A DOE Priority Estates Project training programme and a preparatory two years of joint management preceded the full handover to the legally constituted co-operative in April 1985. Although the co-op has been functioning for little more than a year a number of achievements are already discernible:

1.   A quicker, cheaper and better quality repairs service has been secured, especially for smaller scale jobs.

2.   Voids are now negligible and rent arrears cases have been considerably reduced. Rubbish, litter and vandalism have been reduced.

3.   Community development activity and community self-esteem has risen significantly. Over 80% of the 370 tenants are now paid up members of the co-operative.

4.   The estate's stigma is disappearing. Credit facilities are no longer automatically withheld by shopkeepers, and a small but significant waiting list exists.

These are important and encouraging achievements, but co-op activists are the first to acknowledge that 'much remains to be achieved'. More members are needed to take on the time consuming, difficult and occasionally acrimonious tasks involved in self management. Some co-op members fear that tensions still remaining on the estate may result in divisions, and generate distrust between the organisers and the more passive residents reminiscent of relationships between tenants and council officials before 1981.

The remarkable achievement is the survival of the co-operative despite their own periodic internal crises, and the gradually worsening economic conditions experienced by this and similar working class areas. Perhaps surprisingly a community that had suffered neglect, deprivation, stigma and rejection, does seem to possess the necessary reservoir of management skills that present the prospect of longer-term success for this initiative. The real training for the task is now occurring 'on the job', however the demanding workload makes it most important to heal potential rifts in the community, and ensure a greater involvement by a wider core of actively committed members.

One source of local friction has been allocations policy. Here the co-operative departs from council policy in that it currently does not consider single people. Allegations of favouritism have been levelled by some, who claim that traditional criteria of social need have been over-ridden.

Whatever the rights and wrongs of individual cases, it could be argued that other criteria might well be expected to emerge in this unique situation.

When assessing the appropriateness of applicants, a commitment to the co-operative ideal is an essential requirement. Also any choice between gaining an energetic, potentially activist family rather than a family having to cope with above average problems of its own, poses a real dilemma. Kinship and friendship ties are also very important within such communities.

Another source of friction has been caused by the community learning process undergone as this experience begins to radically change some tenants' lives. A certain amount of 'politicisation' seems to be associated with the process. As there are no communal facilities available on the estate apart from the estate office, fears have emerged that these co-operative facilities might become used for wider political activities. A meeting hall facility, open for all to hire, would be one way of easing such anxieties and plans are in preparation for a community centre.

The co-operative employs a co-ordinator, based on the estate, who acts as adviser, rent collector, advocate and negotiator. He recognises the vital need to extend the involvement of tenants within the co-op, both to spread the workload, widen community learning and 'broaden the mandate' that the co-operative has to sustain to act on behalf of the whole community.

He agrees that issues of fairness, equity and social need are important, but sees the prime need to maintain the full control over estate affairs that tenants have secured. No one should expect the co-op to precisely follow council allocation policies, and even if the co-op did become overtly discriminatory in some way, the local authority should be prepared to tolerate this as perhaps a phase in the learning process. Learning can and often does mean making some mistakes first time around.

This brief summary highlights some important issues relating to local control. Clearly the tenants' co-op makes decisions about allocating properties by using criteria that could be deemed discriminatory - one is reminded of the way in which trade unions in printing, the docks and ship building have traditionally used their power to make sure that jobs are kept 'within the family'. The fear that real local control would prove incompatible with considerations of equity is indeed the rationale behind much of the resistance to a thorough-going democratisation of public service. Whether this is a reason or an excuse for keeping things as they are remains to be seen but a few comments nevertheless seem in order. Firstly, the objection conceals the fact that public services are highly discriminatory in any case.[22] It attempts a false counter-position between 'democratic arbitrariness' and 'technocratic objectivity' which in reality does not exist. Secondly, the objection made to the use of 'ties of kinship and friendship' as a criterion for the distribution of scarce resources needs to be examined as a value statement in and of itself coming as it does from a technocratic elite which has achieved its own position in society as a consequence of considerable social and geographical mobility. Are the highly dispersed kinship and friendship ties of the intelligentsia being unconsciously imposed as a model upon a quite different class and culture? The third objection is so obvious it shouldn't need stating - it is precisely the existing technocratic models of allocating public sector housing that have played no small part in the break up of working class community and kinship systems over the last 25 years. The opportunity costs of such a disintegration - run down and vandalised estates, crime, social isolation and so on - are only now being fully understood.

Infusing representative with direct democracy

The dual nature of democracy

Over recent years we have become dismayed by the monotonous regularity with which councillors and council officers dismiss local community activists with such words as 'you are not telling me that these characters represent anybody but themselves, - or, at best, a very narrow group of interests'. The tragedy is that those holding such views appear quite unaware that the majority of their constituents express exactly the same opinions about them. The problem is that both groups are right -there are real limitations to representative democracy, just as there are real limitations to the system of direct democracy. Traditionally the voice of direct democracy has been much weaker within British society than the voice of representative democracy. In the following discussion we shall consider the complaints that each system makes about the other, but give emphasis to the critique of representative democracy for it is this set of arguments which is less frequently heard.

One criticism made of representative democracy suggests that as national and local government becomes more complex and professionalised so it leads to the 'self recruitment' of a layer of the middle class intelligentsia into the most powerful positions in all the main political parties. The manual working class, the main users of the state's services, become effectively excluded from the main political parties, and hence from government itself. This professionalisation of party politics and its monopolisation by white, middle class men, also leads to the under-representation of disadvantaged groups within society - specifically ethnic minorities and women but also the handicapped, youth and the elderly.

Following from this, the form of democratic involvement offered by the system of representative democracy to the vast majority of people is of a passive and minimalist form (ie it involves 'going out to vote' once in every three or four years). This form of involvement fits neatly with the paternalistic 'leave it to us' approach, it encourages passivity and discourages any form of self organisation other than through the competitive party system. This attitude can be found illustrated in some quite unexpected places - for example, the Militant group of councillors in Liverpool. Finally, there is a suspicion which finds considerable corroboration in contemporary research, that despite the particular social layer from which many local councillors have been drawn, at best they can only effect a fragile form of accountability from service professionals to the electorate.[23] Other than through the medium of the councillor's surgery, virtually no mechanisms exist for 'bottom up' accountability, ie forms of accountability which govern the day-to-day point of contact between service departments and the people and communities that they provide for. As a result, users of public services often feel more powerless in their dealings with the welfare state (and the market monopoly that it holds) than when acting in the open market as a private consumer of goods and services offered by private enterprise.

As we have already noted, defenders of representative democracy in turn attack community organisations for not being representative of the community as a whole. Community groups, quite validly, are often criticised for being sectional and parochial. Tenants' associations are attacked for being white dominated, and not adequately representing tenants with an ethnic minority background, or they are accused of only having tenants' interests in mind and having nothing to say about those without tenancies (eg the homeless). The strength of this critique lies in the extent to which the traditional working class has itself become fragmented and segmented. A sense of the homogeneous, geographical community which still exists in some mining communities has largely disappeared from many of the larger conurbations. A great deal of the work of urban local government can thus be seen as an attempt to manage such intra-class cleavages and tensions - between black and white, employed and unemployed, old and young, men and women, and so on. To this extent local government correctly prides itself on its attempt to be non-sectional and corporate in its view of things - that is, to weigh up and balance the various claims made upon its scarce resources by competing 'consumption sectors'. Of course the problem is that as these resources become increasingly scarce, local government's ability to manage the fight over the crumbs left on its own table becomes increasingly difficult. The whole attitude that this complex management task can be performed 'by us for them' becomes increasingly untenable. Tensions within the community are not resolved, rather they become frozen and institutionalised, festering below the surface and occasionally breaking out with violent ferocity. By taking upon itself the responsibility for the management of urban problems and tensions, local government runs the risk of reproducing in an exaggerated form the problems that it sets out to solve.[24]

The problem for councillors and their officers is that in 'allowing the people to have their say' they frequently do not like the sound of what is being said. In such situations they are faced with two alternatives. They can either put the lid back on the box and hope that the disturbing noises will eventually go away, or they can seek to develop the means necessary to enable a dialogue to take place between all the voices present, no matter how angry and conflicting they may be. Our view is that the conjoining of forms of representative and direct democracy could be mutually advantageous. Clearly there are dangers inherent in this project. Not the least is the possibility that by involving community groups in the process of local government one will end up incorporating them. Nevertheless, over the last few years a number of interesting experiments have begun which have sought to infuse the local representative state with aspects of direct democracy. It is to these experiments that we will now turn.

Co-optation

The strategy of co-opting community representatives onto main council committees has emerged as a way of enhancing local involvement in the planning and delivery of non-facility based services. For example, in recent years, many local authorities have experimented with the creation of area social services and housing committees on which co-opted representatives of community organisations have speaking and voting rights. The impression one gains is that by and large these experiments have not been that successful. The experience of tenants' associations on district housing committees has typically been a quite frustrating one. One of the main complaints resonates strongly with the public criticisms of Birmingham's area committees and Newcastle Priority Area Teams, namely that little thought has been given to changing the style and form of the meetings themselves -'public involvement' but not on the public's terms. The strategy of co-optation appears to have been more successful when applied to the many new council committees which have emerged over the last few years - eg women's committees, police committees, race committees and so on. Interestingly enough, many of these committees have not yet become embroiled in the problems of administering large service departments, their concerns are much more clearly political rather than managerial or administrative. The other key issue facing the credibility of area social service or housing committees in the eyes of the public concerns their relationship to the main service committee. In Birmingham, for example, the area social services committees have virtually no executive powers themselves. In the same manner, very few district housing committees have any real control over capital or revenue budgets for that district.

Hybrid forms of neighbourhood decision-making committees

Perhaps one of the most interesting experiments is currently taking place in Islington with the attempt to establish a network of neighbourhood forums alongside the local authority's 24 neighbourhood offices. The idea has been to try and establish a new form of local decision-making body which involves both elements of the existing council system and elements of direct democracy. A number of principles and objectives have informed the experiment in Islington. Firstly, that each neighbourhood forum should cover an area identical to the catchment area of the local neighbourhood office - only in this way could the administrative and political reforms complement each other. Secondly, no attempt was made to impose a blueprint upon all neighbourhoods. Indeed, if the feeling in the neighbourhood was that they wanted nothing to do with local participation there would be little point in trying to foist a local forum on that area. Thirdly, that whilst local councillors should be involved in neighbourhood forums, it was equally important to provide representation both for the general public and for organised community groups. Finally, the one non-negotiable element of the neighbourhood forums is that they would compensate for the lack of representation of disadvantaged groups by positively discriminating in their favour.

After a prolonged period of public consultation, in November 1985 a day-long conference was organised which was attended by nearly 300 local people, councillors and council staff. The consultation document which had previously been assembled outlined the range of possible executive and budgetary powers that the local neighbourhood forums could have. Not only did the document clearly outline what forms of decision-making power were possible, it also stated explicitly what kinds of decision a neighbourhood forum would not be able to make. They could not, for example, have anything to do with the terms and conditions of employment of existing staff, nor could they take action or make recommendations which were contrary to the council's equal opportunities policy. In terms of the composition of neighbourhood forums, consultation documents suggested that ward councillors would be members of the forum whatever constitution was adopted, and any elections would have to involve a secret ballot. Furthermore, the document recommended guaranteed places on local forums for the following under-represented groups - young people under the age of 21, ethnic minority groups, people with disabilities, and women who look after their relatives or children at home. The document also pointed out that existing, more user oriented, forms of local consultation (eg tenants' liaison forums) would continue to function alongside the neighbourhood forums.

A number of issues emerged from the November conference. Firstly, forums should be as representative as possible and should include people who are not members of groups or organisations. This would appear to imply the necessity of conducting local elections along parish council type lines. Thus there would be three main categories of representation on each neighbourhood forum: local councillors, directly elected members of the public, and reserved places elected by local community groups. Secondly the conference decided that pensioners should be included as an under-represented section of the community. In addition women caring for children in the home and women caring for the elderly or sick relatives had different needs and should therefore be seen as distinct groups. As, quote, 'meetings can be boring and intimidate some people' ways should be found to involve people who would not normally come to meetings. Forums should also have a say in how the local neighbourhood offices work, for example the reception and opening hours. Finally, and perhaps most controversially, councillors should not be able to vote at forum meetings.

As a result of this lengthy programme of public consultation two documents were produced by Islington in early 1986 which provided a framework within which political devolution was to take place. These documents 'Neighbourhood forums: public guidelines' and a 'Model constitution for neighbourhood forums', provided for a range of possible structures rather than the imposition of a single blueprint. To date one neighbourhood forum (Upper Street) has had its constitution rejected by the decentralisation sub committee, three have been accepted (St Johns, Julie Curtin and Durham Road) and two more are coming up for ratification. In all but three of the 22 neighbourhoods progress has been made in establishing neighbourhood steering committees many of which are presently engaged in agreeing upon their own constitution and membership structure.

A few key features of this framework for establishing neighbourhood forums should be noted: local ward councillors do not have voting rights on a forum; places for under-represented groups on the forum have been guaranteed but in practice there have been some difficulties in filling these places; limited budgetary devolution has taken place so that each forum has, on average, just over £60,000 per annum to spend on funding local organisations, environmental improvements and publicity. It is envisaged that neighbourhood bids for traffic and transport, park and playground improvements, area improvement and estate landscaping will get underway in 1987/8.

Clearly we are not yet in a position to give any assessment of how the Islington neighbourhood forums work in practice. All we can do for the time being is to point to some of the parallels between Islington's neighbourhood forums and some other models of local accountability. For example, the idea of a reserved section for voluntary community groups is a principle which is involved in the constitution of Community Health Councils. Another interesting model comes from the experience of neighbourhood government in modern Italy.[25] Here neighbourhood committees are directly elected and they in turn elect a president, but they allow for more direct forms of citizen participation through what are called 'citizens' commissions' (joint officer-community representative working parties) and neighbourhood assemblies (periodic public gatherings reminiscent of the plebiscitary forms of democracy of ancient Greece).

Extending consumer democracy

Having discussed three of the four different approaches to democratisation outlined at the beginning of this chapter (see Figure 2) we now refer to 'consumer' democracy. Our coverage here is very brief as we have already referred to the consumerist approach in Chapter 1.

Developments within the modern consumer movement clearly do have resonance for the public sector. Many of these ideas and their application to local government have been summarised in a recent paper by Michael Clarke and John Stewart.[26] Among the ideas they put forward are the much more consistent use of market research and opinion surveys, customer complaints 'free-phones', the market-testing of all local government information (brochures, notices, etc), the creation of customer panels to monitor the quality of specific services and so on.

One of the particular advantages of marketing techniques is that they enable the organisation to make contact with individuals who are unable or reluctant to make their voice heard through forms of representative or direct democracy. Taking this one step further, some marketing techniques are heavily reliant on forms of group work, thus the boundary between such approaches and more collectivist strategies becomes diffuse. For example, one can see how the development of customer 'circles' or 'panels' for non-facility based public services such as refuse collection could provide the basis for the development of more formal and representative user consultative committees.

Marketing techniques also provide opportunities for developing forms of participation for non-users of services. An interesting example is the 'Gateway Project' organised by Nottinghamshire County Council's leisure services department. The department recognised that many ethnic minority groups made little or no use of the countryside recreation facilities being offered and set about developing panels of 'non users' in order to identify the recreational needs of such groups.

A final development to be mentioned here, and one which has emerged more strongly within the NHS,[27] is the development of advocacy schemes for individuals from disadvantaged groups. Here the aim is to provide a personal advocacy service which aims to intervene on the client's behalf at the point of contact and negotiation between the professional producer and lay consumer of services.

Conclusion

We are well aware of the fact that there is a substantial body of literature on public participation[28] and on the theories which underlie participatory approaches to democracy.[29] We are also aware of the substantial amount of innovation which took place in the early 1970s to develop new and more radical approaches to community work and community development.[30] The decentralisation debates of the 1980s seem to be neglecting this earlier practical and theoretical work on public involvement and there is a good case for reflecting further on the efforts of the 1970s.[31] In this chapter, however, we have chosen to emphasise current approaches to democratisation and we have referred to many practical examples of innovation which are operating today. There is a remarkable diversity of approaches and this is encouraging to all of those who wish to strengthen local democracy. We hope, however, that we have provided some ideas which will stimulate further innovation and experiment by the many decentralising authorities.

Notes and References

1. See Chapter 3 in this volume.

2. **Hambleton, R. and Hoggett, P.** eds (1984) The politics of decentralisation: theory and practice of a radical local government initiative, Working Paper 46, School for Advanced Urban Studies, University of Bristol.

3. **Newcastle Inner City Forum** (1981) A community response to the Inner City Programme, September.

4. **Ibid.**

5. **Hambleton, R. and Hoggett, P.** (1985) Decentralisation in Birmingham, Report to the ESRC Planning and Environment Committee, May. See also Chapter 5 in this volume.

6. Some of these issues have been addressed in a recent pamphlet, **David Clark** (1986) The neglected factor: towards a community strategy for Birmingham, Community and Youth Work Department, Westhill College, Birmingham.

7. **Byrne, T.** (1981) Local government in Britain, Penguin, pp 269-275.

8. **Social Democratic Party** (1985) Decentralising government, Green Paper No 3, pp 51-52.

9. An exception being **Collingridge, J.** (1986) 'The appeal of decentralisation', Local Government Studies, 12.3. See also **Walker, R.** (1986) 'Bring parish councils to the big cities', Municipal Journal, 6 June, pp 894-896.

10. **Amna, E.** (1985) Increased participation and effectiveness through decentralisation and integration: three Swedish municipalities' experiments with sub-municipal councils, unpublished paper for Urban Affairs Project Group on Urban Service Provision.

11. **Nanetti, R.** (1985) 'Neighbourhood institutions and policy outputs: the Italian case', International Journal of Urban and Regional Research, 9.1.

12. **Byrne** (1981) op cit.

13. See the contribution by A. Puddephatt to this volume.

14. **Beresford, P. and Croft, S.** (1986) Whose welfare: private care or public services?, Lewis Cohen Urban Studies Centre, Brighton Polytechnic, pp 185-7, 194-5, 256-8.

15. **Hoggett, P.** (1984) 'Decentralisation, labourism and the professional welfare state apparatus', in Hambleton and Hoggett, op cit, pp 19-22.

16. **Beresford and Croft,** op cit.

17. **Woolley, T.** (ed) The characteristics of community architecture and community technical aid, University of Strathclyde, Department of Architecture and Building Science, Occasional Paper 85/86.

18. **Bishop, J. and Hoggett, P.** (1986) Organizing around enthusiasms: mutual aid in leisure, Comedia.

19. **Beresford and Croft** give some interesting examples from the Social Services field, op cit, pp 249-251.

20. See Chapter 3 in this volume.

21. **Bolan, P.** (1986) The impact of organisational change and innovation in housing management, Dissertation for Master in Public Policy Studies, School for Advanced Urban Studies.

22. **Beresford and Croft** (1986) op cit, p 248; **Harrison, P.** (1983) Inside the inner city, Chapter 12, Harmondsworth: Penguin.

23. **Dearlove, J.** (1979) The reorganisation of British local government: old orthodoxies and a political perspective, Cambridge University Press.

24. See **Hoggett, P.** (1984) op cit, pp 26-27; **Beresford and Croft** (1986) ibid.

25. **Nanetti,** op cit.

26. **Clarke, M. and Stewart, J.** (1986) 'Local government and the public service orientation', Local Government Studies, 12.3.

27. **Cornwell, J. and Gordon, P.** (eds) (1985) An experiment in advocacy: the Hackney Womens' Health Project, King's Fund Centre.

28. **Boaden, N., Goldsmith, M., Hampton, W. and Stringer, P.** (1982) Public participation in local services, London: Longman.

29. **Pateman, C.** (1970) Participation and deomocratic theory, Cambridge: Cambridge Unitersity Press; **Hill, D.M.** (1974) Democratic theory and local government, London: Allen and Unwin; **Lucas, J.R.** (1976) Democracy and participation, Harmondsworth: Penguin.

30. **Jones, D. and Mayo, M.** (eds) (1974) Community Work One, London: Routledge and Kegan Paul; Loney, M. (1983) Community against government, London: Heinemann.

31. Some links are beginning to be made. See, for example, **Hampton, W.** (1987) Local government and urban politics, Chapters 7 and 8, London: Longman.

5

DECENTRALISATION IN BIRMINGHAM: A CASE STUDY

Charlie Barker, Robin Hambleton and Paul Hoggett

Introduction

Birmingham's commitment to decentralising and democratising its services 'began' when Labour took control of the city council in May 1984. The initiative is particularly interesting because Birmingham is the biggest non-metropolitan urban authority in the country and the initiative's objectives, on paper at least, are very ambitious - multiservice neighbourhood offices, devolved local political committees, etc. This case study is based on five months' research undertaken for the ESRC between November 1984 and March 1985 by Robin Hambleton and Paul Hoggett and the more recent personal research of Charlie Barker who, until December 1986, was a member of staff of the city council's social services department.

The general statement on decentralisation in the May 1984 Labour Party manifesto read as follows:

> Labour will seek a partnership with residents of Birmingham by providing greater accessibility to the services of the City Council and by giving residents a greater say in the planning and management of these services.

The manifesto goes on to make separate statements about the 'decentralisation of services' and the 'devolution of power'. By drawing on these statements and on the minutes of the council's Performance Review Committee it is possible to record the stated objectives of the three key initiatives as follows:

Initiative	Stated objective
12 area committees	To involve local communities on a permanent basis in the decisions that affect their lives. (Manifesto).
39 neighbourhood offices	To provide reasonable access to services there will be one neighbourhood office in most district wards. (Manifesto).
Reorganisation of education and leisure services	To obtain a more efficient use of council owned community facilities through the development of a 'dual-use' philosophy and the reorganisation of recreation and community services on an area basis. (Performance review committee).

For the purposes of this chapter we shall consider that 'decentralisation in Birmingham' encompasses all three of these initiatives but one observation should be made. It is by no means clear that this view was shared by many of the relevant actors within Birmingham itself. Only a few of our interviewees perceived the third initiative as an integral component of the Birmingham decentralisation strategy, moreover many construed the area committee initiative as something quite unrelated to decentralisation.

At the outset, then, we are suggesting that 'decentralisation in Birmingham', in common with decentralisation initiatives elsewhere in the country, is an extremely complex and multi-faceted affair. Different actors have different perceptions and different objectives. They are engaged in a political process (or perhaps 'struggle' would be a better word) the outcome of which will determine whether the change achieved is merely a 'rearrangement of the deckchairs' or something qualitatively different from what existed before. The differing perceptions of the different actors have already had and will continue to have major implications for the eventual shape and character of decentralisation within this city council. A primary focus of this chapter will therefore be an analysis of these differences, their political and organisational meanings, and the manner of their interplay and resolution.

In this chapter we attempt to record the unfolding story of 'decentralisation in Birmingham'. Following a brief section outlining the financial, political and organisational setting we discuss the political origins of decentralisation. The next section reviews how the process of decentralisation has been managed. This leads into a discussion of the way the neighbourhood office concept has evolved which, in turn, leads into a review of the current state of the neighbourhood office initiative. In this chapter, then, we concentrate on the ideas underlying the neighbourhood office approach. The parallel, but comparatively disconnected, system of area committees is discussed in Chapter 4.

The financial, political and organisational setting

The history of policy making in Birmingham

Birmingham has a special place in the history of urban political development. In the last quarter of the nineteenth century it was the scene of a wide range of innovations in city government and politics which have since become standard practice in other cities in Britain and elsewhere.[1] However, despite these remarkable achievements of the past, Birmingham does <u>not</u> have a track record as a high spending local authority in the period since World War II. In the period 1950-80 Birmingham increased its spending at <u>below</u> the national average.[2] And, in recent years, Birmingham has continued to be a relatively low spending city council.[3] Table 1 below illustrates the increase in current spending, in cash terms, that has occurred in the period 1978/79 to 1983/84. It shows that Birmingham had the lowest percentage increase in the West Midlands.

Between 1978 and 1983 the council lost 5,407 full time jobs (15% cut) and 810 part time jobs expressed as full time equivalents (10% cut). According to several leading officers and councillors we spoke to the expenditure of the city council as a whole in 1984 was set at 6% under Grant Related Expenditure and in social services it was 12% under target. How do we account for this general history of policy making in Birmingham?

Table 1: Changes in current spending, 1978/79 to 1983/84
(West Midlands metropolitan districts only)

	% increase
Walsall	88.65
Wolverhampton	87.61
Dudley	86.94
Sandwell	81.99
Coventry	73.70
Solihull	67.86
Birmingham	62.45

Source: see reference[2]

We agree with Newton's key finding (based on extensive interviews with Birmingham city councillors in the mid 1970s) that, outside the ranks of a small minority, 'the mood of the council membership is generally cautious, conservative, and suspicious of change'.[4] Linked with this, respondents have suggested to us that the city council has a reputation for 'careful city management' (and the expenditure figures set out above support this) which is coupled to a tradition which has verged on consensus politics. In the period since 1974 political control has changed every few years. The result, so the argument runs, has been that neither party has either desired or felt able to adopt a radical approach.

Our second observation is that local economic trends (discussed below) coupled with the challenge of Thatcherite ideology have shaken this 'cautious balance'. The Conservative administration, led by Councillor Neville Bosworth, which took control of the city council in May 1982 was intent on radical change. It set about cutting the rates and the privatisation of council services. The Conservatives cut £23 million from the Labour budget for 1982/83 and cut the rates for 1982/83 and 1984/85. The latter cut was, in fact, largely financed by appropriating £28 million from balances but few would doubt the ideological commitment of this Conservative administration to 'rolling back the frontiers of the state'. This radical right wing approach was, as we shall suggest later, one of the reasons why the Labour Party adopted an equally radical socialist response in their manifesto for the May 1984 election.

Characteristics of the city

Birmingham with a population of over one million is easily the largest metropolitan district in the country (nearest rival is Leeds with 714,000). A separate point related to size is the burden imposed on elected members. Birmingham City Council has more councillors than any other metropolitan district (117 seats) but this does not compensate for the massive size of the population. If we divide the population by the number of seats we find that the 'average' city councillor has to 'represent' more people than a city councillor in any other city in England and Wales. Wards are, on the whole, correspondingly large in geographical area. The sheer size of wards in Birmingham (average population over 25,000) places an enormous strain on the three councillors who represent each ward.

The most startling facts about Birmingham relate to the dramatic economic decline which the city is experiencing. A review of the Inner City Partnership scheme (published in 1985) highlights some of the key trends:

> .... unemployment in Birmingham has risen by 180% over the last five years. Currently the unemployment rate is 19% in the city as a whole, and 30% in the core area. At ward level, the latest data indicates that Sparkbrook has an unemployment rate of 51%.

> The continuing relative structural decline of manufacturing in the UK, therefore, has clear and serious implications for the future of the city's economy.[5]

By the early 1980s it seems it was clear to radicals on both the right and the left that old approaches could not cope with the new challenge facing the city.

The departmental base for decentralisation

Any local authority embarking upon a strategy of decentralisation will do so from an institutional base which to some extent reflects what had been the tradition for that authority up to this moment of change. In Walsall, for example, the Labour Group faced up to a housing department in 1980 which was almost entirely centralised with virtually all departmental staff operating from offices within the Civic Suite.[6] Islington's Labour Group faced a quite different situation when they came to power in 1982 - a housing department already 'decentralised' into five district offices and a social services department delivering the bulk of fieldwork services from 12 area offices. What then was the institutional base from which Birmingham's new Labour Group had to work in May 1984?

The situation can be summarised in the following way. Whereas Birmingham's urban renewal strategy could, to some extent, be considered as an inspiration for the new initiative and whereas the housing department had been moving in a faltering fashion towards greater decentralisation since the late 1970s, a recent reorganisation within the social services department constituted a major obstacle to decentralisation.

(1)   Urban renewal

Birmingham's urban renewal programme was implemented by eight area-based multi-disciplinary teams containing architectural, planning, surveying, housing and administrative staff. Whilst the programme was managed centrally (from within the environmental health department) the project team staff remained professionally accountable to their own functionally-based parent departments. This form of matrix management has proved effective throughout the decade of the programme's activity.[7]

Perhaps even more important, the urban renewal project teams quickly developed a reputation for community development and consultation. As a direct result of this community development approach the inner city areas of Birmingham are now relatively well endowed with residents' associations. Our respondents suggest that there are now well over 70 of which about 40 are active. Furthermore for some years now the city council has grant aided an umbrella organisation, Community Forum, which represents and services the individual residents' associations.

There can be little doubt that the success of Birmingham's urban renewal strategy has acted as a point of inspiration for decentralisation, indeed a number of ex-urban renewal staff were instrumental in the drafting of key policy papers on the city's neighbourhood office proposals.

(2) Housing

The urban renewal programme should be regarded as the exception to the rule in Birmingham. Virtually all of our respondents from the secretary of Community Forum to the leader of the council described the city council as 'sweepingly centralised', 'one of the most over-centralised boroughs in the country'. The housing department illustrates this tradition vividly. With a public sector housing stock of 128,000 units it is the largest housing authority in England yet only recently has it moved towards a measured decantation of staff and resources to five area housing offices. 'Repairs and maintenance' is performed by the Building Direct Labour Organisation (DLO) which is organised around the same five areas as the housing department. However, the repairs reporting procedure remains very cumbersome with the lines of communication between housing management and the DLO being mediated by a third organisation which contains the professional surveying function (which is responsible for job assessment and specification).

Interestingly enough in 1984 Birmingham began to participate in the DOE's Priority Estates Programme for the first time. The Bloomsbury Project now has a locally based multi-trade repair team operating from the project office. As we shall see, the significance of this development lies in the fact that 'repairs and maintenance' has otherwise remained excluded from the council's decentralisation programme.

The problems of managing a department of this size on a centralised basis have clearly proved enormous. Pressures to decentralise have been growing within the organisation for several years but it is important to understand that such managerialist objectives tend to find expression in forms of decentralisation which are not necessarily compatible with other objectives for decentralisation. Our own case study of decentralisation in Hackney revealed the tensions which result when managerialist and tenant inspired strategies for decentralisation meet head on within the same department.[8]

(3) Social services

Reorganisation of the social services department in Birmingham had been on the agenda since the period 1980/81. The two years of Conservative administration in Birmingham (1982-84) were to prove crucial in the history of the department. The administration's commitment to cost-cutting rationalisation and privatisation found expression within the social services department when a group of commercial management consultants - Price Waterhouse - were brought in 'to review the objectives of the Department and the organisation, structure, resources, systems and information required to meet those objectives in the most efficient manner'.[9] Characterising the department as 'partially centralised' Price Waterhouse came to the following conclusion:

> We see a clear need to make a choice between a centralised or a decentralised structure. We have examined the main alternatives and consider that a district based structure would best meet the objectives of the Department.[10]

Surprisingly enough the Price Waterhouse proposals were not implemented. Instead a set of proposals were pushed through by the then Director of Social Services which drew upon elements of the Price Waterhouse recommendations but used these elements as the basis for implementing a functional and specialist as opposed to geographical and decentralist principle of organisation. Until April 1984 the social services department had a history of decentralised offices (14 in all) from which, with the exception of hospital based services, most services were delivered. The reorganisation discarded the whole concept of 'locality' as being a key factor in service delivery. By May 1984 therefore the social services department was just beginning to adjust to the first few months of a reorganisation which, if anything, had taken it in a direction altogether opposite to that implied by decentralisation - with specialist teams replacing generic area teams.

The inter-departmental base for decentralisation

Besides the particular internal arrangements of key service delivery departments an understanding of the Birmingham tradition of city management, that is, the way in which the authority as a whole has been managed, is essential for an understanding of the emergence of decentralisation in 1984. A flavour of the Birmingham tradition can be obtained from the following extract of an interview conducted with Jim Amos, the city's chief executive immediately after the 1974 reorganisation of local government:

> Although forewarned, I was surprised by the depth of separatism which I found upon my arrival in Birmingham. There was an authoritarian, master/servant relationship both between

chairman/chief officers and between officers/subordinates.[11]

According to Clive Wilkinson, the leader of the Labour Group throughout the period 1974-83:

.... the old system was really outmoded and wasteful .... where powerful Chief Officers and Chairmen did their own thing.[12]

During Wilkinson's first Labour administration (1974-76) considerable efforts were made to undermine this departmentalist tradition by the introduction of corporate management techniques. Our impression is that this attempt to introduce corporate management did no more than scratch the surface of departmental separatism. However, it is clear to us that the ideology of corporate management (of improving inter-departmental working, of challenging narrow professionalism, etc) sunk fairly deep roots into sections of the Labour Party during the mid 1970s. It is not just that the Labour leadership of 1974 attempted to introduce corporate working and the Conservatives threw it out three years later. It is more to do with the local climate of opinion. To use Donald Schon's phrase, corporate working was an 'idea in good currency'.[13] Quite why this might be so is open to speculation. At one level there was considerable discussion within the world of local government. In particular, some writers were arguing that the approach could work at local level as well as at the centre of the authority.[14] These ideas of local corporate planning tied up with the development within the Birmingham District Labour Party of an interest in increasing public participation in local government.[15] The ideas associated with corporate working have been promoted in Birmingham by the proximity of the Aston Management Centre and the Institute of Local Government Studies. Several key political actors had obtained post-experience qualifications or had conducted postgraduate research on public sector management at these institutions.

A number of writers have commented on the close links between corporate management ideology and post-Bains tendencies towards rationalisation and centralisation at the municipal level of government.[16] There can be little doubt that Clive Wilkinson saw the panoply of corporate management as a vehicle for the centralisation of political and managerial authority within Birmingham in opposition to a tradition of fragmented separatism. With regard to the rationalising thrust of corporate management, to cite Wilkinson:

As far as the Labour group is concerned, what they wanted from corporate management was really more efficiency, in the sense of use of resources; that the policies pursued should be reviewed to see whether in fact our theories about what they would achieve in practice did occur.[17]

What is particularly interesting is the way in which this early Labour Party corporate approach of 1974 obtained political expression through the establishment of a performance review committee. This committee along with many of the other elements of corporate management was discarded by the Conservative administration of 1976/80. It is not surprising that one of the first actions undertaken by the new Labour administration of 1984 was the reconstitution of the performance review committee. What was, perhaps, rather more surprising was to find that this committee (a vehicle for centralised management in the past) was for several months given the task of looking after the city's decentralisation initiative!

The political origins of decentralisation in Birmingham

In this section we want to focus on the thinking of the Birmingham District Labour Party. Even within this more restricted arena we will suggest that there were several different political perspectives on decentralisation which were informed by three broad political philosophies at work within Labour politics in Birmingham.

Anti-professionalism

We have referred to Labour's flirtation with corporate management in 1974/76. Interestingly the ideology of corporate management not only provides cover for strongly anti-departmentalist attitudes but, because most local government departments are structured around discrete professional functions, for anti-professionalism also. In the context of city politics in Birmingham this is very important. Unlike many Labour Groups in London, Birmingham's retains a sizeable working class element who refer to themselves informally as 'the hourly paid group'. There can be no doubt that this identification cuts across other forms of more familiar right wing/left wing demarcations which characterise much discussion of Labour Party politics. The working class status of many of Birmingham's councillors does not merely provide a form of emotional identification. More importantly it defines a common proto-political outlook which, without too much exaggeration, can

93

be caricatured as one which is deeply distrustful of local government professionals and, at times, openly contemptuous of their efforts at unionisation. NALGO is not regarded as a 'proper trade union' by this group nor, as several of our respondents testified, does Labour Party membership guarantee officers any form of political credibility.

It is interesting to see how some of these attitudes have found expression through the idea of decentralisation. Speaking at a conference organised by the Birmingham and Solihull Branch of the British Association of Social Workers in November 1984, the leader of the city council spoke of the need to "shake up the grand departments of the city council" and of the need "to get decisions out into the community". He called for a different approach by local government officers involving more emphasis on problem solving 'we need staff who are more interested in the public than they are in their careers'.

Populist socialism

A second political perspective clearly discernible among many leading Labour councillors could perhaps best be described as a form of populist socialism. Whereas the former perspective is managerialist in undertone and hints at the need for a reassertion of control both over professional staff and their departments the primary emphasis of this second perspective concerns the need for greater democratisation within the city council. Again the contrast with boroughs like Hackney and Islington is striking. In these local authorities the language is very much one of 'community control' whilst in Birmingham the emphasis is very much upon 'the people' rather than 'the community'. Several of our respondents who were based in Birmingham's voluntary sector spoke of Labour councillors' traditional suspicion of community organisations. As we shall see later such attitudes probably explain the surprising absence of any community development element within the main thrust of Birmingham's decentralisation strategy to date.

Instead this populism seems to have found policy expression in the concept of the urban parish council. Some Labour councillors view the present area committee system as a transitional step towards the creation of up to 90 parish councils in the city. Whilst such parish councils would have powers to levy an independent precept their decision-making powers are otherwise somewhat limited. A vehicle for influence over strategic decisions they are certainly not.

The 'new' urban left

The third political perspective to be found converging around decentralisation in Birmingham corresponds more closely to that which has provided the political inspiration for decentralisation in several London boroughs. More identifiably 'left wing' than the two other perspectives it seeks to link decentralisation to the struggle for socialism. It recognises widespread public disillusionment with the welfare state in its present form and looks to decentralisation as a way of pre-figuring 'non-statist' approaches to the planning and delivery of public services. It is concerned both to reform the internal organisation of local government and to extend democratic involvement beyond the municipal council chamber. In Birmingham this perspective was put across to us by several backbench councillors and the chairs of some of the main service committees. It tends to be associated with some of the younger, intellectual elements within the Labour group.

The emergence of the decentralisation policy

The above, then, represents a brief description of the main political ideologies at work. Informal debate had begun as early as 1981 and unspecific references to a decentralisation strategy can be found in the 1982 Labour Party manifesto.

Decentralisation figured strongly at the February 1983 city Labour Party policy conference in the form of papers submitted by both the Finance and Housing Policy Groups. As a result a decision was made to establish a Community Participation Policy Implementation Group comprised largely of local party activists, which has played an important role in the development and review of the decentralisation strategy since that date.

During the following two years debate has ranged freely around a number of policy dilemmas that we will refer to further in later sections. Essential questions that had to be answered concerned whether a uniform or selective approach should be taken towards extending democratic involvement, whether the constituency, ward or parish was the proper point at which this extension should take place, and so on. The 1984 manifesto commitment managed to combine elements of radicalism with elements of caution. There was a full commitment "to the decentralisation of services" though it was recognised that "a complete range" could not be made available immediately. It spoke of the "devolution of decision-making functions" to the area committees which it promised would have "real executive powers". Furthermore it gave a clear

95

commitment to involve local residents on these committees and looked towards a long-term integration of area committees and urban parish councils "so that the parish council would elect representatives to the area committee from among its members". Perhaps most radically, it foresaw that the strategy would inevitably lead to a "restructuring of existing committees of the Council". More cautiously the manifesto spoke of giving ward councillors and the community "the responsibility for the management and development of facilities and services for the area" without mentioning any delegated powers which might correspond to such responsibilities. Finally, and perhaps most importantly, the whole strategy was presented very much in terms of 'no cost', the emphasis being on the redeployment of staff from functional departments to neighbourhood offices. Several of our respondents mentioned the exasperation they felt upon first hearing of this 'no cost' commitment. In practice, it is now recognised that an effective decentralisation strategy does cost money, though it is important to recognise that one of the distinctive features of the Birmingham initiative is its attempt to introduce a radical approach at a fraction of the cost of, say, Islington's initiative. However, the fact that May 1984 Labour Party election leaflets suggest that the initiative will cost 'not a penny' remains a source of some embarrassment to some Labour councillors.

Managing the process of decentralisation

Here we review:

(1)   dilemmas associated with decentralisation,

(2)   the speed of change,

(3)   the relationship with the trade unions,

(4)   the factors maintaining political and organisational momentum.

Some common dilemmas

Any local authority embarking upon a strategy involving a multi-service approach to decentralisation faces enormous problems concerning the management of such change, and this is the case irrespective of whether the strategy's prime movers see themselves as revolutionary socialists (as was the case in Hackney) or hard-headed pragmatists (as perhaps is more the case in Birmingham).

There are perhaps two essential difficulties which in our experience play a determining role in any attempt to manage the process of decentralisation. The first problem relates to the lack of precedents. Whilst there are certainly some lessons to be learnt from the area management trials of the mid 1970s and past experiments in community participation[18] those initiatives constitute far more partial and piecemeal strategies than those which are being currently undertaken in Birmingham, Islington, Manchester and elsewhere. It is precisely because there are no adequate precedents that local political parties contemplating multi-service decentralisation have no alternative but to construct the substance of their proposals once in power. This vastly increases the amount of uncertainty which is an inevitable component of any change strategy.

We are not sure however that there were no precedents for Birmingham to learn from. Whilst they consciously used the experience of Newcastle's Priority Area Teams in setting up their own area committee system there is little evidence to suggest any systematic examination of the experience of nearby Walsall or the multi-service initiative in Islington. Birmingham retains a tremendously proud civic culture and whilst this contrasts positively to the tradition of municipal neglect one often finds elsewhere in Britain its negative aspects are expressed in a certain parochialism and unwillingness to recognise that other local authorities may have things Birmingham can learn from.

The second problem refers to the fundamental paradox of decentralisation as a political strategy - a strategy which is about participation, involvement, devolution of power and 'bottom-up' approaches to planning and management which often has to be introduced and, to some extent imposed, centrally upon a recalcitrant local authority organisation. To parody this only slightly, can one legislate for democracy and participation from above or can this only emerge as a result of pressure from below?

If the above constitute the two essential dilemmas facing any radical decentralisation initiative they find expression in a number of more concrete decisions which occur whilst managing the process of change. It is to these that we now turn in the context of Birmingham's commitment to decentralisation immediately after the local government elections of May 1984.

Speed versus dialogue

In May 1984 the Labour Group were returned to power with a two year lapse before the next district council election. Moreover there was general agreement that most of the seats to be contested in May 1986 were Conservative rather than Labour marginals. The city Labour Group therefore had more room to manoeuvre than, say, Walsall. Nevertheless they set about pursuing their initiative with startling speed. The area committee system, for example, was launched immediately after the election (at the performance review meeting of 15 June). This commitment to rapid change has had clear implications for the amount of pre-implementation consultation that could take place between the city council, the workforce and the community.

There was an awareness that the initiative in certain local authorities had become lost in a sea of consultation (Hackney providing the most vivid example) and, whilst rate-capping was not an immediate threat in Birmingham, there was sufficient uncertainty about possible future government-imposed financial targets that speed was made a priority. Furthermore a commitment was made to review the working of the area committees after 'several months' of operation. Nevertheless, despite such explanations, there can be little doubt that even given the most favourable political and financial environment a programme of public consultation parallel to that which occurred in some London boroughs would not have entered the Birmingham agenda. In London many of the leading Labour councillors in pro-decentralisation boroughs were themselves at one time community activists. They brought with them traditions of organisation and procedure which were quite alien to the traditional working class councillors whom they replaced. Gyford, among others, has tried to describe the specific characteristics of this new breed of Labour activists.[19] The phrase 'the new urban left' has been coined and whilst it may conceal more than it reveals, it does draw attention to a new kind of tradition within Labour politics. Interestingly, this 'new tradition' finds only limited expression in Birmingham at present.

Managing relationships with the trade unions

The paradox is that whilst the London boroughs bent over backwards in their efforts to consult the public and their own workforce but encountered formidable trade union hostility in reply,[20] in Birmingham problems with the trade unions have been slight in comparison. There can be no doubt that this is largely a product of the weakening of the trade unions by the Conservative administration of 1982/84. As one union activist put it: "NALGO as a union in this city was brought to its knees". Starting in the early winter of 1984/85 the branch called meetings on three occasions in an attempt to formulate a policy regarding decentralisation but each branch meeting was inquorate.

Consultation with NALGO has, however, occurred on a regular basis from autumn 1984 and departmental consultations with NALGO and, where appropriate, the NUPE Officers Branch got off the ground in early 1985. Virtually all of our trade union respondents were sympathetic to the philosophy of decentralisation but many had grave doubts about the particular form it was assuming in Birmingham. Particularly it was felt that neighbourhood offices may have the opposite effect to that which was publicly espoused - rather than bringing about a more responsive and accountable service they might form a new outer buffer or filter between the city council and the public.

With regard to the process of developing Birmingham's decentralisation strategy, as opposed to the emerging content of the proposals, the unions' main concern has been for the speed at which things have moved. Particularly since early 1985 there has been a feeling that things have moved at such a pace that union representatives have not always been able to consult adequately with their members. Linked to this we have discerned a familiar pair of contradictory attitudes. On the one hand, and this is a view that has been strongly expressed in several London boroughs, the unions can be heard to complain about the lack of 'firm proposals' which they can respond to. On the other hand, the same unions have often expressed the view that they would like fuller consultation with staff before proposals are firmed up. Of course, the problem is that, if one makes room for more detailed processes of consultation, this prolongs the period of uncertainty and delays the production of 'hard proposals' which can become the basis for negotiation. Trade union responses to radical change within Labour controlled urban authorities have been the focus of some debate recently[21] and our own research in Birmingham reinforces much of what has been said about the dilemmas facing unions and employers in such situations.

Having said this, Birmingham clearly could have done more to disseminate information to the workforce explaining decentralisation. Even though it was not possible to provide a single set of clear proposals (given the staffing and evolving way in which such radical plans are necessarily produced) a clear statement of intent could have been produced at a comparatively early stage which may have gone some way to reducing uncertainty within the workforce.

Maintaining the political and organisational momentum

As we have already mentioned, the paradox is that in manifesting a firm political commitment to decentralisation local authorities run the risk of appearing to push through the strategy in a centralised and undemocratic fashion. Our own research on the process of decentralisation in Hackney revealed the alternative danger, for here a local authority embarked upon such a massive programme of open-ended consultation that the political and organisational momentum sank within a miasma of uncertainty.[22] Our experience of decentralisation in Hackney and Islington also suggests that staff very often try to cope with the uncertainty involved in 'change situations' by sustaining an attitude of disbelief until the very last minute. To be successful in such situations the change-agents have to maintain an authoritative profile which nevertheless allows or encourages opportunities for involvement and consultation. Many local authorities have found this to be a difficult, if not impossible, profile to maintain.

Given the above we were particularly struck by a widespread perception, throughout all levels of the city council, of the actuality of decentralisation. Whereas in Islington it was still possible in 1984, two years into their own decentralisation initiative, to find whole groups of staff still convinced that decentralisation was not going to happen, in Birmingham we encountered a more or less uniform perception of the inevitability of decentralisation - and this only six months after the inception of the initiative! How can we account for the perceived strength of the initiative in Birmingham? Clearly the relative weakness of the city's trade union organisation referred to above is a critical factor, but two other sets of factors would seem to be significant - one concerning the political commitment and one concerning the organisational arrangements.

First, there can be little doubt that by initially being entrusted to the performance review committee decentralisation in Birmingham obtained a powerful and resourceful parentage. In some ways one might question the suitability of this committee for this leading role - for example, it has a wide range of other responsibilities besides decentralisation. The key point, however, is that the committee has 'political clout'. It was chaired by the Deputy Leader of the council, a union activist from the Longbridge car plant, who is clearly seen as a powerful exponent of that proto-political outlook which is deeply distrustful of departmentalism and professionalism. The performance review committee also contains several left-wing Labour councillors with a more explicit ideological commitment to decentralisation as a strategy for socialist advance. In November 1984 one of their number was nominated as 'lead councillor' for decentralisation. The composition of the political agency for change therefore reflects a balance between the different political motivations that we described earlier. Furthermore, in January 1985 a decentralisation working party was established which is chaired by the 'lead councillor' and brings together not only representatives from the performance review committee but also a number of key chairs of service committees who are not on the performance review committee. Given, in addition, the strong commitment of the Leader of the city council to a populist form of decentralisation one can see how political commitment has been maintained right across the ideological spectrum of the city Labour Group. This stands in stark contrast to the experience of, say, Hackney, where the differing political inspirations behind decentralisation assumed the form of divisive factionalising which meant unity of purpose was difficult to achieve. However, this formal political unity has not meant the suppression of differences - some policy choices have been kept off the agenda, others have been amended or reversed as differing perspectives have lost and then gained ground.

Now let us turn to the organisational arrangements. In the context of a strategy such as decentralisation one should be wary of establishing neat boundaries between political and organisational arenas - there are overlaps and complex inter-connections. Further, it is dangerous to assume that even very strong political commitment to an initiative will be readily translated into a corresponding organisational commitment. In Islington, for example, where (except for the very earliest stages) political commitment was never in doubt, organisational commitment has been rather more difficult to achieve. Again what is striking about the Birmingham setting is that, with the possible exception of the social services department (which had only very recently undergone a disruptive reorganisation), a significant degree of top level organisational support for decentralisation emerged within a few months of the May 1984 election.

Of particular interest in the Birmingham setting has been the role of the chief executive. After the dismissal of Jim Amos as chief executive in 1977 the city council had no discrete chief executive role until Tom Caulcott was appointed in 1982. Ever since his appointment the new chief executive has adopted what might be called an 'interventionist' role. He strengthened and expanded the chief executive's department and took steps to assert his personal authority over the service departments and their chief officers. Probably in a way closely analogous to the chair of the performance review committee the chief executive has seen decentralisation as a means of tackling problems associated with departmentalism, ie the tendency (common in local government) which some service departments have to take a sectional and narrow approach to their work. Well before the emergence of decentralisation as a high political priority the chief executive's department was being used to monitor and review the performance of service departments through, for example, the work of the management effectiveness unit. The decentralisation initiative can be seen as an additional way of tackling the problems associated with departmentalism. Certainly the chief executive has been happy to see officer responsibility for decentralisation vested in his department. The 'lead officer' on decentralisation is the head of the promotion and community relations unit (within the chief executive's department) and all the four principal neighbourhood officers (who 'oversee' the work of groups of neighbourhood offices) and the neighbourhood co-ordinators themselves (and their neighbourhood assistants) are on the staff of the chief executive's department.

Not surprisingly this rapid expansion of the chief executive's department has created resentment in some quarters. One senior officer described the whole decentralisation initiative as follows: "it's really all about the centralisation of control over service departments and their chief officers". The strong role of the chief executive's department in the decentralisation initiative can be interpreted in two quite different ways. On the one hand, it clearly gives weight and authority to the initiative. As we were suggesting earlier, this helps to reinforce and sustain the political momentum emanating from the decentralisation working party and the performance review committee. On the other hand such powerful backing for decentralisation is not without its problems. Not only has it meant that at times the neighbourhood office concept has been interpreted as a means of asserting greater <u>centralisation</u> of control but it has also meant that this powerful backing has been equivocal in its support for the extension of democracy and devolution of control through the area committee system. With these provisos it is nevertheless possible to point to the key role of the chief executive in guaranteeing organisational commitment to decentralisation - a factor almost entirely missing in any of the radical London boroughs.

Reference should also be made to the inter-departmental officers' working group. This group has met on a fortnightly basis from November 1984 and consists of second and third tier officers from all affected departments. Virtually all recommendations put to performance review committee have resulted from consensus decisions of this group. It has played a vital role in minimising obstructions, thrashing out practical problems and generating a feeling of corporate commitment to the strategy at senior officer levels.

What has been said here should not be taken to mean that 'departmentalism' in Birmingham is now dead: far from it. The social services department has remained fairly aloof from the initiative from the outset nor, to date, has housing repairs been integrally involved.

The evolution of the neighbourhood office concept in Birmingham

The role of the neighbourhood office

Like the overall strategy of which it is a constituent element the neighbourhood office concept is sufficiently general to include (or camouflage) a range of organisational and political objectives. It would be useful to consider what are possibly the three most important roles available to the neighbourhood office.

Firstly it may acquire a problem solving/advocacy role either as one, integrated function of a multi-disciplinary office or 'standing alone' as a minimal form of neighbourhood service. If of the latter character then the neighbourhood office would very much resemble a kind of Citizens Advice Bureau (CAB) operating within the boundaries of the local authority along the lines of a model being developed by Kirklees within its 'priority area' approach. A small group of outposted staff, highly skilled and enjoying access to sophisticated information resources, would be on hand to solve problems, act as advocates for dissatisfied consumers, provide information and act as effective referral agents. Clearly if this role is to be effectively accomplished a number of conditions are necessary: staff need to be highly trained, information resources must be accessible (and if possible computerised) and staff must have power to make the bureaucracy respond. In the absence of these conditions it is possible to envisage how the neighbourhood office may, perhaps unwittingly, assume a quite different role to the one envisaged - rather than providing greater access the neighbourhood office would more closely correspond to an outer earthwork concealing the bureaucratic redoubt, an obstacle rather than a facility, a filter rather than an advocate.

The decentralisation of the main service departments is not a necessary correlate of the problem solving/advocacy role. This function can be performed quite adequately even if the main departments remain tightly centralised - this is the way in which many Housing Advice Centres operate within non-decentralised housing departments at the moment. However, if we turn to the second role for a neighbourhood office, seeing it as a point for the localisation of service delivery, then this can only occur if the services of the main local authority departments are relocated within the new neighbourhood office. This, for example, is one of the main roles of the neighbourhood housing offices in Walsall and of the multi-disciplinary neighbourhood offices in Islington. To use our previous analogy this can be likened to the 'breaking-up' or dismantling of the bureaucratic fortification (ie the local authority). However, as with the advocacy/problem solving role, in certain circumstances it is possible to see how the localised service delivery role might slip into something altogether different. The danger is that if one places staff in accessible outposts, devolves responsibilities to them but not the powers to match those responsibilities, then those staff may become beseiged by demands which they have no power to respond to. In other words their 'power to deliver' has been negated by the organisation's inability to overcome its own hierarchical structure. In such a situation there is little doubt that the neighbourhood office will soon come to play a sacrificial role. Staff will be demoralised, the public will become disillusioned.

A third possible role for the neighbourhood office is a community development role. Essentially here the office and its staff play a key role in resourcing existing local voluntary and community organisations, helping to establish new groups, breaking down the social-psychological boundary between the office and the people it serves so that the community develops a sense of the office as 'its office', helping to establish vehicles for the extension of democracy at the sub-municipal level, and so on.

We suggest, then, that the neighbourhood office concept may serve three explicit and two unwitting purposes. It would be useful now to examine the development of the neighbourhood office concept in Birmingham, for our research suggests a clear shift in the purposes the concept was designed to further. In summary, there was a shift from the problem solving/advocacy role to the localisation of service delivery role. The community development role, despite strong support from the community and youth work department,[23] has been very much in the background - some would say totally ignored.

There can be little doubt that during the initial phases of the initiative's development after May 1984 primary emphasis was being given to the advocacy/problem solving role. The implicit model was therefore one involving little or no localisation of service delivery but an extended ring of small neighbourhood offices pursuing a CAB type function.

By the early autumn however it is possible to detect the emergence of a service delivery role for the neighbourhood office. As was said at a seminar for chairs and chief officers on 15 September 1984: "the neighbourhood office would be service delivery not just service information". However, as late as mid-October it is possible to discern considerable confusion among councillors concerning the character of the neighbourhood office. The minutes of the performance review committee of 19 October, for example, clearly illustrate that councillors from Sparkbrook Ward (the ward which returns the Leader of the council) were acting on the assumption that the housing department was not going to be decentralised.

By the autumn of 1984, two different neighbourhood office models can be observed existing alongside one another. Although quite different the models are not of themselves incompatible, it depends very much upon the political and organisational objectives which find expression in each model. In the Birmingham context this seems to us to be crucial for we believe that the objectives lying behind the original advocacy/problem solving model were actually 'centralist' in character and not 'decentralist'. From speaking to some members and officers one gets a clear impression that the initial model was very much inspired by the desire, a recurring one in city Labour politics since 1974, to undermine the separatist power of the service departments.

Interestingly enough it is this first model which acquires a dominant position in the first major recorded report on the neighbourhood office concept of the performance review committee (5 October 1984). The report envisages a system of 39 neighbourhood offices (corresponding to the city's 39 wards) each one of which would contain three 'basic staff' located within the community relations unit of the chief executive's department. In addition at least three 'specialist' staff would be seconded by the main service departments (housing, social services, environmental health) to each neighbourhood office. One of the three basic staff, the neighbourhood co-ordinator, would have line-managerial responsibility for the two other 'basic staff' but not for seconded staff.

In line with the 'no' or 'low' cost approach to decentralisation the 'basic staff' were to be recruited internally from existing departments. When the first few dozen posts were advertised internally the response was startling - over 1,300 enquiries and 600 applications.

We developed a clear impression that, for some senior officers and councillors, this initial model for the neighbourhood office provided part of a strategy for tackling departmentalism. The main service delivery departments were to be squeezed between the central power of the chief executive and the performance review committee and an outer ring of neighbourhood 'shock troops' and (to a lesser extent) the area committees. From this perspective the neighbourhood office concept was about improving service delivery without necessarily decentralising it. As one highly placed officer put it to us "it's about exposing bad management in service departments". Such an outlook remains fundamentally managerial. One might think of it as a 'radical' or 'enlightened bureaucratic perspective'.

The commitment to the service delivery model of the neighbourhood office appears to have received its impetus from a number of sources - the housing department was particularly anxious to move towards localisation of its service delivery as were many of the councillors on the left of the party. By the late autumn of 1984 it was clear that whilst some neighbourhood offices, particularly in areas of low social need, would contain just the original core of three basic and three seconded staff this would be an exception to the rule. The norm which emerges suggests that a typical office would actually contain between 17 and 23 staff but some would accommodate more than 30. Clearly, then, a standardised approach was rejected in favour of one which was partially responsive to the particular needs of the community. This not only implied that different areas would have different sized offices containing varying numbers of staff, it also implied that the character of the office would vary considerably. Typically in many inner city areas with predominantly private rather than public sector housing, the neighbourhood office would contain large numbers of urban renewal staff but few housing staff; the reverse would obtain in some of the outer city areas dominated by council owned housing estates. Here housing staff would predominate together with perhaps only one or two generic environmental health officers.

Determining the catchment area of the neighbourhood office

The concept of 'neighbourhood' has a long and difficult history. It is not surprising therefore to find that many local authorities have encountered great difficulty when defining the nature of the area to be served by a neighbourhood office. If the idea of neighbourhood has any reality it is clear that this reality is subjectively defined and is unlikely to fit in neatly with what are usually quite arbitrarily defined ward and constituency boundaries. Furthermore it is clear that in some cases the 'neighbourhood' may refer to a small area (of perhaps 3-4,000 in population) whereas only a few miles away, perhaps around a local shopping centre, people define their neighbourhood in terms of an area with 10,000 population. The problem, then, with subjectively defined notions of neighbourhood is their lack of uniformity and their lack of congruence with administrative boundaries. Correspondence with administrative boundaries is of course important if sub-municipal forms of representative democracy are to be established alongside the localisation of service delivery. If neighbourhood boundaries bear no relationship to, say, ward boundaries then the involvement of local councillors in the affairs of such neighbourhoods is made complicated.

Having described some of the choices to be made when determining the catchment area for neighbourhood offices how did Birmingham proceed? Clearly the sheer size of the population covered by the city council rules out the Islington option for this would have entailed around 150 offices! A surprising degree of consensus appears to have been quickly reached that areas corresponding in size (if not according to boundaries) to wards would be the most practicable level to work from. Nevertheless, given that (as described earlier) the wards within the city tend to be very large, this means that each 'neighbourhood' office will, on average, serve an area with a population of over 25,000. Whether this is too large a unit to be identified with remains to be seen.

More worrying is the manner in which the 'neighbourhood' boundaries were constructed. Islington and Walsall began with a notion of the boundaries and then sought to find sites for neighbourhood offices which were central, in terms of the social geography, to those areas. In Birmingham the approach adopted has, if anything, been the other way around - potential sites for offices have been identified and then a catchment area has been constructed around the sites. Some of our respondents have referred to this in terms of 'architectural determinism'. The key point to understand, however, is that this method was not adopted out of choice but was the almost inevitable consequence of the speedy time scale adopted and of the narrow financial parameters within which the search for premises took place. Whereas the average cost of each of Islington's first four neighbourhood offices was in the region of £250,000 the average cost of the first nine neighbourhood offices in Birmingham was projected at around £50,000. As a consequence emphasis has been placed upon redeploying existing council buildings for neighbourhood office use (rather than new-build) and therefore site locations have been restricted by the availability of existing buildings such as area housing offices. This is not to deprecate the approach adopted by the Birmingham City Council. Given the present context of financial constraint any decentralisation strategy is bound to run up against the question of cost. In such circumstances an imaginative usage of existing council-owned office accommodation must figure prominently as a tactic which might further the localisation thrust of decentralisation. The relative ease with which the performance review committee was able to obtain the consent or compliance of departments regarding the use of their buildings for the purposes of neighbourhood offices illustrates the strength of political commitment to the initiative. In both Hackney and Camden main service departments have been able to cling much more obdurately to what they perceive as their territory. The idea that numbers of existing departmental offices might be converted to neighbourhood office use has not even been allowed on the political agenda in Camden!

The final point of interest regarding the construction of the catchment areas for neighbourhood offices relates to the status of constituency boundaries. One can detect a debate within the performance review committee, particularly in January 1985, which was provoked by a realisation that the neighbourhood boundaries which were emerging often cut across parliamentary constituency boundaries. One senses that a strong rearguard action was fought on this issue by what some of our respondents referred to as 'the constituency lobby', that is, those councillors firmly committed to maintaining and strengthening the 12 area committees (whose boundaries match those of the 12 Parliamentary Constituencies within the city). Clearly there was a worry that, if neighbourhood boundaries strayed too far from constituency boundaries the obvious connection between neighbourhood office and area committee would be undermined. As we have noted there were many councillors and officers who saw these two initiatives as quite unconnected, and more still who had virtually no interest in the area committees. That the 'constituency lobby' prevailed was therefore quite surprising. The solution which emerged at the performance review committee on 18 January 1985 was encapsulated in a successful resolution which stated that 'officers be instructed to review the proposed boundaries with a view to these being redrawn as near as possible to constituency boundaries'.

The present state of the neighbourhood office initiative in Birmingham

The scope of the neighbourhood office

We have used the term 'scope' to refer to the range of services obtaining localisation through the neighbourhood office.[24] As the service delivery model of the neighbourhood office began to emerge in Birmingham so it became clear that the initiative was going to be ambitious in terms of its scope. At first sight it would appear that there is one important omission - the repairs and maintenance service - from the list of functions being localised at the neighbourhood office. Several London boroughs during their programmes of public consultation had found that complaints about repairs to council owned properties topped the list of the public's priorities. Unlike Walsall, which created a system of local mobile repairs and maintenance squads, Islington, Lambeth and Hackney set about the creation of a network of permanent local bases (offices and stores) from which multi-disciplinary teams of workers could respond quickly and flexibly to small, routine repairs on local council estates. In fact, whilst neighbourhood office based repair teams do not feature in Birmingham's proposals, attention has been given to the problem of localising and streamlining repairs. What has emerged is the development of a district-based computerised repairs reporting and ordering system (DISOSS) which should enable the immediate ordering of work from neighbourhood offices to repairs depots; however control of repairs workers lies well outside the neighbourhood office.

Another issue concerning the scope of decentralisation relates to the reluctant involvement of the social services department. As our account (earlier) of this department's recent tribulations has illustrated, the department's inhibitions could be viewed as more a result of the recent history than any disagreement with the philosophy of decentralisation. We gained a clear impression that the vast majority of field social work staff had only reluctantly complied with the original plan for a more specialised and less generic structure and practice. But having only just been (more or less forcibly) reorganised, the prospect of being reorganised once more on a neighbourhood basis seemed intolerable to many.

In theory, neighbourhood offices will cover each political ward. In November 1986, 23 offices were open and formal approval had been given to create 45 neighbourhood offices, ie going beyond the 39 envisaged in 1984. There is also a realisation that in areas of high demand there may need to be additional offices and it seems that 67 potential catchment areas have been defined.

The difficulty of catchment area is worth mentioning at this stage, and its effect on the type of service offered in neighbourhood offices. Due to constraints of time and finance, the first neighbourhood offices opened were based in housing centres. In fact some of these offices still have the dual title displayed ie neighbourhood offices were not only undertaking work from the ward that they covered but from the catchment area of the housing centre, which was much larger. This meant, and still does, that the staff in these offices were deluged with work, which has been difficult to manage. Also that work was mainly for housing services, leaving staff with little or no time to introduce the other services of the local authority to the public.

What then are the objectives for neighbourhood offices and how can they be evaluated at this stage? Building on the three potential roles of the neighbourhood office we outlined earlier, we now focus on five specific objectives:

(1)   total service delivery under one roof,

(2)   direct access to information,

(3)   speedier and decisive action,

(4)   new breed of local government officer,

(5)   regeneration of the neighbourhood.

If these are examined in turn it may give some feel of how neighbourhood offices are working at present.

(1)   Total delivery under one roof

This is an ambitious aim; reality is short of that. In practice, in terms of major functions, the neighbourhood office model provides for a neighbourhood co-ordinator, one or more neighbourhood assistants and clerical assistance, (all on the staff of the chief executive's department), three seconded 'neighbourhood advisers' from the main service departments involved (housing, social services, and environmental health) and a range of 'back-up' professional services (varying in accordance with the needs of the area). In 1986 neighbourhood assistants from the treasurer's department were introduced in a selection of neighbourhood offices as a pilot scheme. A major reorganisation of the housing department is taking place which will base most housing staff within neighbourhood offices. However, this is not true of the social services and environmental health departments. It could not be said, therefore, that neighbourhood offices are wholly geared to total service delivery under one roof and it is questionable whether they ever will be. As far as social services is concerned, neighbourhood offices provide service information rather then direct delivery of service. This may change, but this is the present pattern. The issue of repairs poses a major problem for staff and is a source of frustration. While staff can book some repairs they have no control over when repairs will be carried out.

A major criticism is, then, that neighbourhood offices are just a front for a housing service. In no way is there a multi-disciplinary neighbourhood management system in operation. This clearly makes integration of services problematic and there are underlying conflicts between neighbourhood offices and service departments. Some service departments are using the fact that there is no demand for their services at neighbourhood offices to limit the extent to which they provide services for them. This is, of course, a 'chicken and egg' argument in that if services are not being supplied, no demand is created.

However, there are positive aspects in that some services are more local, which is well received by the public and consumers. This is the feedback that neighbourhood staff receive and was confirmed in a MORI poll in February 1986 which showed that 74% of interviewees favoured the setting up of neighbourhood offices.

A lot of work remains to be done to improve the quality of service delivery taking place in neighbourhood offices and a change in management style is necessary towards a much more integrated pattern of service delivery. This can only be achieved if service departments are based in neighbourhood offices or much more closely linked to neighbourhood offices than some are at present.

(2)   Direct access to information

There is a different style of operation within neighbourhood offices, in that they are more friendly and welcoming than traditional service departments. The staff encourage personal contact, will give consumers their names and are less likely to 'fob people off'. Staff are encouraged and see it as part of their role to introduce a whole range of council services to the consumer. They do not deal only with the problems presented.

There are no artificial barriers between service givers and consumers, which encourages the flow of information. For example, consumers can see on the computer screen where they are on the housing list, the number of housing points they have and that their repair has been logged.

A drawback identified by neighbourhood office staff is that their training has not always equipped them for the task they are required to do. Consequently, they are less able to inform the public about appropriate and available services, eg some staff have not completed their training on environmental health, social services or housing matters.

There is direct access to information, even if at times that information is negative. This is a role that neighbourhood staff are enthusiastic about and are keen to develop.

(3)   Speedier and decisive action

In theory, this is a good idea but the reality is more complex. The use of new technology should make decision-making an easier process but there has been a tendency for neighbourhood offices to become enmeshed in bureaucratic systems and paperwork. This makes such things as 'progress chasing' difficult and very little monitoring and evaluation of work is taking place. This is a key concern of neighbourhood office staff and the principal neighbourhood officers.

Where neighbourhood office staff control service delivery, this is carried out quite quickly but there has been great pressure on staff due to demand. This has meant that people have had to wait over two hours to be seen on some occasions but, surprisingly, initial research findings suggest that this has not dampened consumers' enthusiasm for the new style of service. Where the neighbourhood office does not control service delivery speedy action depends on the staff progress chasing. This is not consistently done because of pressure of work. One neighbourhood office assistant made the observation that, on the whole, progress chasing is done by the consumer returning to enquire about their initial request for service. This area requires some attention if the neighbourhood offices are not to become deluged in bureaucratic systems which will inevitably reduce the speed of the service.

(4)   A 'new breed' of local government officer

There were financial constraints on the city council on outside staff recruitment. This has been unfortunate. So far the council has missed the opportunity to bring in people from the voluntary sector who have considerable knowledge in such areas as advocacy and community development. Other viewpoints would also have been of value in challenging the supremacy of service departments. The council may also have missed the opportunity to redress some of the inequalities that exist with regard to the employment of ethnic minority staff. However, the staff that have been recruited have a high level of commitment to bringing services closer to the public, eliminating bureaucracy that interferes with service delivery and making access to services more informal.

This 'new breed' of local government officers is best illustrated by the commitment to an advocacy role. This role is identified with strongly. This is not just simply making sure that people receive benefits to which they are entitled but - because of face to face contact with the public - they are much more committed to pursuing the best interests of the consumer. This is surely a refreshing change within local government services. Part of the change in attitude is due to the intense input of training. Some criticism can be made of the relevance and organisation of training, but it does seem to have played an important role in imbuing staff with the concept of a consumer-oriented service. This is taken very seriously despite the frustrations experienced by staff.

113

As stated earlier, neighbourhood offices could have benefited from voluntary sector influence but, through the input of training, a group of people committed to providing a more open council service is being created.

(5)   Regeneration of neighbourhood

This is the area of most confusion and has not been developed due to pressure of work upon neighbourhood office staff. It is not covered at all in the training programme. Staff have expressed an interest in developing the idea of community regeneration but have no time to do so.

The department of recreation and community services is attempting to promote community development. It has 12 area officers who link very closely to the area committees. It also has 12 community development officers. There is, however, little indication of possible future links with neighbourhood offices. The social services department has made no input at all in this area. It may be unrealistic to expect neighbourhood offices to take on a community development role given the size of the areas they are expected to cover at this time. It remains an exciting opportunity which may well be missed because of lack of direction and time available to neighbourhood staff.

What has surprised us about the reorganisation of leisure services is (with the exception of officers within the recreation and community services department staff) how few of our respondents outside the neighbourhood offices have perceived the possibilities for making connections between community development work and the area committee and neighbourhood office initiatives. Earlier we noted how little emphasis has been given to the 'community development' role of the neighbourhood office and (in Chapter 4) how the absence of a community development approach to the area committee initiative may prove to be the most fundamental weakness within it. Our impression is that the majority of officers and members within Birmingham City Council are deeply suspicious of the notion of community development. There are a few exceptions here -urban renewal and some field social work staff for example - but by and large there appears to be a widespread feeling that the community's attempts at self-organisation can only give expression to naive or unrepresentative demands. Thus, for example, we were struck by the manner in which the undoubted enthusiasm for decentralisation shown by the city housing department evaporated quickly once the issue of organised tenant participation was raised.

The position of social services department

The seeming lack of commitment by some service departments could be exemplified by the social services department staff who are still in the process of working out their response to neighbourhood offices. There has been an improvement in the attitude of the social services department since the appointment of the new director. At the 1985 BASW Conference, shortly after appointment, she stated that:

It seems to me that social services have a great deal to offer in the way of expertise to the council in setting up neighbourhood offices .... There is also a role for us, I believe, in the frontline, wherever that is, and neighbourhood offices are obviously such places ...., let's be in there .... as we can help to facilitate what the council is doing, but at the same time let's recognise that there has to be an evolutionary and incremental approach .... the most important thing from the public's point of view is to have access to services.

This incremental approach is still taking place. A consultation process with staff and trade unions took place towards the end of 1985. Staff were asked to respond to two consultative documents issued by the director. There were numerous responses from which the social services department will produce its strategy on decentralisation and neighbourhood offices. The aim is to produce a service based on localised service delivery with more decentralisation than at present, to enable a better co-ordination with other services, including neighbourhood offices.

It is envisaged that once the full network of neighbourhood offices has been set up the social services department will close down its existing reception facilities and that all new contact with the public will be through neighbourhood offices. This will mean that the public will be seen by neighbourhood office frontline staff and all problems which do not relate to one of the more specialised social service functions will be dealt with by these staff. This will require very close working relationships between the frontline staff. The principle will be to operate a 'core and cluster' model whereby a core base of a number of social service teams will support a cluster of neighbourhood offices.

Social services input to neighbourhood offices is, at present, minimal and the department has been criticised for the length of

115

time it has taken to formulate a response. This accusation could, however, also be levelled at other departments. It can be argued that the decentralisation working group and the performance review committee should be more forceful in demanding a clear commitment to neighbourhood offices by service departments.

Conclusion

From this it can be seen that there are problem areas needing to be addressed. The role of departmentalism is one example. This has not been challenged successfully. For example, the involvement of one of the main service departments (the social service department) has been limited. There is not 'total service delivery' at local level but where neighbourhood offices have opened, there is local access to services and information. Some of these services are delivered more quickly than others.

The attitudes of neighbourhood office staff are refreshing and their commitment to delivering services which are more consumer-oriented is high. There has been little time for 'regenerating the neighbourhood'. Whilst there is a commitment by staff to this role it is not seen as a priority elsewhere in the council.

The key issue for the immediate future concerns the manner in which the two distinct models of the neighbourhood office (the 'problem solving/advocacy' model and the 'service delivery' model) relate to each other in practice. Unless the two models become integrated into the practice of the new neighbourhood offices the danger is that they will begin to contend with one another. There is nothing in the original job descriptions of the neighbourhood co-ordinators which refers to their role vis a vis localised service delivery staff who are neither 'basic' nor 'posted'. How will the neighbourhood co-ordinator and her/his staff relate to such 'back up' personnel? In Islington the nature of this relationship has been subject to a great deal of thought to ensure that the office provides an integrated service. The potential tension between the needs of the neighbourhood office and the requirements of the service departments whose 'delivery end' has been decentralised into the office is very real. If this tension were to find expression within Birmingham's neighbourhood offices rather than between the offices and the service departments we believe this could pose very severe problems for the entire initiative.

The final issue requiring some attention is the possibility of slippage from the ideal of the problem solving/advocacy and service delivery role into an altogether more damaging form of practice. Many of our respondents, particularly those with trade union or community sector backgrounds, have expressed strong anxieties that in reality the neighbourhood offices will become a further buffer between the consumers and producers of local authority services. These anxieties find their parallel in similar arguments which have been made outside of the Birmingham context. It is an unfortunate coincidence (and some would say it is no coincidence) that decentralisation has emerged as a popular strategy within local government at precisely the time when the recession and financial cutbacks mean that the gap is at its widest between the supply of public services and demand for them. Given its tradition of underspending, in a city such as Birmingham this situation is possibly even more severe than elsewhere.

In such a situation it is vital that the resources that are available are fully devolved to the neighbourhood office level and, if the experience of local authorities who have already opened such offices is anything to go by, this Is particularly true for housing 'repairs and maintenance' and housing benefits. As Walsall and Islington have already shown, if the control and delivery of repairs and maintenance can be decentralised then the increase in productivity can be quite startling. A risk for Birmingham is that the neighbourhood offices could come to play the 'sacrificial role' outlined earlier when this is clearly not the wish of the city council.

To conclude, whilst noting a general trend in favour of decentralisation, we emphasised that 'decentralisation' is a term which can be used to provide a kind of camouflage behind which a diverse range (of sometimes incompatible) political and organisational strategies can find cover. Our research in Birmingham has confirmed the importance of avoiding generalising too broadly about 'decentralisation'. It is important to examine the particular practice associated with 'decentralisation' in any particular authority before drawing conclusions.

Birmingham's strategy is, as they put it, about action rather than discussion. In our view a high speed of change is all very well provided the council invests effort in learning and review. A risk is that the sheer pace of change gives insufficient time for thought and that, once established, structures and arrangements become entrenched and difficult to modify.

Notes and References

1. **Briggs, A.** (1952) History of Birmingham, Vol 2, Oxford: University Press.

2. **Bailey, S. and Meadows J.** (1984) 'High spending cities: an historical perspective', Public Money, June, pp 21-26.

3. **Travers, T.** (1984), 'Ranking local authorities: the Lilley league tables', Public Money, March, pp 47-53.

4. **Newton, K.** (1976) Second city politics, Oxford: Clarendon Press, p 241.

5. **Public Sector Management Research Unit** (1985), Five year review of the Birmingham Inner City Partnership, University of Aston Management Centre, January, p 8.

6. **Fudge, C.** (1984), 'Decentralisation: socialism goes local?' in Boddy M. and Fudge C. (eds), Local socialism?, London: Macmillan.

7. Matrix management is discussed further in **Hambleton, R.** (1978) Policy planning and local government, London: Hutchinson, p 300.

8. **Hoggett, P. et al** (1984) 'The politics of decentralisation in Hackney' in Hambleton, R. and Hoggett, P. (eds) The politics of decentralisation, Working Paper 46, School for Advanced Urban Studies, University of Bristol.

9. **Price Waterhouse** (1983) Review of the social services department, unpublished report to the City Council, January.

10. **Ibid** para 6.

11. **Amos, J.** (1977) 'The Birmingham saga', Corporate Planning Journal, Vol 4, No 2, p 13.

12. **Wilkinson, C.** (1977) Ibid p 20.

13. **Schon, D.A.** (1971) Beyond the stable state, London: Temple Smith.

14. **Stewart, J.D.** (1974) The responsive local authority, London: Charles Knight; **Hambleton R.** (1978) Policy planning and local government, London: Hutchinson.

15. Evidence for this is anecdotal, but it is supported by a couple of dissertations: **Bell, J.** (1976) A case study in the application of contingency theory: the management of Birmingham City Council 1961-76, M Soc Sci Dissertation, Institute of Local Government Studies, University of Birmingham; **Baldwin, W.S.** (1984) Area approaches to local government in Birmingham, M Sc Dissertation in Public Sector Management, University of Aston, Birmingham.

16. **Dunleavy, P.** (1980) Urban political analysis, London: Macmillan.

17. **Wilkinson, C.** (1977) op cit reference (12).

18. **Hambleton, R.** (1978) op cit.

19. **Gyford, J.** (1983) 'The new urban left: a local road to socialism?' New Society, 21 April, pp 91-93.

20. **Hambleton, R. and Hoggett, P.** (eds) (1984) The politics of decentralisation: theory and practice of a radical local government initiative, Working Paper No 46, Bristol, School for Advanced Urban Studies, University of Bristol, Chapters 4 and 5.

21. **Wolmar, C.** (1984) 'Divided we stand', New Society, December, pp 13-15; **Sharron H.** (1985) 'Overcoming trade union resistance to local change', Public Money, March, pp 17-23.

22. **Hoggett, P. et al** (1984) op cit, reference (8).

23. **Clark, D.** (1986) The neglected factor. Towards a community strategy for Birmingham, Community and Youth Work Department, Westhill College, Birmingham.

24. **Hambleton, R. and Hoggett, P.** (eds) (1984) op cit, Chapter 1.

6

AREA REPAIRS : A NEW DEAL FOR TENANTS OR PAPERING OVER THE CRACKS?
Edward Pilkington and Tim Kendrick

Since 1980, an ever increasing number of left-wing local authorities have adopted decentralisation as a means of defending local government against central government cuts. They have begun by recognising that council services are often bad and at worst hardly worth defending. To this extent, advocates of decentralisation bear something in common with Conservative critics of the welfare state. But whereas the government or Tory local authorities such as Wandsworth use arguments against public services to justify privatisation, the decentralisation camp calls for radical reforms which will improve public services and make them worth defending.

The phrase 'going local' has been employed by its supporters as shorthand for the reforms that they propose - a convenient phrase which obscures the fact that decentralisation has many different aims and objectives. On the one hand it aims to improve services by attacking bureaucratic delay, by cutting through red tape and by creating more 'indians' and fewer 'chiefs'. On the other hand, decentralisation is also about redistributing power within the local authority, both to subordinate officers and workers and, politically, to the wider public.

Housing repairs provides one of the best examples of decentralisation, both in theory and in practice. After all, many local authority repairs services epitomise what is wrong with local government - they are often highly centralised, inaccessible to the public, unaccountable, slow and poor in quality. What this amounts to in practice is that council tenants have virtually no control over repairs and hence their own living conditions. They are severely disadvantaged in this respect compared with owner occupiers. They are pushed into a form of dependence and impotence by institutions that are supposed to be a locally responsive limb of the welfare state. As the Hackney Federation of Tenants' Associations put it:

We believe that the housing stock provided by Hackney Council primarily belongs to the people who live in it. After all they pay for it. Yet tenants are treated as second class citizens and denied many rights allowed other people including non-council tenants.[1]

Central government has played upon the grievances generated by tenants' experiences of council house repairs to justify cuts and privatisation of the service. The Local Government Planning and Land Act 1980 (Sections 8-21) enabled the DOE to make regulations requiring council builders - or Direct Labour Organisations (DLOs) - to compete with private contractors when tendering for contracts and to show a 5% profit at the end of each financial year.[2] The legislation aimed to put an end to the unfair competitiveness DLOs were felt to enjoy as a result of their non-profit making structure supported by subsidies from the rates. However, it has been pointed out that the legislation goes much further than redressing any supposed imbalance between DLOs and private contractors by imposing a profit margin on DLOs which private contractors are currently finding it impossible to meet.[3] To give an indication of how severely the new regulations are likely to affect DLOs, Hackney council has estimated that its DLO must increase its productivity by 15-20% by November 1986 if it is to survive.

In addition, regulations came into effect in January 1986, under Section 24 of the Housing and Building Control Act 1984, giving tenants the right to carry out their own housing repairs and to claim reimbursement from the council.[4] Once a tenant has told the council that she/he wishes to carry out a repair, the onus will be on the council to either carry out the repair within six weeks or come up with a legally valid reason why the tenant cannot do the work. Although it is hard to assess how effective the regulations will be, due largely to their enormous complexity for both tenants and landlords, they are likely to provide another strong incentive for councils to improve the efficiency of their DLOs.[5,6]

The housing led approach to decentralisation

So the general context within which decentralisation is operating embraces poor repairs services, a lack of tenant control and DLOs threatened with extinction. Area repairs initiatives set out to tackle some or all of these issues. Advocates claim that area repairs can improve the service whilst both strengthening the DLO and increasing tenant involvement. With so much expected of it, no wonder then that the reorganisation of repairs has become a number one priority in many authorities committed to going local.

Only a few councils, such as Islington and Birmingham, have opted for a comprehensive and interdepartmental approach to decentralisation. Many others, like Lambeth and Walsall, have concentrated from the beginning on housing and the repairs service in particular. Others still, intending originally to follow the interdepartmental model, have prioritised housing in the last 18 months as shrinking resources have forced them to moderate their proposals. Sheffield and Hackney are examples of this. Consequently, the majority of local authorities are now pursuing a housing led approach to decentralisation, often prioritising the localisation of repairs.

The typical area repairs team

Traditionally, repairs services have been operated from centralised depots. In these depots, craft workers are organised into specialised teams - for example electricians, plumbers and carpenters. These teams are managed by their own specialist supervisors and are responsible for carrying out work throughout the borough. Advocates of area repairs say that this centralised system is inefficient and provides an unsatisfactory service to tenants. If work on a repair involves more than one craft, for example both plastering and carpentry, then time will be wasted as one specialist team waits for the other to finish.

The system of area repairs, like patch in social services, does away with centralised, specialist teams. Instead, all the main crafts are brought together within multicraft or 'generic' teams at the local level. An average area repairs team (ART) would consist of plumbers, carpenters, plasterers, labourers and bricklayers, with maybe glaziers, electricians and gas fitters as well.

The teams are managed not by specialist supervisors, but by multitrade supervisors who are responsible for the work of all crafts represented in their teams.

One of the most problematic issues that decentralisation raises for both theoreticians and practitioners is how to define the neighbourhood. This is no less the case with area repairs, as different solutions to the problem illustrate. In Islington, for example, there are now 16 ARTs with eight to 10 operatives in each. Each team covers a patch of about 2,000 council dwellings. In Lambeth there are also 16 ARTs, but here the similarity ends. The ARTs have 16 to 20 craft workers in them and cover about 3,500 dwellings. In other words, a 'neighbourhood' in Lambeth is 'worth' two in Islington. These conflicting ideas about what constitutes a local area can largely be explained by the fact that the new area repairs systems have generally been built on top of old political and organisational structures. Departments have tended to adapt area repairs to their existing boundaries rather than vice versa.

However, this has not always proved successful. Different localities generate different levels of demand for repairs, according to the nature of their housing stock - a factor that is rarely reflected within ward or departmental boundaries. As a result, one ART might be swamped with day-to-day repairs whilst another stands idle. This is a problem that is facing all area repairs systems at the moment. In Hackney, for example, there are 20 ARTs each covering about 2,000 dwellings. The management believes that there are too many areas and it is now proposing that they reduce the number of ARTs to increase the viability of the system. In Lambeth, on the other hand, the council suggests that instead of changing boundaries, labour should be shifted between ARTs to ensure that the workload is more evenly spread.

Lambeth's approach illustrates one of the most important features of area repairs - flexibility and a mobile workforce.[7] In Walsall they have taken this to the extreme. In 1981 the borough council set up an area repairs system based in eight mobile caravans. Each of the caravans covers approximately four of the 32 neighbourhood offices in the borough. The teams travel around their patch on a cyclical basis, dealing with one neighbourhood office per week. The craft workers are therefore highly mobile, but there is also considerable flexibility between teams, with labour being frequently shifted according to the amount and type of work needed in each area.

Flexibility has also been built into area repairs in another form - 'generic' work. Here, workers are encouraged to take on new responsibilities and to widen their job descriptions. An example of this is the multitrade supervisors already mentioned. Walsall again has taken this principle furthest. Emergency repairs in Walsall are now done by 'mobile technicians' - salaried workers who are capable of carrying out any work required, even if this means doing plastering, carpentry and plumbing. It is as if all the craft workers have been rolled into one.

Another essential feature of area repairs is that greater communication is encouraged between the housing and building departments. In the old centralised systems, an order for repairs work can take weeks to pass from a housing officer who records the complaint to the building worker who carries out the work.

Sometimes the order gets lost altogether in the town hall corridors. Area repairs aims to cut through the red tape and provide a direct line of communication between local housing officers and the ARTs. The most advanced form of this involves the introduction of a computerised repairs order system with direct access to information on both the housing and building sides.

Does the reorganisation improve services?

A typical area repairs system consists, then, of locally based, multitrade teams, with built-in flexibility and mobility supported by new technology. But how does this improve services? Area repairs has many advantages, the most obvious of which is that the system is more accessible to tenants. Where the localisation of repairs has been most successful, it has been accompanied by the decentralisation of housing services into neighbourhood offices. In Lambeth, for example, the 16 ARTs work closely with 32 local housing offices, all of which have been set up in the last two years. By giving tenants the chance of reporting their repairs complaints more quickly and easily, decentralisation has in effect released suppressed demand for repairs. In Lambeth this has been dramatic - since decentralising housing the council has seen a 20% increase in requests for repairs in only a year.

To an extent, this increase in demand has been matched by an increase in supply, due largely to greater productivity on the part of the Direct Labour Organisation. With operatives based locally, less time is wasted travelling to jobs. The area repairs teams can also complete individual jobs more quickly because of their multitrade team approach. Productivity improvements have been dramatic in some cases, most noticeably in Islington. The building department claims that, as a result of introducing area repairs, the average time to complete a repair has been slashed from 15 weeks to 1.5 weeks, with the number of jobs carried out each week almost doubled.

Statistics such as these are clearly impressive and, if accurate, would denote a radical improvement in the repairs service. A faster turnover for repairs is of obvious benefit to tenants. It is also of benefit to building workers. Area repairs has given operatives the chance of demanding better pay and working conditions. In Islington, for example, the DLO unions used the negotiations over decentralisation to do away with the much hated bonus system, replacing it with flat-rate salaries. In Hackney the trade unions and management have also agreed to scrap the sliding bonus system and in its place they now have stable earnings. Moreover, any 'profits' that are generated within an area repairs team are shared amongst the operatives within that team. These reforms have been generally welcomed by the blue-collar unions who see them as a means of reducing differentials between white and blue-collar workers.

At best, the decentralisation of repairs has strengthened the DLO at a time of shrinking resources and central government attacks. In Lambeth, for example, the council has reacted to the rapid increase in demand for repairs by recruiting 200 new operatives - at a time when most DLOs are issuing redundancy notices. Islington has also taken on around 250 new operatives to service its area repairs.

So the potential is there for area repairs to benefit both workers and tenants. But there are also potential disadvantages. A question mark hangs over the financial viability of the system. Certainly, in Islington the building department is now showing a weekly surplus of about £2,000 which means they are keeping well within the financial restrictions imposed upon them by government legislation. A similar turnaround has been achieved in Walsall DLO's financial fortunes - the DLO made a 'profit' of £1.4m on a turnover of just under £12m in 1984. Elsewhere, however, the financial performance of area repairs has been less impressive. The director of building in Camden, for example, has criticised the pilot local repairs service in King's Cross, saying that "it has not been successful either in management or in economic terms", although he did have to agree that it had increased tenant satisfaction.

At worst, area repairs can increase bureaucratic confusion and delay, as Hackney council has found out the hard way. In Hackney, the new system was introduced with virtually no communication between the housing and building departments, which is an essential factor in any successful scheme. There are now 30 local housing offices and 21 local building bases, but they are often not situated at the same sites. Moreover, the two departments still do not share the same boundaries. Repairs tickets are still passed up from the local housing office to the district level, a process which can take weeks. If the tickets are not lost, they pass back to a local building base which may not even be on the same estate as the housing office where the repair was originally reported. As a result, red-tape has arguably been multiplied by the number of new offices - 30 times! According to a joint union report, area repairs in Hackney, though a good idea in theory, has been so badly implemented in practice that it amounts to "an unmitigated disaster .... the service provided is nowhere near to meeting tenants' needs".[8]

The response of the unions

The trade union response to decentralisation is often portrayed as being negative or obstructive. This has certainly not been the case with area repairs, where blue-collar unions in particular have been at the forefront of developing the ideas behind the reorganisation, as shall be seen. However, housing decentralisation in general has raised a number of legitimate concerns and anxieties for the unions. It is perhaps no coincidence that the essential characteristics of area repairs reflect changes in management techniques that occurred in the private sector some 10 years ago. Local cost centres, flexibility, generic working, interdepartmental communication, increased productivity, new technology are all familiar concepts in private enterprise. Indeed, area repairs is as much about introducing new managerial procedures as it is about improving services to tenants.

Some of these procedures have caused alarm amongst town hall trade unions. Many unionists believe that decentralisation in both the housing and building departments is an attempt to increase workloads without increasing pay. Generic work is regarded with particular suspicion for this reason. Critics have argued that if decentralisation involves increasing workloads for staff without providing adequate financial or staffing resources to run a proper service, then it amounts to do-it-yourself cuts. In some cases these suspicions may well be justified. In Wandsworth, for example, privatising authority par excellence, the housing policy committee produced a report in February 1986 proposing decentralisation to the neighbourhood level in order to achieve 'greater effectiveness in service delivery'. The report implies that this can take place through a redirection of staff involving no extra posts.

Some trade unionists also believe that decentralisation will give management greater control over the workforce. On the one hand, there is a real danger that the power of the unions will be reduced as the workforce becomes locally fragmented, although the unions are trying to prevent this by reorganising their own structures. In addition, they fear that management will use its power to shift labour between areas as a means to further divide and rule.

The introduction of new technology has been problematic in many areas. In Sheffield, for example, NALGO members came out on strike for four months over the way that new technology was being introduced for decentralisation. Manual unions also have their fears in this area. One specific worry is that new technology will allow management to monitor the productivity of not only individual ARTs, but of individual operatives as well. This illustrates one of the paradoxes of decentralisation. Although some responsibility is devolved locally, the centre still has responsibility for overall co-ordination of the service and also controls most of the information required at the local level. Some would argue that because of this power at the centre is increased.

The views of the tenants

Tenants may have a completely different view of area repairs from the council officers who developed them. Whereas council management normally regards area repairs as a means of achieving greater efficiency within the building department, tenants often have far greater expectations, especially in terms of the extent of their own involvement in the management of the service. High levels of tenant dissatisfaction with council repairs services have meant that tenants' own demands have often played a large part in bringing about the changeover to local repairs. In 1981, for example, Hackney Tenants' Federation produced the Hackney repairs report along with council building workers and local estate managers. The report arose as a result of tenants' anger with the time it was taking to get repairs done, as well as the building workers' own frustration with the existing system.

A number of deficiencies were identified, including: too few depots; lack of co-ordination; a deteriorating bonus scheme and, perhaps more significantly, a lack of tenant involvement in the management of the repairs service. The report pointed out that a failure to involve tenants and local estate managers in consultation over repairs had led to a failure to respond to longstanding grievances.

The report came up with a number of proposals which included the setting up of a local repairs service. It also called for the improvement of job security and wages for building workers through the replacement of the bonus system with salaried earnings. The report also argued for the introduction of a system of planned maintenance and cyclical repairs and the setting up of estate joint management teams. It was proposed that these teams should have control of area budgets and include tenants, local estate superintendents, district office staff, cleaners, maintenance workers and local councillors.

Proposals put forward by tenants and trade unionists in the London boroughs of Islington and Camden followed roughly the same pattern, seeking to defend and strengthen the DLO at the expense of private contractors while at the same time creating as strong a link as possible between tenants and building workers.[9, 10] One of their common overriding aims was set out in the Islington report:

> Our proposals are about more than a change in the organisational set-up. They are about upgrading the status and priority given to running council estates, to the people who live on them and the people who work on them (Islington Tenants and Trade Unions, 1981).

Similar tenant demands have preceded the setting up of area repairs in other authorities.

However, in spite of the widespread involvement of tenants in the development of these ideas, very little has been done to assess how well the resulting schemes have lived up to tenants' expectations. Any monitoring normally takes the form of a largely passive reaction to complaints made by individual tenants or tenants' associations. As a result, there are often marked differences between some of the claims being made by councils and the improvement to services actually perceived by tenants.

The same old mistakes?

Interviews carried out with tenants' representatives in a number of authorities have, however, revealed a number of general points which should be of interest to any authorities contemplating decentralising their own repairs service. The most frequently quoted advantages of the new initiatives concern improved accessibility to, and greater familiarity with, local housing officers and repairs workers. In most cases, these benefits are rapidly appreciated by tenants and workers alike. However, even in this area tenants have voiced reservations. Sheffield Tenants' Federation, for example, have pointed out that having a few shorter queues rather than one long one may well have been the only benefit of area based management in Sheffield so far.[11]

The extent to which these benefits are felt also appears to be highly dependent on the level of commitment shown by management in maintaining staffing levels and ensuring continuity of staffing within local offices and depots. One of the most common criticisms of area teams is that they are understaffed and exclude some of the most essential crafts for a particular estate, notably glazing. Tenants also complain that housing officers and building workers are frequently shifted to other areas just as they have built up a relationship with local tenants.

Many tenants also feel that the structures being set up at the local level merely duplicate centralised structures and actually prevent direct communication between tenants and building workers. Where local tenant forums have been set up, for example, these normally involve tenants and housing officers and exclude building workers. This is often resented since many tenants feel that these are the people who know most about the repair needs of estates. Building workers themselves often resent the fact that their relationship with tenants is mediated by housing officers who, they feel, typically blame the DLO for the deficiencies of the repairs system.

The acid test for local repairs is clearly whether or not they lead to quicker and better repairs. In many cases, council claims for improved response times for repairs have been backed up by the tenants themselves and the changeover to local repairs has led to a dramatic increase in the number of repairs requested. This has been most clearly illustrated in Walsall and the London boroughs of Islington and Lambeth, as well as in pilot schemes in other authorities such as Tower Hamlets.

However, proponents of planned maintenance point out that this rapid increase in the demand for repairs should not be used as a measure of the success of the new systems as, ideally, proper maintenance should remove the need for repairs in the first place. As the Hackney DLO convenor recently pointed out, local repairs systems per se do not signify a departure from the traditional 'fire brigade' approach to maintenance.

Lack of involvement

In many instances, claims made for general improvements in response times have not been wholeheartedly endorsed by the tenants themselves. It is claimed that repairs reporting is still difficult and response times still inadequate. To get an idea of why this is often the case, it may be useful to look at some of the areas which tenants feel have not been adequately addressed in the new initiatives.

A common criticism is that there is still too much bureaucracy at the local level. Complicated lines of reporting mean that tenants may still have to go through several officers before they can get anything done. Tenants may also feel that they are not given enough information, especially about how a complaint is progressing and when a repair is likely to be done. However, the main criticism of area repairs initiatives is that they do not tackle the primary issues of tenant involvement and the inadequacy of resources of housing maintenance.

Since the changeover to locally based management is taking place at a time when finance for improving services is more restricted than ever, many argue that tenants' expectations can never be satisfied unless there is a significant transfer of resources to housing maintenance. The latent demand being unleashed by the localisation of housing offices and building depots will simply serve to put even greater pressures on an already overstretched system.

Similar reservations are being voiced about the willingness of councils to devolve any power to tenants. Although estate joint management teams have been set up in some local schemes, notably in the DOE co-ordinated Priority Estate Projects,[12] so far, no borough wide schemes have involved the devolution of any real control to tenants. A number of authorities are, however, moving slowly towards this goal by developing consultative forums at the estate level. In Lambeth, for example, local tenants' associations are encouraged to organise estate strategy meetings where tenants, councillors and officers can discuss specific problems relating to estates. Any issues that cannot be resolved locally can then be referred to district committees at which tenants are again represented. Islington council is also trying to involve local service users in the management of services by setting up 24 neighbourhood forums. Although these forums will be largely advisory to start with, the council is committed to devolving as much power as possible to the local level.

In most schemes, however, tenants still feel that locally based officers and building workers lack accountability. Many tenants object to the widely held view that only 'professionals' can have a say in how repairs are managed. Hackney Tenants' Federation,[13] for example, argue that the decentralisation of housing services in their borough, as organised at present, offers no solution to current problems. They claim that Hackney's present system of area housing bases is not truly 'local' since it has not shifted any power away from the centre. Indeed, power at the centre may actually have increased due to its important co-ordinating role for many functions. The Tenants' Federation insists that decentralisation must be accompanied by the devolution of financial control along with a major shift of resources to housing maintenance.

In this context, they argue that the housing stock can only be properly maintained if all money collected as rent is reinvested in the improvement of tenancies. They want an end to the present system whereby part of the rent income is used to pay for general work carried out on estates which tenants have already paid for in their rates. To do this, they propose the establishment of a 'landlord account', whereby rent income can be used to finance a network of largely autonomous area bases which would administer, with the minimum of bureaucracy, traditional landlord functions such as housing maintenance, lettings and allocations and voids.[14]

Unless the underlying financial contradictions are resolved, Hackney Federation argues that changes in management practices, of the type carried out so far, will have only strictly limited long-term benefits for tenants.

In Hackney, therefore, the council's failure to deliver the goods in the area of local repairs has done lasting harm to council/tenant relations. Despite management's best intentions, it is likely that similar frustrations will arise from decentralisation initiatives in other authorities. Only by making a genuine commitment to devolving control over the day-to-day management of services, backed up by the provision of adequate resources, can councils hope to take sufficient account of the needs and expectations of both front line staff and tenants.

Notes and References

1.   **Hackney Tenants and Building Workers** (1981) Hackney repairs report.

2. **DOE** (1980) <u>Local Government Planning and Land Act, 1980</u>, HMSO.

3. **Gillon, S., Dorfam, M. and Moye, A.** (1981) <u>The Local Government Planning and Land Act 1980 - a layman's guide</u>, TCPA, Planning Aid Unit.

4. **DOE** (1984) <u>Housing and Building Control Act, 1984</u>, HMSO.

5. **Hinchcliffe, P.L.** (1986) 'The statutory requirements of the government's right to repair scheme', <u>Housing Review</u>, Vol 35, No 1.

6. **Youngs, R.** (1985) 'Complexities of right to repair', <u>Local Government Chronicle</u>, 25 January.

7. **Gosney, J.** (1985) 'Walsall's caravan squads repair DLO's image', <u>Surveyor</u>, 18 April.

8. **Hackney DLO Unions** (1985) <u>Building division reorganisation - joint trade union proposals</u>.

9. **Islington Tenants and Trade Unions** (1981) <u>A new deal for council housing</u>.

10. **Camden Tenant/Trade Union Working Party on Repairs** (1983) <u>Repairs, repairs, repairs</u>.

11. **Sheffield Federation of Tenants' and Residents' Associations** (1985) <u>Housing area based management in Sheffield - assessing the problems and proposing alternatives</u>.

12. **DOE, Priority Estates Project** (1984, 85, 86) <u>Peptalk</u>, Issues 1-6.

13. **Federation of Hackney Tenants' Associations** (1984) <u>Proposed structures for landlord area bases</u>.

14. **Federation of Hackney Tenants' Associations** (1984) <u>Landlord account proposals</u>.

7

THE DECENTRALISATION OF LOCAL SERVICES: RHETORIC AND REALITY

Peter Arnold and Ian Cole

Introduction

The growth of interest and support for the development of decentralised services over the past few years is encouraging in its commitment to create more responsive local services and to devolve genuine power away from the Town Hall to the neighbourhood. Let us state from the outset our belief that this positive impulse needs to be enhanced and developed, in the face of so many constraints, difficulties and obstacles. However, the alluring objectives of decentralisation should not blind us to the fact that the actual impact of such initiatives has often been limited or fragmented in practice, and we wish to explore some of the reasons for this disappointing outcome in this chapter.

We feel it is essential to start measuring the rhetorical claims made on behalf of decentralisation against its actual achievements. The time has passed when all the various conflicts and problems arising from these initiatives could be dismissed as mere teething problems. We need to begin the task of confronting the difficulties of programmes for decentralisation in order to achieve a more balanced assessment of their potential. Above all, we need to understand why decentralisation has generally promised far more than it has actually delivered in different services and areas of the country.

Our overall approach to 'going local' initiatives has been prompted, therefore, by a growing unease about the prevailing conventional wisdom as to their value. We feel that the beguiling themes of 'participation', 'responsiveness' and 'democracy' have been interwoven into programmes for decentralisation in such a way that many initiatives have been launched under the shadow of ambiguous, vague and often contradictory objectives. We now sense a growing level of disappointment about the rather limited gains being made by some of the very local authorities which were being heralded as bold pioneers a few years ago. It is not our intention to be unnecessarily defeatist or negative. Yet if the initial enthusiasm for decentralisation has been overstated, there is now an equal danger that the reaction to the perceived failure of the programmes to achieve these objectives will be all the greater. We are fearful that the current sense of the disappointment in several local authorities might develop into wholesale disenchantment and that many of the genuinely valuable ideas and principles behind decentralisation will be summarily dismissed or abandoned.

There have already been occasional warnings that conflicts may arise in the development of proposals for going local:

> There is no single recipe for a local authority to use which will enable it to achieve decentralisation without hiccups.[1]

This might now appear as a rather mild appraisal to those authorities currently suffering from severe bouts of indigestion as they attempt to make progress over schemes for decentralisation. What has happened to the confident scenarios of a few years ago? Is it any longer tenable to describe decentralisation as 'a new vision for local government'?[2] What gains have been made and what lessons can be learned? Answers to these kinds of questions are immediately hampered by the rather loose and limited analysis of initiatives which have been undertaken so far.

The need for critical evaluation

The debate around the decentralisation of local services has been weakened by several factors. First, a London-centred approach has skewed the terms of the debate. Decentralisation initiatives by Hackney, Islington, Camden and Lambeth are of major interest, but these programmes have been shaped by a quite distinctive political, administrative and professional culture which has little resonance elsewhere. Let us take the example of local housing services. The housing profile of many London boroughs is unusual for its highly urbanised environment, the large proportion of flats and the distinctive patterns of tenure. These factors give the organisation of services and the role of housing management a particular emphasis which renders their application to geographically, politically and administratively diverse areas elsewhere very problematic. Several London boroughs have also benefited from financial support from the Greater London Council for decentralisation programmes on a scale unparalleled elsewhere.

A second weakness of earlier debates is that crucial conflicts between the political and managerial aims of decentralisation have been neglected. In particular we sense that a strategy of centralised management control might quite plausibly evolve from a decentralised network of neighbourhood offices and participatory mechanisms. The initial proclamations of the virtues of going local often failed to appreciate that the anticipated political opportunities could be undermined or cancelled out by the managerial response to these proposals.

The provisional and preliminary nature of most decentralisation initiatives undertaken so far has been reflected in largely descriptive and exploratory case studies, which have skirted round awkward problems such as resource allocation, direct and indirect revenue and capital costs, training, professionalism and the changing relationships between consumers, elected members and officers. As a number of local authorities - such as Birmingham, Bradford and Manchester - progress further with their plans, this evasion of key issues and the lack of a comparative dimension is likely to inhibit the development of a genuinely critical approach towards both the managerial and the political consequences of decentralisation.

The political, managerial and professional differences between services now require more detailed consideration. In housing and social services, for example, the status of the two professions, the extent of elected member intervention, the potential for user control and the degree of managerial autonomy are all sharply different. The type of conflicts and pressures emerging from decentralisation initiatives will take on different attributes as a result. The distinct traditions and organisational cultures of local authority services can obviously pose acute difficulties for councils pursuing a multi-agency approach in decentralisation - but these differences need to be elucidated rather than evaded.

Overall, the specification of ambitions, hopes and long-term objectives has completely overshadowed the empirical analysis of the outcomes of different programmes. In view of the often overheated claims about the cultural revolution of going local, the dearth of any systematic research material on a comparative basis is striking. Accounts of different decentralisation initiatives have rarely been set in a broader national framework to permit a fuller assessment of its impact on the mainstream culture and practice of local government.

Symptomatic of the dominant tendency in research is the absence of detailed qualitative or quantitative information on customer or client responses or attitudes to decentralised provision. In one particular case, community reaction was elevated to a mystical, almost spiritual, level of re-awakening.[3] We suspect that a less impressionistic analysis than this might urge a less euphoric view of the gains of decentralisation for tenants and residents, as the intended benefits founder amidst resource constraints. The political consequences of decentralisation have similarly eluded probing analysis. Nicholas Deakin, for example, has questioned the assumption that 'decentralisation is socialist by definition'.[4] We feel this comment needs to be elaborated to balance some of the rhetoric of decentralisation with a clearer account of its political impact - in terms of voting behaviour, party membership and activity, community action and the extent of neighbourhood solidarity. We suggest that one of the ironies of the political support for localised provision is that in practice many a blue cuckoo resides comfortably in decentralisation's apparently red nest.

In short, if the aims of decentralisation have been eloquently stated, analysis of actual performance and managerial or political outcomes has been far less impressive. Paul Hoggett, for example, has noted the sense in which:

> .... decentralisation is an almost 'empty' term, a kind of camouflage behind which a diverse range (of often incompatible) political and organisational strategies can find cover.[5]

The time is surely ripe to penetrate this camouflage - and to reveal the conflicts which lie behind it.

The legacy of the corporate approach

Looking back, one is struck by the parallel between the debate on decentralisation now, and the position of corporate planning ten years ago, offering its own 'new vision' for local government. In many ways the appraisal of corporate management in 1976 was poised at a similar stage to the discussion of decentralisation in 1986. The first flush of enthusiasm was over, and a period of more critical analysis was beginning. Benington,[6] for example, had started to reshape the focus of the debate about the corporate approach and it became clear that the reality of corporate planning and management in local government had not attained the heady heights mapped out for it. As we know, this period of reassessment soon gave way to an all-out assault by critics such as Cockburn[7] and in the withering dismissal by Dearlove.[8] While the legacy of the corporate approach is still nevertheless evident in the attitudes and structures of many local authorities, its potency as an idea has now evaporated. Does a similar fate await decentralisation ten years hence?

The parallels between corporate planning and decentralisation are not merely fanciful. The corporate approach was seized on as a panacea in a period of deep crisis in local government, following the disruption and traumas of reorganisation in 1974. It offered the prospect of altering the balance of political and managerial control and of reorganising the internal structures of local authorities to make service provision more effective. The corporate perspective espoused a new relationship between the council and its local community, under the banner of flexibility and innovation. The Bains Report - the bible of the corporate approach - waxed lyrical about local government extending beyond the 'narrow provision of a series of services' to encompass the 'overall economic, cultural and physical well-being' of the community.[9]

It is striking that all these themes - reorganisation, flexibility, innovation, relationships with the community - find clear echoes in current debates on decentralisation, even if the language of technology has now been dislodged by the language of democracy. If we take the overriding objective of decentralisation - to make services more responsive - we should perhaps also recall that 12 years ago the guru of corporatism, Professor John Stewart, was editing a series of papers on the corporate approach entitled The **responsive** local authority.[10] Although the impetus behind the corporate approach was solely managerial - whereas decentralisation uneasily embraces both political and managerial dimensions - in their different ways, these approaches seemed to offer potential solutions to crucial dilemmas facing local authorities. The confident assertions of the corporate approach were welcome to local government during a period of severe organisational confusion and uncertainty 10 years ago, and the image of political regeneration and managerial responsiveness through decentralisation is similarly appealing now.

The corporate approach is now considered to have failed. However we disagree with those who suggest that it has "faded into the distant memory".[11] We view corporate management as having had a profound effect on the management ethos in local government which constantly recurs in the local debate over decentralisation. With hindsight, it would probably be agreed that the major factors contributing to the failure of the corporate approach were both external - for example, the implicit assumption of growth which foundered on the reality of cutback and contraction in local government - and internal - for example, departmental and professional interest and a resistance to corporate values. We suspect that the debate on decentralisation has so far begun to appraise the external forces, but has seriously neglected internal dynamics and barriers which have in fact exerted a profound effect. Analysis based on the experience of London boroughs, for example, has tended to emphasise elements of conflict with Labour Party and trade union organisations rather than conflicts within the corporate structures of the decentralising authorities themselves.

Our own experience of work with local authorities indicates that the inter-departmental rivalries and antagonism which undermined and irritated the past generation of corporate planners continue to dog the progress of decentralisation, particularly in the provincial setting. The inter-departmental response to initiatives in local estate management such as the Department of the Environment's Priority Estates Project has underlined these difficulties (Department of the Environment, 1984).[12] However, these tensions between different professions and departments are compounded in more comprehensive programmes to decentralise across service boundaries.

One of the great dangers of decentralisation is that it will over-run its potential and that the debate around principles and intentions will set a political and managerial agenda which simply cannot be realised. From a political perspective, the objectives of mobilising neighbourhoods, creating new forms of democratic control and transforming service provision are, in the face of the continued financial and legislative attack on local government, already beginning to wear thin. From a managerial perspective, the objective of changing the culture of a profession or service by bringing together front-line and senior management teams is becoming equally questionable.

The present stage of development suggests quite plainly that decentralisation is, to use David Peryer's phrase, a "high risk business"[13] which must be analysed in much greater depth to avoid its rapid degeneration into engaging but elusive catchwords, catchphrases and caricatures. The two images which emerge as one from decentralisation - of housing repairs clerks transformed into potential freedom fighters and social workers into super general managers, equipped with the full battery of audit, personnel and counsellor skills - send a cold shiver down the spine.

A characteristic of the analysis of decentralisation, therefore, which harks back to discussions of the corporate approach, is the extent to which the debate around principles has become divorced from the realities of going local. Ideas about the corporate process, founded on a rationalist model of decision-making, soon became seriously out of touch with the more prosaic realities - the more established art of 'muddling through' undertaken by management teams, policy committees and so on. Similar difficulties may now beset the developing debate on decentralisation unless a clear-headed empirical analysis is made of the pitfalls, difficulties and obstacles.

The decentralisation of housing services

It was our interest in the extent to which the experience of decentralisation in practice matched the expectations set out for it which prompted a project group at Sheffield Polytechnic to undertake a sample survey of local housing authorities in England and Wales.[14] The survey covered 80 local authorities (18 London boroughs, 16 Metropolitan Councils and 46 non-Metropolitan Councils) and was an attempt to remedy the lack of systematic research on a national scale.

Of the 53 local authorities responding to the survey, 21 were already operating some kind of decentralised service, eight were in the process of introducing plans for decentralisation and the remaining 23 had centralised systems. (One council had recently centralised its service to save costs.) The national survey covered a broad range of subjects - in terms of the objectives of going local, mechanisms for participation, the distribution of housing department functions, links with other services and methods of monitoring. Clear differences emerged between local authorities with established decentralised services (usually a form of area management, often based on pre-reorganisation boundaries) and those authorities currently in the midst of introducing proposals.

We have suggested that decentralisation embraces both political and managerial objectives, often in a rather uneasy combination. When asked to specify the aims of their decentralisation programmes, most respondents referred to managerial aspects such as providing a 'personal' service, improving liaison with tenants and increasing effectiveness. Only two respondents couched their aims in explicitly ideological terms - one referring to 'restructuring the tenant/landlord power relationship' and 'raising political consciousness'.

In ranking the importance of different potential objectives (Table 2), managerial concerns again predominated. While these results may have reflected the fact that questionnaire respondents were senior housing department staff rather than elected members, we suspect that the replies might suggest a process in which politically inspired ideas became incorporated within conventional managerial priorities.

The results in Table 2 show that the most prominent objectives in decentralisation are 'internal' organisational factors concerned with the image and effectiveness of the service. Broader political aims, such as democratising services, were only considered as an important influence by a minority of local authorities, though a degree of political commitment was more evident among those councils in the process of introducing programmes. Certainly, it seems that decentralisation has not been introduced in response to public clamour for local offices - only two authorities mentioned tenant demands as an important factor. The tenor of the responses suggests that decentralisation has been adopted as an internally-generated strategy for survival rather than as a direct response to external economic and social pressures.

The extent and pattern of decentralised service provision varied widely among the 22 local authorities with established systems. In these cases, the issue of decentralisation was first raised by officers in seven local authorities, by the Majority Group in a further six instances and for six councils decentralisation was simply a by-product of local government reorganisation. All but one of the local authorities with decentralised services had an area-based management tier, with areas generally covering from 1,000 to 7,500 council dwellings. Four authorities had just one office, while at the other extreme four authorities had between nine and 12 offices in their system.

12 of the 22 local authorities incorporated neighbourhood based provision into their system, with offices covering around 1,500

Table 2: Objectives of housing decentralisation in 30 local authorities

Objectives		Very important	Fairly important	Not important	No answer	Total
(i)	to improve the effectiveness of the service	22	2	-	6	30
(ii)	to improve accessibility	22	1	1	6	30
(iii)	to improve public relations	15	6	4	5	30
(iv)	to prevent environmental decay	9	8	7	6	30
(v)	to increase cost effectiveness	8	8	8	6	30
(vi)	to make services more democratic	8	10	6	6	30
(vii)	due to the political commitment of the Majority Party Group	8	5	11	6	30
(viii)	to reduce bureaucracy	6	6	11	7	30
(ix)	to increase job satisfaction	5	8	10	7	30
(x)	to improve security on estates	2	10	12	6	30
(xi)	due to tenant demands	2	8	14	6	30

council dwellings on average, though five councils had provision for less than 500 properties. Seven of the local authorities had less than four neighbourhood offices, while, at the other extreme, three councils had more than nine offices.

In the majority of cases, the area and neighbourhood boundaries were determined by council officers, usually following 'common sense' criteria rather than ward or administrative boundaries, though in five local authorities elected members decided the boundaries. In terms of the properties used for office accommodation, 14 of the 22 councils had purpose-built offices, 12 used pre-1974 Town Hall buildings, 11 used prefabricated properties and 10 converted existing houses for use.

The advantages of decentralisation for officers in local government have been presented in terms of devolving power to front-line staff, creating more autonomy and control and maximising staff participation in decision-making about service delivery. The survey results show a different picture. Eight of the 22 local authorities had consulted senior housing staff only and only three consulted all staff in the housing department. There was no example of a staff ballot being held over proposals for decentralisation. Although the majority of local authorities introduced new job descriptions due to decentralisation, only five of the 22 councils had accompanying training programmes for their staff. Only five local authorities had instituted formal negotiations with non-manual and manual trade unions, though the majority of respondents reported general union support (or indifference).

One of the implications of decentralisation in terms of the division of labour in a housing department is the shift from functionally specialised to area or neighbourhood-based management, centred on more generic forms of practice. Seven of the local authorities had introduced generic work at area level, and four at the neighbourhood level, while a further four councils had combined certain specialisms in the process of decentralising. However, the majority of survey respondents had maintained existing specialisation within the service. A fairly common pattern emerged in terms of those aspects of housing management devolved to a local level and those functions retained centrally. Dealing with waiting list and transfer applications, rent arrears, housing welfare, caretaker/warden supervision, and repairs and maintenance were predominantly locally-based; housing benefit, urban renewal, homeless lettings, Right to Buy, liaison with housing associations, project planning and control, capital programme work and research and development functions remained centralised. The decentralisation of housing services is, clearly, functionally selective in practice. The balance of the survey results suggests that the prospects for greater participation and radically different working practices are over-shadowed by other factors involved in the organisational change wrought by decentralisation.

One or two local authorities, notably Islington, have embarked on ambitious schemes for decentralisation, extending reorganisation across a range of council departments. Our survey suggests that such programmes are very much the exception rather than the rule. In nine of the 22 authorities departments other than housing had introduced a degree of decentralisation - primarily social services, environmental health and technical services. However, the same area boundaries were being used by these departments in only four cases, and there was not one example where common neighbourhood boundaries had been adopted by different services. If liaison across departmental boundaries in the local authority was tenuous enough, links with other services outside the council - such as health or probation - were non-existent, according to our survey.

The decentralisation of service provision had often carried with it a strong commitment to the devolution of power and control - as a political parallel to the managerial impulse.[15] For example, Peter Hain, doyen of community politics, has stated that decentralisation:

> .... means offering people services over which they have some direct control, whether through neighbourhood social services or neighbourhood housing offices .... the aim would be to create an alternative socialist network and political culture which the Tories or Alliance would find very difficult to dismantle.[16]

This intoxicating vision, however, remains a very distant prospect indeed. Even on the most elementary level, setting up area or neighbourhood committees, only six of the 28 local authorities had set up area committees, and only one a neighbourhood committee, with a further council establishing a special decentralisation committee. 15 local authorities retained a centralised committee system. Equally illuminating is the finding that, in half the local authorities with decentralised housing services, elected members still direct their enquiries to the central office, rather than the area or neighbourhood office - and councillors knew, more than most, where to go to in the structure to get results.

The setting up of area-based committee structures is, of course, only a small and preliminary step towards the creation of genuinely participatory services at the neighbourhood level. It is here, above all, that the gap between the hopes and the reality of decentralisation opens up into a chasm. All but four of the 22 local authorities with decentralised services had no formal tenant representation on area committees, and in only one case was there equal representation with elected members. Only two of the local authorities provided area budgets specifically for local tenants associations. Furthermore only two councils had consulted tenants groups prior to introducing the programme to decentralise.

An analysis of the eight local authorities in our survey which were in the process of decentralising their housing service suggests a rather different profile from the above picture. While the number of local authorities is too small to permit more than a preliminary appraisal, it is evident that in these cases the decision to decentralise was more often politically inspired and controlled. Similarly, the aims of decentralisation were phrased in terms of accountability and neighbourhood-based participation. Five of the eight authorities had introduced new job descriptions for staff and four had combined certain specialisms in favour of more generic work. These councils were also more likley to devolve a greater range of housing department functions to the area and neighbourhood level. A firmer commitment to staff and union consultation over decentralisation proposals was also evident among the eight local authorities.

Nevertheless, this perceptible shift in emphasis should not be mistaken for a total transformation in outlook. Only two of the local authorities were establishing specialised staff training programmes. Only three of the authorities were to introduce a formally constituted area or neighbourhood committee to parallel the devolution of managerial responsibility and only one local authority was planning to introduce a specific area budget. Formal tenant representation on committees was still strictly limited and the multi-service approach to decentralisation was very much the exception rather than the rule.

The survey results suggest that more local authorities than one might expect are moving away from centralised service delivery in housing towards area-based management in various guises. However, progress in realising the political vision for responsive, participatory local services remains slight. The question remains how far these findings are unique to the housing service, or whether similar dilemmas and problems arise elsewhere. The shortage of comparative data on a national basis prevents a conclusive answer. Nevertheless, while we would not expect a precisely similar profile of conflicts and problems in the personal social services, for example, we sense that our broader claim - about the gulf between the rhetoric and reality of decentralisation - would still prevail.

The decentralisation of social services: different demands, different dilemmas

As in the housing service, the decentralisation of personal social services embraces political and managerial dimensions. However, due to the complexity of social services, in terms of the range of groups and problems it addresses, the balance between fieldwork, residential and voluntary effort and the contemporary importance of the 'care in the community' ethos, one distinguishing characteristic of its decentralisation has been the noteworthy balance struck between political and managerial elements. In the London boroughs, where traditions of neighbourhood action and participation have been well developed, the political imprint has been the strongest; in provincial settings, such as East Sussex and Humberside, the managerial design has been dominant.[17] Social services' capacity to absorb and respond to seminal reports such as Seebohm[18] and Barclay,[19] which have emphasised the need to break down bureaucracy, democratise and provide community based services, is evident. Indeed this marks off social services from housing, for which no such erstwhile pronouncements exist.

Since the late 1970s the growing politicisation of local government has affected social services at the same time as the equally influential, if largely unresolved, debate over genericism versus specialism. While these are both important and relevant to decentralisation, it would be wrong to bind them in a cause and effect relationship with it.[20] To evaluate properly the impact of decentralisation, it is important to recognise that some social services departments have taken up several of the themes of decentralisation without formally accepting it in toto. The presently highly selective accounts of social services departments experiencing change emphasise a holistic approach which we believe has been the exception rather than the rule.[21,22] We suggest that a wider empirical evaluation of social services would indicate: first, that the switch to patch or neighbourhood based work has occurred for many authorities without any deeper perception of the principles of decentralisation; and second, that decentralised provision has not signalled the demise of central and hierarchical management.[23],[24] In respect of this last point, while initial evidence suggests greater professional autonomy for social workers, ultimately management control and power remain centralised and firmly in place.

Critical comment on patch and neighbourhood based services has pointed to the gulf between the aspirations and realities of patch and has emphasised the importance of appraising these initiatives in terms of the broader ideology of community care.[25] As local authorities move further forward with plans to implement 'care in the community' schemes, we believe that the already evident contradictions of decentralisation will be compounded further. For example, conflicts may arise between clients and social workers, social workers and their social work managers, and the competing demands of different client groups, due to an inadequate resourcing of care in the community initiatives. Robert Pinker has already warned that "inadequately-funded decentralisation will almost certainly founder and the only positive result will be a shift in opprobrium from the centre to the periphery of local government services".[26] The consequences of this failure occurring in parallel to failure in care in the community might undermine the whole credibility of community based social work, community care and decentralisation at one go.

It is only recently that the debates on decentralisation and care in the community have merged. One contributor has addressed different strategies for decentralisation and its problems and potential and concludes that "decentralisation seems to be a necessary but not sufficient condition for care in the community".[27] While there is undoubtedly a direct relationship between the two initiatives what may be most evident is that those social services organisations which have experienced structural change occasioned by decentralisation merely respond more swiftly to the requirements of community care. This need not, however, imply that decentralisation is necessary for community care, though it may be beneficial.

To develop a more complete appreciation of decentralisation and care in the community it is necessary to recognise the impact of changes on consumers of the service and on inter-agency relationships and structures. In a recent criticism of decentralisation, Howard Glennerster has noted that in issues of resource bargaining and planning, social service organisations may have to develop centralist techniques and strategies, particularly in negotiations with the Regional Bodies in the National Health Service. The situation clearly reveals several paradoxes:

How does this pull to more centralised strategic discussions link up with the patches which have to pick up the consequences? Just how autonomous can a patch be when decisions that will decisively affect the demand for its services and the number of extremely vulnerable people in the community are taken far away and with little or no reference to it.[28]

The goal of creating a comprehensive network of local services within a single organisation has proved difficult enough in the context of social services without their pressing on too far with mechanisms for collaborative work and joint planning. On this theme Glennerster has sounded an important note of warning, that concentrating managerial attention on decentralisation may draw attention and enthusiasm away from improving the links between personal social services and the health services on which community care primarily depends.

In view of the rapid rate at which care in the community initiatives will now have to develop particularly for groups such as the mentally handicapped and the mentally ill, the immediate prospect is that the major impulse for structural change in social services will be derived from this source. Until there is a clearer identification of the relationship in policy and practice between decentralisation and community care, there may indeed be dangers of making 'yet another well meaning mistake'.[29]

We have argued that in housing internal and external constraints have often been neglected in discussions of decentralisation. Similarly, in the case of social services internal factors - such as staff and client attitudes, managerial and fieldwork responsibilities - and external factors - such as government policies on community care - have generated a more varied experience than is suggested in the literature. In reviewing more widely the decentralisation of social services there is a need: first, to assess empirically the scale and extent of decentralisation of social services and the various motives behind it; second, to evaluate the impact of decentralisation on management and fieldwork structures and the extent to which decentralisation has shifted division of labour from functional specialism to area-based generic practice; third, to assess the implications of decentralisation, in the context of care in the community, for the allocation and rationing of resources;

and, finally, to consider the extent to which decentralisation of social services has actually improved accessibility, responsiveness, social work effectiveness and public credibility. This heavy agenda for evaluating the impact of decentralisation can only be achieved by developing a different analytic framework which can embrace hitherto neglected ares of research.

Priorities in evaluating the impact of decentralisation

As a starting point for a more focused evaluation three dimensions of decentralisation in particular require more study. The first is alluring but difficult to achieve, the second and third are more apparent but still under-developed propositions. The first would concern resistance to decentralisation - eliciting information on the flavour of the political and managerial opposition to decentralisation. The second would focus on decentralisation and management control - analysing how the radical principles of decentralisation may have been subverted or incorporated by managerial control. The third aspect concerns continuous monitoring and appraisal of the progress of decentralisation.

In assessing resistance to decentralisation a preliminary orientation concerns the extent to which decentralisation cuts across paternal and authoritarian traditions of representation and management and the established sanctity of departmental independence in local government. Given this, it is likely that principles emphasising the breaking of bureaucratic power and the changing of professional and managerial values will meet with resistance. As we have suggested earlier, the corporate approach in local government foundered partly on departmental isolationism: we believe that empirical evidence from those authorities which have made slow progress towards decentralisation - Sheffield, Kirklees, Southwark, Hackney - demonstrates that organisational obstructions have not been eradicated by the more direct and less technocratic purposes of decentralisation. Other processes have also been at work. For every proposal to decentralise, there seems to be a countervailing argument emphasising wider financial, managerial and political implications and this has resulted in plans for decentralisation often being stalled, or moved back into the less risky world of traditional service management. Furthermore, in those authorities where individual officers have been specially appointed to separate units as the staunchest advocates of decentralisation, there is evidence of their professional marginalisation. These patterns suggest that an inquiry into internal resistance to decentralisation is both tenable and necessary if we are to understand why progress has so often been disappointing in practice.

Resistance to decentralisation has not only come from management - though arguments referring to disruption of career patterns, prohibitive capital and revenue costs, the need for more education and training and front line staff are now part of decentralisation's stock in trade. Resistance has also come from local political and trade union sources. The experiences of some of the London boroughs especially have underlined how trade union resistance can prove decisive, while at the party political level decentralisation has not always won unanimous approval in local party structures. Our analysis of the local politics of decentralisation would incorporate assessment of the grass roots appeal and the potential (if sometimes empty) radicalising effect of decentralisation. However, in contrast to the original intentions of a broadly-based strategy the political leadership of a few - the Leader of the council and chairs of major service committees, such as housing or social services - has often proved ultimately the most effective influence in the political dialogue. While the initial involvement of those ideologically committed to decentralisation has been clear, very often a more pragmatic route - reconciling managerial and political considerations - has eventually been selected.

In stating that the theme of <u>decentralisation and management control</u> merits systematic attention, a clearer account of the structures and organisational frameworks which have emerged with decentralisation is required. One of the ironies of the current local debate on decentralisation is that it has occurred at the same time as an equally important call for effective management in local government. With its emphasis on a complete shake up of managerial and fieldwork responsibilities, the political requirement for decentralisation can ironically create the scope for a 'Rambo' style of local government management which takes out tiers of functional responsibility and rolls them together, and secures the dominant position of central management with the added justification of political support. If a critical eye is cast over the network of decentralised offices which has generally emerged, there is little doubt that service provision has been moved further forward. However, one of the chief complaints of neighbourhood workers is that their powers and responsibilities are still circumscribed by the centre - the only locus now capable of taking the wider strategic view and legitimising its control over neighbourhood officers in the process.

In analysing the structures and organisational frameworks which have been established for decentralisation in various parts of the country, one of the initial impressions gained is of the limited extent to which the devolution of power has accompanied the decentralisation of management. We believe it unlikely that this has occurred inadvertently and suggest that this impasse may reflect the success of managerial controls in diluting political proposals (assuming they were sincere in the first instance). Several authorities have established specific working parties or committees to discuss decentralisation, and specialist units to promote and serve them. Each of these measures has, however, often combined to keep the political debate about decentralisation at the centre, where managerial control is also at its most effective. We are not suggesting that senior management in decentralising local authorities has consciously conspired to perpetrate a cruel hoax on local politicians, other local government workers and members of local communities. However, in advancing the view that in many decentralised systems a management strategy to control decentralisation from the centre has almost effortlessly evolved, we feel that the suggestion of intent merits more systematic consideration than it has received so far.

The third aspect of decentralisation which urgently requires more attention is the monitoring of its impact by local authorities embarking on these programmes. In many areas, support for decentralisation has revolved around anticipated improvements in the quality of the service provided, yet it is striking that very few local authorities have even rudimentary systems of monitoring and appraisal to assess how the service is changing. We would not underestimate the difficulties involved, particularly in measuring less tangible, more qualitiative aspects of service delivery. In fact we would urge caution against the uncritical application of performance measures - such as those suggested for housing by the Audit Commission[30] - without careful regard to the interpretation of changing trends. However, at the moment, the diffuse and imprecise objectives of decentralising services are compounded by a sheer lack of information - whether at senior management level or at the 'front line' - on how changes in structure percolate through into the service provision.

Due to lack of an adequate information base in most local authorities, basic questions about decentralisation - the costs involved, the additional level of demand caused by localising services, changes in consumer response or staff attitudes - can only be assessed intuitively. The initial managerial and political investment in the idea of decentralisation is simply not matched by a parallel degree of attention to the progress, problems, costs and benefits once the programme is underway. Those local authorities planning to embark on a strategy of decentralisation therefore find that the impact of initiatives undertaken elsewhere cannot be applied to their own context.

The themes of internal resistance, management control and monitoring in decentralisation are illustrative of a wider problem. The current state of progress in many programmes suggests that the mercurial concept of decentralisation has become beset with confusion and contradiction. Underlying assumptions need to be subjected to effective empirical analysis, to anchor some of the more elusive claims made for going local.[31] To indicate the manner in which this appraisal might be developed, five such assumptions about decentralisation are considered below:

(1) **Decentralisation breaks bureaucratic power** As we suggested earlier, many of the delays in implementing proposals indicate that the capacity of local government bureaucracy to frustrate and incorporate innovation is not diminished with the challenge of decentralisation. Furthermore, many local authorities have in fact set up rather <u>clumsy</u> organisational structures - often led by a small, and centralised, unit - to promote decentralisation.

(2) **Decentralisation changes officer values** While we accept that the impact of decentralisation may be difficult to evaluate here, we wonder whether initial changes in attitude are often fairly transient, particularly if localised provision is contained within relatively unchanged hierarchical management structure at the centre.

(3) **Decentralisation increases job satisfaction** While going local seems to offer the prospect of greater autonomy and more flexible working conditions, it can also create new pressures, due to the demands of generic practice, or the increasing numbers of inquiries, or the more exposed conditions which place staff at greater risk of physical assault. The debate in these early stages of decentralisation has often been framed by the content of trade union negotiations over gradings and job descriptions. The broader parameters of the officer response to new practices now needs to be brought into account.

(4) **Decentralisation redistributes resources** The redistributive potential of going local, focusing more resources on priority areas (however defined), has been proclaimed far more than it has been evaluated. When more information is available on access to services and community responses to decentralisation,[32] the argument for redistribution may look firmer. Until then, we need to be convinced that the gate-keepers have not just been moved further down the line. We suspect that the growing literature on the unintended differential outcomes of service provision[33] may prove unsettlingly relevant to the debate on decentralisation.

(5) **Decentralisation is politically regenerative** This assumption is, of course, another which defies firm acceptance or refutation. However, we might wish to counterbalance this view with an alternative account, which suggests that local residents and tenants may be taking an instrumental, rather than politically inspired, approach to neighbourhood provision when they leap to the defence of their local offices, as happened in Walsall.[34] It is not necessarily the dawn of a socialist renaissance at the local level.

While these five assumptions about decentralisation are by no means a comprehensive statement of the outstanding issues for further evaluation and scrutiny - the potential agenda is much larger - they do help to indicate the direction we think that future analysis should take, if a more critical perspective is to emerge. But, whatever the approach, the paucity of detailed research on the issues arising from decentralisation is quite astonishing when one considers the prominence of the idea in debates and proposals for the future of local services and local government.

Conclusion

There is a clear danger at present that many of the expectations of the decentralisation of local services have been set too high, without due regard for the professional, political, managerial and economic pressures and constraints which apply. It is, of course, often only too easy to puncture over-inflated ideas without presenting alternative ideas or proposals. However, we hope we have suggested here positive ways in which the ideological commitment and vision necessary to sustain the belief in decentralisation can be balanced with a firmer analysis of the practical difficulties of such initiatives. While a number of local authorities such as Islington have made considerable progress in building on the Walsall initiative, these advances should not blind us to assessing and acknowledging failures and conflicts. Unless a clearer understanding of these problems is reached, we are concerned that the 'bandwagon effect' of decentralisation may be halted, or even start to move in the opposite direction, as the idea becomes unjustly discredited.

Decentralisation has been variously projected as a strategy to revitalise local communities, regenerate local government and instigate a broader political movement for the future. Decentralisation, it would seem, is local government's last chance. Therein lies our greatest fear. If, for whatever reason, decentralisation is perceived to 'fail' - just as the corporate approach is now considered to have failed - then the current threats to local government will loom even larger. At present, the attack on local authorities - through privatisation, expenditure cutbacks, central government control and the intrusion of non-elected bodies - is virulent enough, without local government being unintentionally weakened even further by those who attempt to save it.

Notes and References

1. **Hambleton, R. and Hoggett, P.** (1984) The politics of decentralisation, Working Paper No 46, School for Advanced Urban Studies, University of Bristol, p 97.

2. **Polytechnic of Central London** (1985) Going local Nos 2 and 3, Decentralisation Research and Information Unit.

3. **Seabrook, J.** (1984) The idea of neighbourhood, Pluto.

4. **Deakin, N.** (1984) 'Two cheers for socialism' in **Wright, A., Stewart, J. and Deakin, N.** (eds) Socialism and decentralisation, Fabian Tract 496.

5. **Hoggett, P.** (1985) Political ideology and the nature of decentralisation, ESRC/Rowntree Housing Studies Seminar Report, Sheffield.

6. **Benington, J.** (1975) Local government becomes big business, CDP Occasional Paper No 11.

7. **Cockburn, C.** (1977) The local state, Pluto.

8. **Dearlove, J.** (1979) The reorganisation of local government, Oxford University Press.

9. **Bains Report** (1972) The new local authorities: management and structure, HMSO.

10. **Stewart, J.** (1974) The responsive local authority, Charles Knight.

11. **Clapham, D.** (1985) 'Management of the local state: the example of corporate planning', Critical Social Policy, Winter.

12. **DOE, Priority Estates Project** (1984) Peptalk, Issues 1-6.

13. **Peryer, D.C.** (1985) 'Neighbourhood teams and neighbourhood management: the decentralisation of social services'. Transcript of Paper presented at Conference on The decentralisation of local services: managerial and political perspectives, Humberside College of Higher Education, September.

14. **Bentley, H., Button, C., Elliot, T., Hortop, G., Morris, A., Reynolds, G. and Wormald, K. (et al)** (1985) Decentralisation of housing services: a national survey, Sheffield City Polytechnic.

15. **Blunkett, D. and Green, G.** (1984) Building from the bottom: the Sheffield experience, Fabian Trust 489.

16. **Hain, P.** (1985) 'Socialist vision and Labour strategy', The Chartist, No 109, November.

17. **Community Care** (1985) Down your way: special issue on decentralisation, 18 April.

18. **Seebohm Report** (1968) Report of the committee on local authority and allied personal social services, Cmnd 3703, London, HMSO.

19. **Barclay Report** (1982) Social workers: their roles and tasks, London: Bedford Square Press.

20. **Pinker, R.** (1985) 'Against the flow', Community Care, 18 April.

21.   Hadley, R. and McGrath, M. (1984) <u>When social services are local: the Normanton experience</u>, Allen and Unwin.

22.   Hadley, R., Dale, P. and Sills, P. (1985) <u>Decentralising social services: a model for change</u>, Bedford Square Press.

23.   Beresford, P. and Croft, S. (1982) <u>Democratising local services</u>, Battersea Community Action.

24.   Brownlow, J. (et al) 'Hackney goes local', <u>Community Care</u>, 7 April.

25.   Croft, S. and Beresford, P. (1984) 'Patch and participation: the case for citizen research', <u>Social Work Today</u>, 17 September, pp 18-24.

26.   Pinker, R. (1985) op cit, p 21.

27.   Hatch, S. (ed) (1985) <u>Decentralisation and care in the community</u>, Policy Studies Institute.

28.   Glennerster, H. (1985) 'Decentralisation and inter-service planning' in Hatch, S. (ed) <u>Decentralisation and care in the community</u>, Policy Studies Institute.

29.   Ibid, p 57.

30.   Audit Commission (1986) <u>Managing the crisis in council housing</u>, HMSO.

31.   Labour Co-ordinating Committee (1984) <u>Go local to survive</u>, Labour Co-ordinating Committee.

32.   Beresford, P. and Croft, S. (undated) <u>Perspectives on patch</u>, Lewis Cohen Urban Studies Centre.

33.   Le Grand, J. (1983) 'Making re-distribution work: the social services' in H. Glennerster (ed) <u>The future of the welfare state</u>, Heinemann.

34.   David, J. (1983) 'Walsall and decentralisation', <u>Critical Social Policy</u>, No 7.

PART 3
MANAGING CHANGE

8

GOING BEYOND A 'REARRANGEMENT OF THE DECKCHAIRS': SOME PRACTICAL HINTS FOR COUNCILLORS AND MANAGERS

Paul Hoggett

During the last few years, as an increasing number of decentralisation initiatives have come on stream, it has become clear that many organisations are making a bit of a hash of things. Such criticisms have emerged particularly strongly from front-line staff who have been at the spearhead of such initiatives. Typically, they argue that whilst they now find themselves in new local offices nothing else has changed. Indeed, in some respects things have worsened - they have been made more accessible to service consumers but have few powers to match consumers' increased expectations. Worse still, far from being empowered by their own organisations many front-line staff feel that since localisation their management has trusted and supported them <u>less</u> than before.

If one studies the history of many of these organisations one is struck by the amount of fudging that has been going on.   In particular one is struck by the existence of an often unexamined assumption, held by councillors and senior officers alike, that real change is possible without real pain. We shall examine some of the effects of this assumption in more detail later but it will be useful to summarise the most important consequences here:

(1)   the 'buying off' of resistance has produced accommodation to change but not commitment;

(2)   senior and specialist staff tend to introduce forms of decentralisation which leave them untouched: this has brought about the 'localisation' of 'going local';

(3)   changing structures and procedures is one thing; changing attitudes, values and behaviours is another.

Therefore the first question that those contemplating decentralisation must ask is "What game are you in?" The creation

of neighbourhood offices, in and of itself, is likely to change
nothing. Paradoxically enough several organisations, even some in
rate-capped local authorities, have found it easier to find the
capital to open neighbourhood offices and the revenue to create a
few more posts than to tackle the thorny organisational issues
involved in delegating real powers to front-line staff, overcoming
organisational rigidities embodied within the specialisation of roles
and functions, or introducing new forms of democracy and
accountability.

It is as if decentralisation were some kind of limb which could be
grafted on to the existing organisation. It is well known that
organisations very often try to cope with the threat of change by a
process of marginalisation and isolation. Thus one finds many
organisations who say they are in the business of decentralisation
yet are actually in the business of damage limitation. Figure 3
describes one typical strategy here:

Figure 3

Here the organisation is divided into two zones; change is focused
upon 'public contact staff' (which tends to be the 'low status' bit of
the organisation in terms of the proportion of highly paid posts) as
if one bit of the organisation could change its approach while the
other bit remained the same. What this often leads to is the
creation of decentralised teams who do not even have control and
responsibility for their own administrative staff let alone anything
else! The assumption is that financial management, policy
development and co-ordination, capital programming, specialist

services, etc are not really in the front-line of decentralisation. Interestingly enough one often finds exactly the same method of marginalising the impact of change at work within organisations which say they are in the process of introducing equal opportunity policies.

If decentralisation is to be anything more than simply an attempt at localising certain bits of service delivery then it will require changes to the structure and practice of the whole organisation. Localisation of service delivery, if it occurs unaccompanied by any efforts towards greater delegation and reintegration, simply creates a 'neighbourhood buffer' between consumers and the local authority resources they require. Real delegation requires a fundamental break with the management structures and practices which characterise most local authority departments. It requires a fundamentally different approach to, among other things, financial control, staff development, recruitment and service-evaluation. Yet one can count the number of so called 'decentralised' organisations with, say, devolved budgetary or personnel practices on one hand. To an outsider it seems quite absurd that many recently created 'neighbourhood teams' have no say whatsoever over the appointment of new team members, yet many departments for whom decentralisation is just another thing to be 'grafted on' see no paradox in this at all!

Of course if an organisation is to face the issue of delegation and sevice reintegration squarely there will be losers, and many of these will be located at senior managerial and professional levels of the organisation. We argue in the final chapter of this volume that decentralisation can be seen as an expression of a much broader paradigm of organisation which has been emerging within both private and public sectors over the past decade. Taking advantage of developments in information technology the new paradigm seeks to achieve the goal of better management by getting rid of managers, just as the automated factory achieves higher production by making many of its producers redundant. The perception that local government is over-managed but underled is as accurate as it is hurtful. If real change is intended then organisational decentralisation must mean fewer managers, flatter hierarchies and a shift towards more self-managing and self-monitoring work units.

This must lead to major changes in the way in which traditionally centralised functions are organised. Whilst it is impossible to be prescriptive (as each organisation needs to work out a structure which meets the specifics of its own environment) logically it does lead to something of the following order:

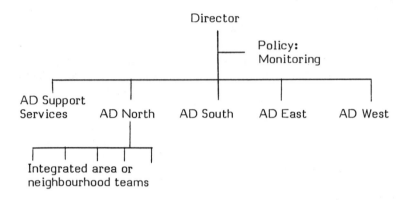

In other words a reorganised top-management structure should reflect the priority given to 'spatial' over 'specialist' principles of organisation. The bulk of financial, administrative, personnel and specialist functions would be delegated to the newly constructed area teams. In the context of social services departments this would necessarily imply the abandonment of specialist divisions based upon residential, day care, domiciliary and fieldwork functions, and their reintegration at neighbourhood team level (eg Islington, Humberside). In the context of housing departments this would necessarily imply the abandonment of public sector, private sector and technical/development services boundaries and their reintegration within local multi-disciplinary (eg Newham) or generic (eg Walsall) teams.

The role of the centre

Clearly there is still a role for some residual financial and specialist functions at the centre of the organisation. The whole problem of agreeing and adhering to standards of service delivery becomes critical under a decentralised system. Paradoxically experience suggests that non-decentralised systems were actually very bad at setting and evaluating standards of service delivery. The rule was that everything seemed like a priority and therefore no real priorities existed in many organisations. Despite their apparent obsession with management control effective centralised approaches to priority setting and the establishment of performance indicators, etc were rare. In many respects decentralisation should lead both to a strengthening of the 'centre' and the 'periphery' of an organisation and this is particularly crucial where a local authority also has a commitment to equal opportunities policies. In such circumstances there is clearly a need for a kind of centrally located conscience or super-ego from which considerations of equity can be lodged against considerations of democracy.

The issue is not the need for financial and managerial control within a decentralised organisation but how the control function is exercised. Nor is the issue the need for centrally enshrined service delivery standards and performance indicators but how these are developed, decided upon and implemented. The issue of service evaluation is critical here, for clearly evaluation of service delivery is crucial in enabling us to understand whether and how decentralisation works, yet traditional forms of evaluation tend to assume a centralised and bureaucratic model of organisation and are obviously inappropriate.

Evaluation for decentralisation must be:

(1) **Pluralistic and democratic** If the redistribution of power is central to the reorganisation then it is no longer adequate for a small group of senior officers (and possibly a few councillors) to set service standards and performance indicators from above. Such criteria must emerge from a much wider group of actors, crucially involving front-line staff and their managers but also service users and trade unions. The whole problem of management control under the old model was that it failed to appreciate that workers will not be committed to standards and indicators that they have had no say over. Public sector organisations are currently riddled with policies and objectives which in practice are inoperable because those who have conceived of them have never engaged in a dialogue with those who are assumed to be implementing them. A pluralistic and democratic approach would also inevitably involve a willingness to confront conflicting perceptions, priorities and values within the organisation and between the organisation and its environment. Democracy is fundamentally about conflict; those who shy away from conflict should reflect upon their commitment to democratic values.

(2) **Quantitative <u>and</u> qualitative** The old model, in so far as it was concerned with evaluation at all, gave primacy to quantifiable measures of throughput and output (voids, levels). Very often it tended to confuse evaluation with accounting by comparing the unit costs of, say, residential care for the elderly in different establishments in the belief that this would provide the basis for evaluation of service delivery. Decentralisation, on the other hand, gives questions of quality the same status as questions of quantity. It is as concerned with effectiveness as with efficiency, with staff and consumer satisfaction as it is with the control of limited resources. The evaluation of quality of service or product has long been practised within the private sector using market research techniques but it has virtually no echo within the public sector. Some public sector organisations (eg North Warwick Health Authority) are experimenting with 'quality circles'; some (eg the Gateway Project run by Nottinghamshire leisure services department) are experimenting with 'customer circles'; some (eg Newham housing department) are trying out the use of customer questionnaires and programmes of staff interviews to monitor and develop 'quality of service'. However such experiments are few and far between. Again there is a danger of 'grafting on' market research techniques to organisations whose management style and culture are fundamentally antithetical to thinking and reflecting upon what they are doing.

Structure and culture

This brings us to the problem of managerial style and organisational culture. Put most bluntly, it is quite possible for an organisation to change its structures and procedures quite radically yet leave its style and culture (ie the values, attitudes, assumptions and behaviours of workers and managers) relatively untouched. It was mentioned earlier that the issue is not <u>whether</u> management control is exercised under decentralisation but <u>how</u> it is exercised. My own work with team leaders in several decentralised departments suggests that traditional approaches to management have persisted within apparently changed organisations. A typical complaint from team leaders is that very often meetings with their own managers assume the form of an inquisition in which they are interrogated over minor procedural lapses (eg letters to councillors), berated for not meeting targets that they had never been consulted on, and so on. Such clumsy attempts at the exercise of management control are only too frequent and accurately portray a whole generation of public sector managers who think that management is all about targets and objectives and forget that it is also about communication between people.

Of course 'communication', like the term 'decentralisation', is such a 'big' word that it conceals almost as much as it reveals. One thing is clear however: open communication is just not possible within what some writers have termed 'power cultures'.[1] Within 'power cultures' differences and conflicts are latent and suppressed, 'bottom up' communication is almost entirely absent and as a result the people at the top of the organisation (and very often this includes councillors on the relevant committee) are the last to know what is really going on. Like Hitler's bunker, because messengers bringing bad news have always been shot, people quickly learn that 'speaking truth to power' is a risky business. Many organisations seem to think the answer lies in meetings - weekly DMT meetings, weekly divisional or district meetings, weekly team meetings, and so on. The problem is that simply establishing meetings is a procedural solution to what is a cultural problem - if people at the bottom of an organisation feel powerless, distrusted and unvalued no amount of meetings are likely to get them to 'speak up' to managers who do not trust or value them. I once worked with a group of 18 highly talented and experienced area managers who were very perceptive of the failings of their own organisation, yet when we put them in a room with their own divisional manager they were completely unable to articulate to him the criticisms they had expressed so competently to us.

At this point it is worth spending a few moments looking at the 'back-line/front-line' concept of working which has been pushed strongly at Walsall.[2] The essential point being made here is that everyone within a local authority service department should see themselves as engaged in service delivery, not just front-line staff. The difference being that whereas front-line staff deliver services to the public the task of centrally based (ie back-line) staff is to service the front-line staff. Clearly if the role of the back-line changes in this way it would entail a fundamental shift in the attitude and behaviour of middle management and many centrally based staff. The question constantly on their lips would be "how can we best serve our front-line staff?" Not only does this entail the development of 'user friendly' finance, admin and personnel systems, intelligible procedure manuals and policy summaries but moreover it requires a change in the very concept of management. To give a practical illustration of the change required think of a typical meeting between a manager and her/his subordinates: who sets the 'agenda'? Who asks the questions and who is asked questions? Who feels accountable to whom? Who most frequently feels the need to justify their actions? Answering such questions enables us to see how most management meetings are designed to satisfy the needs of managers rather than the managed, moreover they assume an absence of trust and the impossibility of any pattern of accountability other than a hierarchical one (of course councillors are as much to blame for the reproduction of such bureaucratic and hierarchical cultures as senior officers).

How then do you change the culture of an organisation? The first thing to realise is that individual change is insufficient and therefore if training efforts are targeted at individuals little organisational change is likely to be achieved. Change interventions must therefore be aimed at groups who share common functional or geographical locations or who 'interface' with each other in a way which is critical to the organisation's behaviour. An example of a group sharing a common functional characteristic would be one comprising all the neighbourhood or area managers within a decentralised organisation. It is interesting to note that very often where such training interventions have occurred these first-line managers have continued to meet afterwards. If the training event was one which allowed and encouraged them to identify their own needs it has often acted as a means whereby they have become aware of a common identity and hence of their potential power. Some organisations have stepped on this very quickly, demonstrating their zero-sum assumption about power (eg "if they've got more of it we've got less of it"). Others have permitted such developments and have sought to take it further, first by enabling all layers of the organisation to join in this way, then by developing training interventions aimed at the boundaries or interfaces between such layers (eg running events exploring the relationship between senior management and first-line management).

Working on the interface between such managerial strata is also vital because of the way each layer of the organisation tends to reproduce, in its dealings with the layer below, the way in which it is addressed by the layer above. I have been struck repeatedly by the way in which local authority organisations tend to reproduce patterns of powerlessness in this manner. The pattern goes something like this: the chief officer and the departmental management team feel they have been rendered powerless by their political members; middle managers feel powerless to do anything about what they feel is an inept and indifferent group of senior managers; neighbourhood team leaders feel they get no support from middle management; neighbourhood staff feel suspicious of their team leaders and doubt their competence; tenants, clients, customers experience front-line staff as remote and unsupportive; councillors in turn feel only nominally in control of an organisation which appears incapable of responding in a way which is congruent with their political objectives. Indeed the reality is that although virtually everyone in such organisations feels powerless they do have sufficient power to silence the layer below. In such organisations there is no open conflict because the exercise of power prevents open communication; instead there is a regime of covert back-stabbing, resentment, low morale and absenteeism.

A key means of intervening in organisational cultures such as these is to enable staff at any level of the organisation to perceive how they reproduce in their own behaviour the very things that they criticise their own managers for doing. Logically, if organisations are to move away from 'power cultures' towards 'democratic cultures' then they must move towards an ethos similar to that adopted by Newham's housing department where the organisation seeks to promote relationships between managers and managed that mirror the new staff-customer relationship which it has adopted as an ideal.

It might be useful at this point to compare some of the values and assumptions implicit in the old model and the new:

Bureaucratic Paternalist	Democratic/Consumerist
1. 'keep your head down'	1. encourage risk and allow for failure - how else do people and organisations learn?
2. 'do the work' (more or less efficiently)	2. don't just 'do the work' but think about how the work is done
3. 'always have an answer ready'	3. asking the right questions may be more important than having a ready answer

4.	an 'accounting' approach to 'evaluation'	4.	evaluation as an integral component of organisational development and learning
5.	communication - telling people to do things they have no ownership of	5.	communication - listening to things you'd prefer not to hear
6.	management is: (a) impersonal, reliant upon written rules, objectives and procedures. As a result many managers have no <u>skills</u> in working <u>with people</u>, they are socially incompetent (b) control via inspection and interrogation (c) intrusive and distracting	6.	management is: (a) personalised - hence managers must be socially competent (b) staff enabled to set own negotiated standards and to hold themselves accountable to these (c) supporting and 'servicing'
7.	organisation is: hierarchical, the key terms are 'top' and 'bottom'	7.	organisation is: lateral, the key terms are 'centre' and 'periphery'

Methods of tackling traditional organisational cultures

Finally it would be useful at this point to summarise some of the principles which might inform an effective approach to organisational change:

(1) Training is vital but one must also recognise its limitations.

(2) Above all it is necessary to go beyond an idea of training which involves taking individuals out of their work situation to be placed on a course. Real organisational change can only be achieved if the trainer works with whole groups of individuals who work together - neighbourhood or area teams, layers of middle management, the top management team, etc.

(3) The change agent needs to work 'vertically' through the organisation as well as horizontally. In other words, only by

166

getting different levels of the organisation together can 'truth be spoken to power'.

(4) Training is often a useful vehicle through which people can acquire new sets of values. But one needs not just to change workers' 'espoused theory', one also has to tackle their 'theory in use' which may be quite different.[3]

(5) The change agent needs to be considered as a kind of trouble shooter or trained subversive. Her essential role is to be disturbing, to force workers and managers to reflect critically upon their behaviour, to keep them on their toes so that they don't fall back into old ways. They must have the personal capacity to be disturbing, confronting and yet also supportive. They will need support themselves. Moreover it is vital that they have the backing of members and senior managers otherwise they will very soon become marginalised.

(6) If organisations are serious about changing rather than tinkering with their structures then they must give time and priority to non-task oriented forms of training - ie training for cultural change.

Notes and References

1. **Reason, P.** (1984) 'Is organisational development possible in power cultures?' in **Kakabadse, A. and Parker, C.** Power, politics and organisations, Chichester: Wiley.

2. **Baddeley, S. and Dawes, N.** (1986) 'Service to the customer', Local Government Policy Making, 12.3.

3. **Argyris, C. and Schon, D.A.**(1978) Organisational learning: a theory of action perspective, London: Addison-Wesley.

9

TRAINING FOR CHANGE IN NEWHAM'S HOUSING SERVICE

Adrian Rivers

Introduction

This is the story of the development of a new training unit within a decentralising housing service. It tells of the struggle to identify a clear role for training and to establish a strategy which would most effectively facilitate the process of radical organisational change.

Brief details of the model of decentralisation adopted by the London Borough of Newham's housing service are set out in the Annex to this book. However, it should be noted that the service is being decentralised phase by phase. Each phase consists of several district offices. A typical district office comprises several new teams - a public sector housing team, a private sector housing team, a technical team and a district resource unit comprising allocations, administration and 'rents and benefits' teams. When all phases are complete there will be a total of 12 district offices, with an average of 30/35 staff per district. This chapter describes the situation relating to training for Phase 1 of decentralisation.

The training unit was established as a direct result of the decentralisation proposals. The unit consists of two training officers who have responsibility for a training budget that, while limited, is three times the size of the 'pre-decentralisation' budget. The training unit's activities which do not relate to decentralisation are not commented on in this chapter.

My background is in housing, but this was my first job as a 'trainer'. Initially I worked with Barbara Lane, who had previously worked as a training officer within the health service, and as a housing officer within a local authority. Barbara left and was replaced by Louise Fox, who had extensive experience in the field of training in counselling skills.

The establishment of the 'Training Unit' - facilitating the process of change

We arrived at Newham's housing service in January 1985. There was no act to follow as we were the first 'in house' trainers to be employed within the department. And there was no detailed strategy for training that had been developed. What to do?

Everywhere around us there was hectic activity. Negotiations for the final staffing structures for the soon to be decentralised service were under way. Valiant attempts were being made to keep the building programme for the new district offices on schedule. We felt confused and isolated. Clearly the focus of our work had to be around the issue of decentralisation, and the first local office was due to open in a few months' time. But where to start? There was certainly no time to carry out a detailed study of training needs, and then set up a series of skills based training courses.

In a state of slight panic we started by reviewing why the training unit had been established.

The rationale for training

It was clear the unit was set up as an integral part of the decentralisation programme. The basic aim of the unit should, therefore, be to help the organisation complete the process of development in a way that ensures that the original objectives of decentralisation are met. So in order to determine the objectives of the training unit we obviously needed to be clear about the reason why the service was embarking on such a radical and extensive period of change.

It seemed to us that the council was working from the following premise:

> Local government is under attack. Cuts in central government funding and increasing constraints are making it more and more difficult for local councils to provide a decent service to their customers. This trend will continue unless our customers decide that the service is worth defending. This is not happening.
>
> Why is the destruction of local government not opposed by the recipients of council services? Clearly the accent in the past has been on local authority rather than local service.

We have not been responsive to the demands of our customers. Indeed we have been perceived as authoritarian, bureaucratic and inefficient. Hardly worth defending!

Decentralisation provides an organisational structure that allows for the development of a service that can respond to the demands of the local community. This can be developed through the establishment of smaller local offices, where the customers can develop a closer relationship with the neighbourhood office staff. In addition, structures of local control can be developed through local forums and area committees which include co-opted representatives of the local community as well as councillors.

Decentralisation aims, therefore, not only to achieve a more efficient form of service delivery. The objective is also to develop a service that is seen by our customers as being responsive to their needs. It is only by achieving this goal that the service has any chance of arresting the decline in its ability to provide for its customers.

So decentralisation can be seen as an <u>accommodation to a change</u> in an environment which is increasingly hostile. However, it is also a <u>commitment to a change</u> in values, with the organisation shifting from a professional orientation to consumer orientation.

But changing the structure of the organisation alone will not develop the changes that are required. We need a radical change in <u>the way</u> in which people working within the organisation relate to the public, to their customers and to their job. If this does not happen we will simply set up a series of 'mini town halls' - which will be seen as equally bureaucratic, authoritarian and inefficient.

It was in recognition of this need to change the <u>culture</u> as well as the structure of the service that the training unit was established. Its role and objectives must be intrinsically linked to the demands of an organisation which has established a new set of objectives and values.

Departmental objectives

So the training unit was established to help the organisation change its relationship with the consumers of the service. Much work had been done in developing an organisational structure. The training unit therefore needed to focus on the organisational culture - the way things were done; how it felt to work within the service or to be a customer of it. The issues we needed to tackle related to the processes of the organisation - issues of style and approach.

While the multitude of council reports on decentralisation did not discuss these issues at length, we did find some clues to the direction that the service should take within the written material that was available:

> The chain of command should be short between the member of the public and the person able to make the decision.
>
> Those responsible for providing a service should be in control of it.
>
> The service should .... allow the greatest possible degree of local control over decision-making, involving customers, councillors and staff.
>
> Each local office should be organised so as to encourage the development of staff skills which lead to a broad view of the inter-related elements of the service, and the withering of specialisms so as to:
>
> - minimise red tape and bureaucracy,
> - break down problems of scale,
> - integrate rather than separate service delivery.

So by this stage the direction in which the department wanted to go was becoming clearer, and we were starting to formulate ideas about the role that the training unit should adopt. But I still needed to find out the degree to which these departmental objectives were understood and shared by staff within the service. In addition, before going any further, we needed to find out what their hopes, fears and expectations of decentralisation were.

Staff views

We spent a couple of week roaming the department, talking to individuals and small groups. We wanted to know:

(1)   How they saw their present job and how they thought this could change with decentralisation?

(2)   What they saw as the objectives of decentralisation and whether they were realistic?

(3)   What would need to change in terms of their relationship to their job, colleagues, boss, subordinates and customers in order to help them do their job better?

(4)   What they wanted from the training unit?

Following this investigation it became clear that staff had concerns in the following areas:

(1)   Realism
    -   Is decentralisation just change for change's sake?
    -   What are the motives of the managers?
    -   Will there be enough money for full decentralisation?

(2)   Effectiveness
    -   How will decentralisation be effective when the quality of key parts of the service (eg repairs/housing benefits etc) are still reliant on outside agencies?

(3)   Uncertainty
    -   How will it work?
    -   What will my job be?
    -   Who will I work with?
    -   Will I be able to cope with the extra demands that will be placed on me?
    -   What will the office be like?
    -   Will there be barriers between us and the public?

Throughout these discussions we suspected that many of the staff we spoke to who were critical of decentralisation were concerned about their ability to cope within an unknown future environment - an environment which they felt powerless to influence. We felt that this fear led to a level of defensiveness and cynicism being expressed by these staff.

We decided, therefore, to attempt to develop a training strategy that would involve staff gaining a clearer picture of the operation of their future office. Indeed, a training strategy that allowed them to have some influence over that picture!

At last we began to feel confident about our role and able to develop a strategy.

Role

There is no one 'role of the training officer'. In different contexts and situations different roles become necessary. The role that a trainer can adopt could be described as:

(1)   Managers of training
- Organising sending people on external training courses
- Organising external trainers to provide internal courses
- Organising internal courses with internal staff acting as trainers

(2)   Direct trainers
- Providing training to staff to develop skills and knowledge

(3)   Trainer trainers
- Providing training on training skills to staff who will then carry out direct training

(4)   Internal consultancy
- To assist managers and their staff to determine their objectives; how they should work to achieve these objectives and how they should evaluate whether they are achieving these objectives

In many organisations the role of training is limited to (1) and (2), or just (3). But to limit ourselves to the role of direct trainer would in no way lead us to tackle the huge task that lay ahead.

In order to generate the kinds of change that were required, we needed to develop an ethos where training and staff development were seen as the responsibility of every manager and specialist within the service. There was no way that two trainers with a limited budget could fulfil the training needs of the whole department, so 'trainer training' was clearly going to be one priority.

Perhaps more importantly, it was clear that we were going to have to operate in the role of 'internal consultants' if we were to confront the real problems of the organisation in transition.

173

We felt both excited and apprehensive about undertaking the 'consultancy' role. We knew we had to force the staff groups who were coming together for the first time to establish a clear vision of the kind of service they wanted to establish. This meant <u>clarity about values as well as policy, about management style as well as procedures.</u>

We knew that we would be asking managers to explore their relationships with their staff, as much as we would be asking staff to explore their relationships with their customers.

We knew that it would not be our role to determine how the organisation should run, but that we would have to confront staff at all levels when we felt that <u>what they were doing</u> conflicted with <u>what they said they wanted to do.</u>[1]

To undertake the role of 'internal consultant' would never be easy. In order to help the organisation change its culture, we would need to be able to observe the culture, the way things happened, with a degree of perspective and distance. This would mean "being in the workplace, but not of it" and being able to "speak truth to power".[2] Would the managers within the service allow us to have such a role?

Strategy

So with a broad role developed, it was time to put this to the test. We needed a simple initial training strategy for Phase 1 of decentralisation, covering the first three district offices, with about 35 staff to each office.

We came up with this basic model:

(1)   Informing We needed to make sure that staff had as much information as possible, presented in a way that reduced fear or uncertainty. This had to be done quickly, as we were approaching the time when people would be able to indicate which of the posts in the new structure they wanted to be 'slotted' into.

(2)   <u>Team building</u> As soon as people had been 'slotted' into their new posts we needed to start developing a shared vision of what the new service would be. And of course, as far as we were concerned this meant exploring values and philosophy as much as practice and procedure.

(3) <u>Skills development</u>   Once clear objectives had been developed, we could build the skills in order to achieve the agreed goals.

(4) <u>Trainer training</u> We could not achieve all this on our own. We were clear that we needed to develop a network of staff with an understanding of the role of training and organisation development, and the skills and enthusiasm to act as trainers within the department.

(5) <u>Evaluation</u> If our goal involves a total change in the culture of the service, we needed to find ways of measuring this abstract concept.   We needed to find a way of deciding whether we have reached our goal, and if not, deciding in which direction to go to get there.

Experience with training for Phase 1

Looking back now it is easy to kid ourselves that it was all quite organised! In fact we made many mistakes, attempted sessions that did not work, took too much time over some areas of work and not enough over others. Still, let's explore how our simple strategy turned out in practice.

(1) <u>Informing</u>

Before we arrived at the department a regular newsletter to all staff was already established.   Normally a single sheet circulated every six weeks or so, the aim was to keep all staff informed of the progress towards decentralisation.

This newsletter was vital in keeping staff informed of the slow progress towards the reorganisation.   However, it was now important to increase the level of communication. Presentations were made in all sections of the department. This gained the grand title of the 'Decentralisation roadshow', with representatives of the decentralisation project team (responsible for developing the new structure), the personnel section and the training unit, along with local managers, running 'question and answer' sessions in each section.

Following these initial presentations, regular briefing sessions were held for all managers within the first phase of decentralisation. In addition 'briefing' on progress became a regular part of later training sessions.

(2)   Initial team building

(i)   <u>Initial team building - managers' workshops</u> In order to start the process of team building we decided to hold two one-day workshops for the three district managers and 12 team leaders within Phase 1.

Following individual pre-interviews, held with the managers before the workshops, it became apparent that a spectrum of views existed both in relation to the objectives of decentralisation, and as to how these objectives should be put into practice. In addition, there was a range of concerns which required discussion. These concerns focused on the need to clarify specific objectives, and for individuals to understand their role, responsibilities and relationships to other managers in achieving these objectives.

We worked in a variety of ways during the two workshops, utilising questionnaires and instruments, and providing brief inputs on issues such as 'organisational culture'. Essentially, however, we were trying to get the managers to explore some basic questions, such as:

- Why decentralisation?
- How are you going to work together?
- What changes are required of staff and the way teams are organised?
- What changes are required of you personally?
- What are the criteria for success?

Perhaps the key outcome of these initial workshops related to the issues of management style.

One of the objectives of decentralisation was seen to be to:

.... change the relationship we have with our customers, so that they have a friendly responsive service over which they feel they have some control. Our staff can't always say yes, but customers should be able to make demands, and if the demand cannot be met, they should leave understanding why not.

176

We then explored how these managers should manage their staff if they are to start to achieve these objectives. After discussion the answer came back:

The relationship between manager and staff member should model the ideal relationship between staff member and customer.

In other words, staff should be valued in the same way as customers; they too should have some control over the service. And they should be provided with a friendly responsive service from their manager. Indeed the notes from the first workshop state:

It was agreed to establish a style of management within Phase 1 that reflects the philosophy of decentralisation. This style should be consistent with the approach that we wish to see developed between our staff and the public. In general terms this means a more collaborative and participative style of management which enables ideas and change to be initiated from all levels of the organisation.

Whether these words would end as empty rhetoric was still to be seen, but they provided an important basis for future work with other 'Phase 1' staff.

(ii)   Initial team building - staff workshops 'Face to face' course. This two and a half day training course was aimed at all 'non-managerial' staff in the first phase of decentralisation. Run in conjunction with the School for Advanced Urban Studies, the purpose was twofold. Firstly we wanted staff to be offered a forum to explore what they wanted from decentralisation. In addition we aimed to help staff develop the skills in interpersonal communication which would be essential with customers and with other staff members if 'collaboration' and 'participation' were to become a reality.

For many staff this course provided the first experience of in-service training. The course was successful in providing a forum for staff to consider their role and to be introduced to techniques in interpersonal communication. However, there were a number of learning points:

Group size For many staff it was extremely stressful to work in a group of approximately 18 members, even though we were working with three trainers and much of the time was spent in small groups. For future phases of decentralisation we will run this initial training session with smaller groups.

Focus Most staff did not perceive there to be any problem in relation to their dealings with the public. The training programme was seen as an implied criticism, which they resented. For future phases of decentralisation we need to put more care into the initial presentation of this course.

However, after a shaky start to each course, we did find that by the end we had succeeded in providing staff with an opportunity to develop some of the 'interpersonal skills' that were explored. More importantly, the programme provided the first opportunity for staff to consider the same basic questions relating to decentralisation that we had asked their managers.

A senior manager attended on the last day of each course in order to get direct feedback from staff about what they wanted from the new service. This was an important element in the design of the course, as it was the first explicit practice of the 'management style' that had been discussed, and it was a chance, often for the first time, for staff to express their needs directly to their manager in a clear way.

The feedback from staff was used by the managers in the development of the new offices, and this process was found to be of use to both manager and staff member.

(iii) Team building - preparation workshops The main area of training activity that took place focused around a series of 'preparation workshops'. This would involve all the staff from each district working together for one afternoon per week. The programme lasted for between 12 and 15 weeks (depending on the district).

178

Essentially these events were about team building. We wanted a clear distinction to be made between the organisation before decentralisation, and the new service. We wanted all staff to reassess their aims and objectives, and to develop these with all their new colleagues within the new district, not just their own teams.

We tried to introduce a wide variety of activities which would help achieve the overall objective of these workshops including:

Whole group activities Meetings for all the staff of the district were held to:

- Introduce all staff to each other and develop district identity.

- Facilitate the briefing of staff on progress towards decentralisation.

- Enable staff to take responsibility for the planning and conducting their own training within the embryonic district structure (eg each team within the new structure organised a 'presentation' for the other teams as a way of explaining its role and function).

- Allow grievances/questions/suggestions to be raised.

Team meetings Time within the preparation workshops was set aside for the individual teams to meet in order to:

- Develop team identity and reporting relationships.

- Establish team objectives and targets - and strategies for achieving those targets.

- Carry out skills related training specific to the needs of the team - eg unified points scheme, technical training etc.

<u>Project groups</u> Individual projects, such as development of publicity, local directory and reception design, were undertaken by small groups of staff. The objective in establishing these groups was to:

- Develop inter-team relationships/understanding.

- Develop functional improvements within the district which may not otherwise have been achieved.

These preparation workshops were critical in determining how staff would approach their new work place. They were essentially run by the managers of the new offices, with the Training Unit providing a supportive and consultative role.

Running workshops was not easy. While staff found it useful to get to know others members of the district, many found it stressful to be expected to contribute to large group discussions. In addition the lack of imposed structure led to a perceived waste of time by some staff.

<u>There was a dilemma here. If we had imposed a strict programme of activity, this would not have involved a change of ethos. Yet staff who were not practised in taking control of their own time found the programme difficult to manage,</u> and therefore of limited use.

We persevered with the preparation programme in spite of initial criticism. By the time the offices opened there was a clear shift in prevailing views, and staff were starting to take an interest in establishing <u>their</u> new offices.

I now think that the major contribution of the preparation workshops was that they allowed for the establishment of various specific agreements relating to details of how the new service would operate. These agreements seemed to be of little importance, for they did not directly affect any policy or procedure. Yet they were critical to the establishment of the new culture, for they dealt with the very symbols that 'shout out' the values of the organisation. Some examples:

Car parking   In the 'old' organisation senior managers automatically got a parking space near the main office. In the first new office too, there were not enough spaces to meet the needs of all the staff. Who was to get the prize?   The issue was discussed within one preparation workshop, and it was agreed that those staff who had to use their car for visits would be allocated a car parking slot. The district manager has to park in the street.

Meeting room   The new office did not yet have a meeting room available for staff and team meetings. The senior manager therefore sat in the open plan area with his staff, and his office was used as a meeting room.

Generic working   It was agreed that it was important that staff should provide cover to other teams. Rather than negotiating this practice in detail, the district manager simply stated that he would be willing to cover reception when there were staff shortages. Other staff followed suit without question.

Role of reception staff   In the 'old' organisation receptionists found that they were being treated as a 'buffer' between the specialist staff and the customers. The preparation workshops provided an opportunity for receptionists to state how they felt about 'being left in the lurch' by their colleagues. There has never been any problem getting staff to come to reception in the new offices!

Within these examples the importance of 'modelling' is shown. Managers do influence what happens within organisations. But what they do is far more influential than what they say. I remember the style of dress within a section of the department changing radically within a week of the arrival of a new senior manager who did not conform to the existing norms, though he had said nothing about this issue. If managers would model the kind of behaviour that fitted with the values that they advocated we felt change would follow.

(3)   Skills development

Some people were surprised that we did not put more
emphasis on skills training. Our view was that we had to
start with the establishment of clear shared objectives.
From this the appetite for skills development would come.
Outlined below are brief details of some of the skills based
courses that have been developed in response to the needs
consequent to decentralisation.   With the exception of
'technical training for non technical staff', all courses were
held shortly after the new offices had been opened to the
public.

'Technical training for non technical staff' This five day
course focused on the needs of the local housing officers who
had increased responsibilities for repairs reporting. Run by
the Department's technical services division, the course
proved very popular and useful to those attending. Follow up
modules covering specific areas in more detail are being
developed.

'One to one interviews' for managers This was a two day
course for staff with supervisory responsibilities. The aim
was to explore the skills required to conduct 'one to one' staff
interviews.   The course was requested by managers who
wanted to explore the skills that they would need to acquire
in order to fit with their objective of developing 'a more
collaborative and participative style of management which
enables ideas and change to be initiated from all levels within
the organisation'.

In some districts this course has led to regular 'one to one'
meetings between staff and their line managers.

'Teamwork skills'   This three day course was held for
members of the three Phase 1 district management teams. It
focused on the need to help managers develop more effective
collaboration within their management teams, and to develop
greater understanding of group processes which would make
them more effective within their own teams.

At the moment we are developing further skills based courses
for reception staff, who are key to the establishment of the
new relationship with our customers, and for first line
managers, who are often taking on supervisory
responsibilities for the first time and need particular support.

182

The focus on training managers was deliberate. Within the time available we could not provide sufficient direct training for all staff. We believed that it was important to concentrate on those staff who would have most effect on the culture of the organisation, and this is clearly the managers.

(4) Trainer training

Having carried out the initial training programme for the first three district offices we needed to continue to provide follow up training and start our programme for the next nine districts. There was no way that two trainers could carry out such an intensive programme on our own. The next part of our strategy was therefore to develop a network of staff within the department who could act as trainers.

We started by inviting representatives from the different sections within the department to attend a 'Trainer training course in written communication'. This was a three day course held during the week, which aimed to give staff the skills and confidence to run courses in correspondence and report writing. This initial course was well attended, and led to a number of successful short courses run by these representatives within the department.

Suitably encouraged, and with financial and practical support from the Local Government Training Board, we organised a weekend residential 'Trainer training' course. To our delight 20 staff attended, with a good spread of senior and middle managers, as well as specialist non-managerial staff. It is hoped that this 'Training and development network' will continue to develop, with the aid of regular informal sessions for further training, discussion and experimentation.

(5) Evaluation

The final stage in our strategy is evaluation.

If the organisation has set out on a journey it must be able to know whether it has arrived! Clearly we will know that the structure has been changed when people turn up to work having accepted their new job descriptions. We can attempt to measure whether the service is more efficient, by measuring such things as the number of repairs that are carried out and the number of empty properties that we own.

183

But how do we measure whether we are really achieving our objectives, when these objectives relate to all aspects of the organisation's culture? Those aspects of the service that could be quantified were being measured. We wanted to find ways of evaluating those aspects that cannot be quantified.

We carried out a pilot project within the first decentralised office six months after it had opened. Individual interviews were carried out with every member of staff in order to find out how they felt about their past training and their new relationship to their job, their manager and their customers. In addition we asked them what they wanted for the future.

Clearly this project was not an adequate form of evaluation. No attempt was made to consult the customers of the service, and no criteria were established. However, it was absolutely clear that attitudes within the office were radically different to those that were expressed to us before decentralisation.

Much progress had been made, and it seemed to us that it was even in the right direction! But we need to establish better methods of evaluation, and this is an area that we want to develop with the School for Advanced Urban Studies.

Conclusion

This chapter has outlined the first tentative steps in developing a training strategy for a housing service that was in the process of radical change. Our approach was not based on any particular theory of organisational behaviour. We essentially tried things out, and repeated the things that we felt went well.

Our approach was both 'top down' and 'bottom up'. We encouraged managers to be both firm about the overall goals of the service, and flexible about the route taken to those goals. We tried to encourage staff to look at the way they related to each other, as well as to their customers, and to live out the values of the service in all their activities. And we tried to model these same values in the way we worked within the training unit and with our customers, the staff of the London Borough of Newham's housing service. Finally, the approach was specific to Newham. We started by looking at what this department was trying to achieve and worked from there.

Has our approach been successful? We have said that evaluation of cultural change is difficult, and that we have to do more work in this area. And it is difficult to assess how much the specific activities of the training unit have been instrumental in promoting the changes that have occurred. But change there has been. Certainly staff within the decentralised service are clearer about what the department is there for, and of their role within that service. And the way things are done, the culture, is substantially different.

Has the service reached its objectives? Certainly not. Organisational change must now be seen as a continuous process, not just linked to changes in the organisational structure. We have travelled, but we have not arrived.

Notes and References

1. **Argyris, C. and Schon, D.A.** (1978) Organisational learning: a theory of action perspective, London: Addison-Wesley.

2. **Wildavsky, A.** (1979) Speaking truth to power: the art and craft of policy analysis, Boston: Little, Brown.

PART 4
REFLECTIONS ON
CURRENT DEVELOPMENTS

10

LOCAL STATE AND LOCAL COMMUNITY:THE HACKNEY EXPERIENCE

Andrew Puddephatt

Communities are not just physical neighbourhoods, although these can still be important. There are communities of work, of social and political activity, of culture, sex, religion, sexuality and education. A community can best be understood perhaps as a set of reciprocal social relations that provide an identity and mutual support. Community development implies that local government has some role in enabling communities to develop, either for their own good or in the interests of maintaining social order or to relieve pressure on resources. Community development draws on at least two separate strands in its recent history.

The political movement of the late sixties and early seventies gave rise to various forms of community politics. There is no coherent overall view of community politics but there are several elements that can be distinguished.

Antagonism to the state

Much of the political influence on community politics was libertarian rather than 'orthodox' socialism. Many community activists saw all state institutions as the enemy; as constituting an oppressive weapon hanging over the heads of the 'people'. State activities were seen in opposition to the self-activity of the people. Alongside the 'hard' repression of the police was the 'soft' repression of the social worker. Some came to believe that activities of local groups were intrinsically superior to the activities of the state because they were under the direct control of the 'people'. There are of course many interesting questions to be asked about the accountability of such groups and from which social layers they are drawn. Nevertheless, such a view cut across municipal socialism and some views of state socialism as much as it did of the right.

Gaps in service

Community GPs identified major gaps in services where the local state was choosing not to exercise its role. At the same time it was widely felt that many state services were inadequate or needed to exist under different forms of control. Claimants' unions took an uncompromisingly hostile view of the benefits system. Under-fives provision was seen as completely inadequate and, after much struggle with the Labour controlled council, community nurseries and playgroups appeared (around half of Hackney's provision is in the community sector). Free schools came into existence. In fact a whole parallel network of groups came into existence, particularly in London, carrying out functions traditionally associated either with the local or the national state.

Community development also had its roots in various managerial initiatives. In the late 1970s it became widely recognised that there appeared to be an increasing separation of local authorities from the communities they purported to serve. The heady days of pioneering municipal socialism of the 1970s seemed to have long passed. The image of a local authority was conservative, unresponsive, indifferent to people's needs. They were the institutions which demolished communities through comprehensive redevelopment, not built them. In Hackney, the National Dwelling and Housing Survey reported Hackney's residents expressing the highest levels of dissatisfaction with their environment in London (over 40%). The Institute of Community Studies' 'Report from Hackney' (1982) documented the nature of this dissatisfaction - there was a sense of people who were unable to influence either what services were delivered or how they were delivered. It revealed serious concerns both about the content and the control of services.

Community development in Hackney

This was the origin of Hackney foray into community development. After several officer papers which also examined the role of the 'voluntary' sector in Partnership, a community development committee was set up with extensive terms of reference. It was seen as the cutting edge of more open access to services, as an instrument of opposing departmentalism, of improving information flow and of co-ordinating grants to the voluntary sector through a code of practice for funding. A small unit was transferred to the chief executive's office with this ambitious brief, worthy of the PR for the Titanic. The unit itself soon became embroiled in internal conflicts not of its own making but stemming largely from political and managerial confusion. It was soon marginalised by those departments whose professional barriers it was meant to dissolve. In many ways it was a classic local authority approach of superimposing a new - and usually badly resourced - answer onto an old problem. The new answer tends to rapidly experience all the same devastating contradictions of the old problem it was meant to overcome.

The problem experienced by the unit had several strands. It was very difficult for a small centrally based unit to tackle its full brief without the staff resources and without substantial political backing. The problem had been identified but not the political solution. A frequent plea from the officers was for someone to tell them what the members wanted. The committee and much of the unit became bogged down in funding issues and internal conflicts inside community groups. Many community groups wanted an increasing say in how both the statutory as well as the voluntary sector of the services were run. The policy of co-opting representatives of disadvantaged groups onto council committees began with the social services committee where it was originally perceived in a fairly limited way, in terms of the specialist expertise such representatives could bring to the committee. After a while those representatives began to play a more active political role on the committee. In 1982, when the new Labour council was returned, we realised that the composition of the council failed to reflect the proportion of black/ethnic minorities and women in the community so we embarked upon a systematic process of co-optation of representatives of these groups into all main council committees. Their political importance has steadily developed, indeed I have chaired committees where they have been in the majority! At the same time the groups wished to maintain their distance and therefore their political purity from the difficult decision, such as prioritising grants. Despite these problems a substantial block of money, something like over 400% increase over two to three years, was pushed towards the community sector, the largest real growth area of the council.

Regarding Inner City Partnership Hackney's councillors originally gave this a low political profile. Their disinterest created a vacuum that a number of community groups then sought to fill. A large number of community groups saw this pool of resources which had suddenly become available as an opportunity for them to develop their own projects. At the same time they got involved in the development of the objectives of the Partnership Programme.

189

As a result effective control of several areas of the programme became genuinely shared between the council and the community. Recently it has been the community groups themselves who have been pushing the strongest corporate view (often against their own sectional interests) that the focus of the programme should shift towards housing related issues - it was the members who took the sectional view, bidding for growth in their own departmental areas. Behind all these problems however lies the deeper problem - what kind of relations exist and are possible between the people and state apparatuses?

Reflections

At one level the task of changing local government resembles the problem of moving a monolith so it would seem important to reach a common understanding of what we all mean by the 'monolith' and how much of a monolith it really is. The state acts as a condenser of the various interests of society on behalf of the dominant class/group. Classic socialist analysis tells us that there is anarchy among competing capitals and that a state body is necessary to provide the stability that avoids loss of class power. A prime function of any state apparatus (and there are many) is to unify those who dominate by virtue of their economic power and to cause disunity among the dominated. Of course various apparatuses exist to serve the people - education and health for instance - but they are not autonomous and are 'allocated' a specific role to play within the overall structure of the state. An apparatus is not fixed in time, nor should it be confused with particular institutions, buildings or people. It is primarily a set of social relations. It is both the expression of the clash of social forces and the outcome of such a clash. Surface appearances aside there is no such thing as a monolith - state apparatuses constantly change, are constantly in ferment - the apparently bizarre obsession of many local authorities with organisational change is perfectly normal. As soon as new central government legislation is enacted we devote all out attention to how to get round it which produces new forms of activity. The 'monolith' is actually quite a dynamic structure.

Of course contradictions exist inside and between apparatuses because political power is not unitary. To many participants in any bureaucracy, be they councillors or officers, the 'real' struggle is inside the apparatus, not between the apparatus and those it is meant to serve, who are often the helpless spectators of such conflicts. Over the past few years a bitter and protracted struggle has developed between central government and local government.

It has seriously affected the room for manoeuvre that many local authorities have. But this struggle has had contradictory effects. In some sense it has constrained local authorities but in another sense it has liberated them and led them into uncharted territory. One effect has been to define a new role for local authorities and a new relationship with its community - that of defender against a hostile central government and a campaign focus against government policy (viz the role of many councils during the miners' strike). A distinct element in the national political struggle has appeared, one with profound consequences for the monolith. Local authorities have openly backed groups and organisations whose purpose is to attack the government of the day. Central government doesn't like that, they like to reward their friends and penalise their enemies, they don't like to see local government do the same. This 'politicisation' of local authorities opens up possibilities of change despite government restrictions.

What implications does this have for the relation of community and local state? Looking back over the last 30 years we can see how local authority responsibilities have constantly changed. The utilities have gone; education, economic development and personal social services have come to the fore. Thus the nature of the responsibilities of local government changes over time. A local authority does not have a simple relationship to local communities, there are many different kinds of community requiring different forms of relationship, and thus there can be no simple view of community development.

A local authority is a transmission belt for government policies. When councillors vote to implement cuts in housing benefit that are determined by central government but administered by themselves they hurt those sections of their communities least able to endure it.

When a local authority accepts that it must manage scarce resources it often has to convince communities to accept less than they aspire to. They have to prioritise and bring a degree of social order to their communities. If the local authority simply cannot tackle a problem, as is increasingly happening in housing, then it risks demoralising communities, leaving them feeling powerless to change their lives. Such management of scarce resources creates a great number of complex problems in terms of local authorities' relationships to their communities.

Local authorities can be a powerful weapon in political struggle. They can take sides in their communities, legitimising some issues and undermining others. It is a myth to believe that you are there to serve the whole community. The development of equal opportunities policies and contracts compliance are good examples of policies which favour some in the local communities but not others. Obviously they arouse tremendous opposition but that has to be faced head-on and not ducked.

A more complex role lies in dealing with what Mao called "contradictions among the people". There are many such contradictions - between black and white people, between women and men, between people with disabilities and others, between providers of services and consumers. The local authority has a specific but delicate role to play in choosing sides, not to create a more localised 'inverted' oppression but to promote the positive virtue of equal opportunities in enriching the life of all. Contradictions do exist between workers and consumers even though many socialists would like to believe in a mythical unity.

A brief example from our own experience in Hackney illustrates this. At the beginning of 1984 an area housing management base with a maintenance base attached in Shoreditch (one of the most deprived areas of Hackney) was occupied by a group of building workers and tenants against the workers of the local housing staff. The tenants were demanding a locally managed and controlled area housing base with its own budget directly employing staff. The trade unions had made it clear that there was no way that they were going to work for a local authority which fragments into 30 or 40 separate employers, each possibly insisting on different working conditions. There were genuine virtues in the arguments of both sides in that particular battle. Although tenants, building workers, housing staff and councillors were all members of the Labour Party the Party was quite incapable of playing any mediating role in bringing the various sides together.

A solution was put forward by Hackney council which sought to preserve a commitment to common conditions of employment throughout the borough whilst moving towards a greater degree of local autonomy and tenant control over the Shoreditch base. The solution broke down partly because of the council's inability to proceed with the required organisational change at a rapid enough pace to satisfy the tenants; partly also because the local tenants couldn't organise themselves into an elected management committee which could control the development of that area base. This is an important issue: it seems that communities coming together for the first time have great difficulty in producing democratic and accountable structures. I think one of the lessons for us was that accountability is not just a problem for local authorities but for groups operating in the local community as well.

At the root of all these issues is the question of who controls and in whose interest, which are the real concerns of 'community development'.

Power is not a zero-sum game. To gain political power you don't have to take it off somebody else, you don't have to take power away from central government and the state to discover new areas of power for yourself. If local authorities simply concentrate on administering what they have they will inevitably enter into serious conflict with their local communities. No authority-wide community development strategy will be able to avoid it. In fact it will become a face saving exercise tacked on to the existing structures which will be directed at co-opting the community on the council's terms rather than with the development of that community. Community groups for all their faults have shown us how to expand into new areas. The success of many authorities' economic development strategy, often developed (as was Hackney's) in real partnership with the community has begun to show the way. The technology and employment networks created by the GLC offer new possibilities. It is time to campaign for the return of the utilities to local government control (as they are in Denmark), time to campaign for a thorough democratisation of state provision. Institutional reform alone cannot be effective. Only an alliance between communities and those apparatuses which are able to listen and respond can produce such a seismological change. But the rewards are worth the struggle and at the end community development will take on some tangible meaning at last. Such a struggle will also require that a local authority recognises it is only one agent - however strong and purposeful - of change. People tend to take a very fashionable view that the officers are like a 'secret club' who jealously preserve their power: my experience is that many councillors behave very similarly, they often are very resistant to devolving power to others. Socialist led local authorities do not have a monopoly on political change or political control: we must recognise that such processes of change are essentially pluralistic ones which involve a whole number of different organisations and groups.

[This chapter is based on a talk Andrew Puddephatt gave at a seminar at SAUS in September 1985.]

11

A COMMON LABOUR MOVEMENT? LEFT LABOUR COUNCILS AND THE TRADE UNIONS

Edmund Heery

The purpose of this article is to account for a seeming paradox: why is it that in the current period of pressure on local government it is those authorities which are most committed to the preservation of jobs and services which have encountered most resistance from local government trade unions? In the past few years there has been a series of major disputes in authorities controlled by the Labour left.[1] In 1984 there was a 13 week strike of NALGO members in Sheffield over the introduction of new technology in the housing department; in the same year Islington NALGO went on strike for 14 weeks to secure better pay and staffing levels for nursery workers; in Hackney a series of disputes has blocked the council's plans for a far-reaching organisation of services; in Liverpool there have been disputes over the appointment of Samson Bond and over proposed changes in services; and in the GLC the normally staid Staff Association refused to process job applications for six weeks in 1983 in response to the council's unilateral imposition of a new grading structure. Survey data, recently published by Ingham[2] supports the impression given by these examples. The propensity of local government workers to take strike and other industrial action is positively associated with the proportion of council seats held by the Labour Party. 'Local socialism', it would appear, is more effective in prompting trade unions into defensive action than cuts or privatisation.[3]

There are a number of reasons why this should be the case. The first is that trade union organisation tends to be stronger in the large cities typically controlled by Labour. Ingham's survey data, for instance, shows an, albeit rather weak, relationship between the percentage of Labour councillors and trade union density.[4] It also reveals an association between the level of unionisation and the incidence of industrial action by manual, though not white-collar, workers.[5] A second reason, ironically, is that Labour-controlled authorities have tended to be relatively generous employers.[6] Central government pressure on their expenditure, however, has limited their ability to grant concessions. Although Labour councils have been fairly successful in protecting jobs and services, their room for manoeuvre on issues such as staffing levels and regrading has diminished. Despite this, trade union expectations of relatively sympathetic treatment remain high. There is tension, therefore, between buoyant aspirations on the union side, possibly supplemented by a desire for compensation for parsimonious national pay settlements, and a diminishing ability to pay on the part of the authorities. This was illustrated most clearly by the Islington nursery workers' dispute. This arose from a claim from the union for salary increases and the appointment of 70 extra staff, at a cost of £800,000 to which the council responded with an offer worth £15,000. Throughout the dispute, the union used Labour's manifesto commitments to improve services and combat low pay as a weapon against the council.[7]

A third reason is that left Labour councils have proved determined innovators. They have been eager to develop radical policies, to experiment with novel organisational forms, and achieve a much fuller subordination of the routine practice of local authorities to political strategy. This appetite for innovation has led to conflict with trade unions, in the first place, because it has increased the sheer volume of negotiation and hence the possibility of conflict, and in the second place, because certain of the changes advocated have directly challenged the interests of local government workers and trade unions.

Left Labour councils, therefore, have embarked on ambitious programmes of change in a context of relatively well organised trade unions and a diminution in their own ability to engage in productivity bargaining. The result, in many cases, has been an unlooked-for determination in industrial relations and occasional disputes. In the rest of this paper I want to look in detail at the implementation of two such programmes, the GLC's equal opportunities policy with its commitment to 'positive action' to improve the situation of female and black workers, and the London Borough of Islington's policy of decentralising services to local neighbourhood offices. For each case I hope to demonstrate the origins of policy in the left's political evaluations of the problems and opportunities facing the Labour Party and to trace its implementation through conflict and accommodation with the trade unions.

The political strategy of the Labour party

The political strategy of authorities like the GLC and Islington is founded on a particular diagnosis of Labour's declining electoral fortunes. Labour's crisis, it is held, arises in large part from the inadequacy and insufficient radicalism of the policies the party has followed in the past. The new left has been prepared to cast a critical eye over what a rather self-congratulatory Labour movement has viewed as its finest achievements, the welfare state and the nationalised industries. Too frequently, it is argued, Labour administrations, at both local and national levels, have created highly centralised institutions which are remote from those they formally serve and which treat those they employ in a manner not dissimilar to that of a private corporation. The new left accuses the party of offering only a bureaucratic and authoritarian socialism.[8] The institutions which Labour had built in the name of the working class, it contends, have become distant and operate too frequently as agencies of social discipline rather than as means of emancipation. Alienation from those institutions has led, in turn, to alienation from the party which created them.

A second element in the left's critique of Labourism is that its policies have been framed primarily to serve the interests of the skilled, white, male working class.[9] Such a position, it is felt, has become increasingly intenable because of changes in the occupational structure and in the social composition of the cities. Ken Livingstone, for example, has argued that:

> The organised working class, industrial, skilled, trade unions have left London .... and that means a considerable weakening of the base here. Now, it is not a question of recreating the base because there's no prospect of skilled crafts moving back into London at all. It's a question of building on this new sort of alliance .... we have to start to articulate the needs of the minorities and the dispossessed in a way that Labour governments and the Labour Party never have in the past.[10]

The thinking of the new left, therefore, resembles that of the 1950s revisionists in its conviction that the shrinking traditional working class provides an insecure foundation for the establishment of a powerful party of the left.

The first part of the left's diagnosis of Labour's difficulties has led to a commitment to alter the form of the welfare state. The welfare bureaucracies must become more accountable and the influence of the recipients of services over the nature of those services raised. In the first instance, this is said to require more responsive institutions which meet genuine needs efficiently and do so without stigmatising those who receive assistance. In the second place, it is said to require popular control of the running of welfare services wherever this is feasible. These two connected avenues of reform, it is believed, will create effective institutions of social service and render the welfare state more securely the property of ordinary people.

Islington's policy of decentralisation embodies both kinds of initiative. Open plan, multiservice neighbourhood offices are being established throughout the borough in an attempt to improve the efficiency, accessibility and integration of the council's services. This ambitious reorganisation has been accompanied by a programme of community development. In time, it is intended to establish a neighbourhood forum for each of the 24 offices, which will be composed of local residents and representatives of service users and which will participate in local decision making.[11]

The left's concern at the erosion of the party's traditional support has led to attempts to build a broad, progressive alliance, Labour's own 'rainbow coalition'.[12] Policies which have been implemented to further this aim include the establishment of women's committees and the funding of minority groups. It has also led to interventions in the labour market to redress existing patterns of discrimination and disadvantage. The GLC's equal opportunities policy is an intervention of this type. Through monitoring the characteristics of its workforce, through altering recruitment and promotion procedures and through special training programmes, the GLC is striving to make the sexual and ethnic makeup of its own staff reflect that of the working population of the Greater London area.[13]

The selection of policies like decentralisation and equal opportunities can be viewed, to a large exent, as adaptations on the part of Labour to a more uncertain environment. They clearly also arise, however, from significant ideological shifts within the party itself. A commitment to equal opportunities, for instance, is a manifestation of the greater involvement of feminist and black activists in the party in recent years. Islington's decentralisation policy has emerged from a widespread preference on the left for less hierarchical forms of organisation and participative decision-making. It has been framed by those previously involved in various forms of community action and embodies the typical concerns of such movements to mobilise communities and subordinate officialdom to popular decision.[14]   The political strategy which guides the left local authorities, therefore, is a response to Labour's crisis shaped by the experience and beliefs of those who have entered the party since the 1960s.

Equal opportunities and trade unions: the GLC[15]

The starting point of the GLC's equal opportunities policy was a conviction that racial and sexual discrimination are enduring features of the labour market and can only be combatted by 'positive action', a concerted attempt to tackle the effects of past and present disadvantage. Such a commitment necessitated, in the first place, the establishment of a system of monitoring to ascertain the percentage of female, disabled and ethnic minority staff in the various departments and levels of the organisation. This was necessary to guide future policy and provide proof of discrimination and justification for targeting jobs for minorities. A second series of measures were designed to improve the position of these groups within the GLC's internal labour market. The council has conducted a review of its training policy and instituted a number of training initiatives.   These are intended to equip minority groups with skills and are linked to counselling programmes designed to stimulate the career aspirations of those in low paid work.   Other measures are intended to raise the numbers of blacks and women drawn from the external labour market. Job vacancies are now advertised in the ethnic minority and women's press and there has been a standardisation of recruitment procedures to minimise the risk of discriminatory practice at departmental level. This has had most impact on manual worker recruitment which, in many cases, was previously done informally through personal recommendation.

A principal obstacle standing in the way of these policies was the council's existing agreements with the trade unions on grading. These were effective barriers to the aims of opening up the internal labour market for women and ethnic minority groups and of increasing the percentages of such workers by direct recruitment from outside the GLC. The grading structure for white collar workers, for example, consisted of five classes, clerical, executive, technical, administrative and professional. Movement from the lower grades to the higher, from clerical and executive to administrative or from the technical grade to the professional, was extremely difficult. Workers in the lower grades, where the majority of women and ethnic minorities were concentrated, were effectively locked into lower paid, lower status positions with limited opportunities for career development. There were also strict vertical divides between the professional and technical streams and the administrative and executive. Each grade, therefore, constituted a largely selfcontained system of recruitment and promotion. This obviously militated against the GLC's desire to push members of minority groups up the hierarchy through its training programme and to end the sexual stereotyping of different categories of work (seen, for example, in the reservation of technical jobs primarily for men). Accordingly, the Labour Group came to office committed to 'open-grading'. Its manifesto recommended that:

> GLC grading structures should be reorganised so as to create an integrated service-wide salary and career structure, with no artificial departmental, professional or blue collar/white collar barriers.

An additional feature of the old grading structure was that many positions could only be filled internally. This was particularly true of senior posts. The opportunity to apply for many managerial jobs was confined to those who had come into the GLC through administrative or professional points of entry. Abandoning this system, it was felt, would permit the recruitment of qualified women, ethnic minority and disabled candidates directly from the external labour market into these relatively senior positions. There were other reasons, however, why the administration was keen to move to a system of open recruitment. Integral to its wider strategy was a desire to reform the county hall bureaucracy. It was considered that many managers were of inferior quality. An equal opportunities adviser who was interviewed, for instance, described many of the authority's chief officers as 'time servers' who would not have risen to such a level if there had been greater competition for posts. It was also felt that many officers were hostile to the administration's programme of radical change. A repeated theme in Ken Livingstone's discussions of the problems encountered in office has been the conservatism of the County Hall bureaucracy.[16] Throwing all positions open to both external and internal candidates, therefore, was seen as a means of renewing the authority's management and of obtaining staff more sympathetic to Labour's policies.

The response of the trade unions to the equal opportunities policy has been varied. The manual unions initially were rather apathetic. According to one interviewee, they viewed equal opportunities as a 'bourgeois deviation'. The benefits which have accrued to their members through the training programme and the equalisation of manual and white collar conditions of service, however, have swung them behind the policy. Despite central support, though, opposition has been encountered from manual groups at the workplace, in particular to the implementation of new recruitment procedures.

The reaction of NALGO, the minority white collar union with about 3,000 members, was generally favourable. The branch is dominated by the left and many of its activists are recent recruits to the GLC attracted by the council's radical policies. Criticism from NALGO has tended to take the form of complaints that the equal opportunities programme does not go far enough. It was objected, for example, that the reform of the grading structure would not improve the position of typists who would remain on a separate system of salary scales.

A much more equivocal position was adopted by the majority white collar union, the GLC staff association, which has about 17,000 members and which dominated the GLC's Whitley council machinery. The GLCSA did not accept that a major programme of 'positive action', with movement towards 'equality targets' for black and female employees, was either necessary or desirable. It welcomed the expansion of training opportunities for minorities but was suspicious of the overall thrust of council policy which it believed favoured recruitment on the grounds of race or sex rather than on merit alone.[17] Despite these misgivings the staff association co-operated in the setting up of the council's ethnic monitoring system and agreed to participate in the GLC's equal opportunities monitoring groups. According to councillors and equal opportunity officers, however, the GLCSA has played a largely passive role and has not been active in using the monitoring information in claims for regrading or promotion.

The GLCSA's equivocation over the equal opportunities policy was most apparent in its response to the proposals for the reform of the grading structure. Its opposition to the GLC on this issue eventually led it to take industrial action. The GLCSA was prepared to accept some erosion of the barriers between grades but it did not want to proceed to a single, authority wide structure for the majority of white collar workers.[18]

The old grading and recruitment structure, therefore, acted to shield many managerial positions from competition, both from the external labour market and from lower graded workers already employed by the GLC. According to a councillor who was interviewed, an effective seniority system operated at certain levels of the organisation. The Labour leadership, in the pursuit of equal opportunities and a wider reform of the County Hall bureaucracy, wanted to remove these shields. This generated conflict with the GLCSA. An important element in the situation, however, was the distribution of influence within the trade union. Although the GLCSA represents white collar workers from all levels of the organisation, its leadership is drawn primarily from the ranks of relatively senior officials. Much of its policy reflects the interests of those occupying the positions the GLC wanted to expose to new sources of recruitment.[19] It tends to favour percentage wage settlements, for example, and has opposed the GLC's policy of narrowing differentials.

The GLCSA's dispute with the GLC arose not so much over the substantive content of the GLC's proposals for grading structure, as with the manner in which the council chose to proceed. In 1983 the chair of the GLC's staff committee took advice as to the legality of the authority's recruitment and promotion procedures. He was informed that they constituted a 'discriminatory practice' under the terms of the Sex Discrimination and Race Relations Acts. Accordingly, on 4 July 1983, at a meeting of the staff committee, he told the trade unions that the existing arrangements would be replaced by a single, authority wide grading structure and the external advertisement of posts.[20] The reason for this unilateral action was that after two years in office the GLC had not succeeded in removing what was seen as the principal obstacle to its equal opportunities policy. The blame for the delay, the council felt, rested squarely with the GLCSA. "They were never going to agree to it", one councillor stated in interview, "It ended 50 years of a corrupt practice".

The response of the GLCSA to this announcement was to register a dispute with the council and to instruct members to refuse to co-operate in the proposed changes. This action lasted six weeks before it collapsed. There then followed several months of negotiation during which the union secured a number of compensation payments and regradings in return for accepting the new, unified structure. The GLC's tough stance, therefore, was effective in accelerating the pace of innovation and in compelling the GLCSA to negotiate over, and ultimately accept, the bulk of its equal opportunities policy.

201

Decentralisation and trade unions: the London Borough of Islington

The ruling Labour Party in Islington included a pledge to decentralise services under community control in its manifesto for the local elections in 1982. Since then, the new left wing council has embarked upon the transfer of a number of its core functions, such as housing, social services, environmental health and building repairs, out of centralised departments and into 24 neighbourhood offices. This is a substantial organisational innovation: in the region of 1,000 staff are being relocated. The first neighbourhood offices were opened early in 1985. Islington intends to complete its decentralisation programme in time for the 1986 elections.

The decentralisation policy constitutes a limited departure from three principles of administration widely encountered in public service bureaucracies. The first of these is the centralisation of executive decision-making. In local government departments all significant, innovative decisions are taken by councillors in conjunction with their chief officers. It is the duty of those below this upper tier to implement these decisions in accordance with written instructions. A second principle is the strict definition and limitation both of individual jobs and of departmental functions. A third principle is administration according to universally applied rules. Local government bureaucracies are legalistic organisations. The individual cases which come before the bureaucracy, applications for housing, improvement grants, or whatever, are judged and processed by set procedures which are meant to ensure standard treatment for all.

The aim of the reorganisation of the council's work in Islington is to make services more accessible and increase the speed of service delivery once need has been identified. To achieve this the council is advocating, in the first instance, a partial reversal of the bureaucratic tendency towards centralised decision-making. Obviously, major policy initiatives will continue to be the prerogative of councillors. An element of neighbourhood control, however, will augment the established system of representation and, it is intended, will permit local needs and wishes to influence the nature of council services. In addition, each neighbourhood office has been given its own budget with some opportunity for virement at the local level. Most importantly, however, there has been an attempt to increase the autonomy and decision-making capacity of those staff dealing directly with the public. The key professional groups who staff the neighbourhood office, environmental health officers, housing managers and social workers, have all been given additional responsibilities and freed, to a degree, from the need to refer to superiors. The scope of manual jobs has also been widened. Caretakers, for example, have been given more responsibility for the running of estates, while home helps are now given a caseload and are permitted to plan their own timetable.

Decentralisation is also intended to modify the bureaucratic attachment to strictly delimited, specialised functions. It has not been feasible for Islington to break with the established division of council departments and occupations. Greater flexibility and better communications between specialisms, however, are major means by which the authority is aiming to improve service provision. This has been attempted, firstly, by housing different specialisms in the same office in the expectation that more co-operative working relations will develop and, secondly, by the creation of new generalist positions. The most important of these is that of neighbourhood officer who will head the office and be responsible for its overall management. The principal task of the neighbourhood officer is to weld the various specialist staff into a unified team. He or she, however, only exercises direct management control over administrative support workers.

Decentralisation also represents a departure from the practice of standard provision. Across the borough, under decentralisation, it is recognised that the style and method of service delivery in each neighbourhood may well differ. The intention is to match services much more flexibly to local requirements, as these become apparent to staff in the neighbourhood office and are expressed by the new neighbourhood forums, which the council is eager to establish. Standardised provision of services is closely linked to a conception of the client as an essentially passive 'case'. Giving the community some influence over services, therefore, implies a relaxation of the principles of standardised allocation.

Negotiations with the trade unions over decentralisation proved to be difficult. After two years agreement was secured to staff neighbourhood offices, though a number of grading disputes remain to be settled. Some unions adopted a harder line than others, but the general response to the proposals was defensive and wary. This was disappointing for the council. It had offered assurances to the unions that there would be no cuts in jobs and stressed that decentralisation promised greater job satisfaction for their members. The council believed that these commitments provided the basis for drawing the units into open ended and informal discussions on how decentralisation could be effected. Councillors were keen to hold workplace meetings at which staff could express their views on decentralisation and which would permit the workforce's intimate knowledge of council operations to be fed into the policy forming process. The council, in effect, hoped to replace the conventional, adversarial system of industrial relations with a more co-operative relation between employer and trade union.

The unions, however, refused to countenance such a change in the nature of industrial relations. They insisted that they must be the sole channel for communication with the workforce, that discussions should be formal and that the council should provide detailed descriptions of the decentralised structure to which the unions could respond. This latter point almost led to the collapse of negotiations and an attempt by the council to impose the new working arrangements unilaterally.

The council was eager to make early appointments to the positions of neighbourhood officer and head of social services, housing and environmental health in the first four neighbourhood offices to be opened. It was envisaged that these staff would play a part in finalising the decentralisation plans and training the remainder of the neighbourhood office workforce in new working methods. NALGO, the major union involved in negotiations, however, was not prepared to accept these appointments until the council had finalised its proposals. The council, therefore, accused NALGO of unreasonably delaying its policy and advertised the posts without union agreement. NALGO responded by blacking the posts and withdrawing from negotiations. At the union's instigation the two sides then went to the Greater London Whitley council for conciliation. After a series of meetings with the Joint Secretaries of the Whitley council a compromise was reached in which NALGO accepted the new appointments in return for more information. A total breakdown was avoided, then, but negotiations remained difficult and the first offices opened without social services due to a dispute with NALGO over staffing levels.

As with the GLC case, it was the manner in which the council sought to introduce change which generated a crisis in industrial relations. Behind the unions' cautious response and the insistence on more information, however, lay a concern about the substantive content of the policy. It was appreciated that change in the three directions intended by the council could have deleterious effects on the working conditions of local government staff.

The council's commitment to devolve decision-making, for instance, implies greater discretion and more flexible work roles for the borough's employees. It was anticipated that this would be welcomed by staff and indeed some groups such as building tradesmen, and estates managers, responded positively to the promise of greater autonomy. Amongst other groups, however, change in this direction generated concern. It was feared that more autonomy would in fact mean heavier workloads as staff were expected to assume additional responsibilities. Amongst some groups such as environmental health officers, housing benefit and housing advisory staff this fear was allied with a concern over being isolated in local offices without the support of colleagues. There was concern also among professional workers that flexible working would lead to a dilution of their skills. Social workers, for example, feared that a greater proportion of their time would be devoted to dealing with off-the-street enquiries at the expense of preventive social work.

In articulating these concerns the unions have attempted to minimise disruptions to existing job descriptions. There has been opposition to the council's plans to compress the division of labour. NALGO, for instance, has successfully opposed the merging of housing advisory with housing transfer and letting work and has insisted that additional administrative support workers be appointed to prevent professional staff being over burdened with reception duties. The unions have demanded that extra staff be appointed to guard against an increase in workloads and have been keen to ensure that adequate managerial support is available to staff in neighbourhood offices. Where they have acceded in the alteration of work roles they have attempted to secure regrading. Virtually every position in the neighbourhood office has been the subject of a regrading demand.

The unions have also responded cautiously to the council's proposals to secure a closer integration of functions through the erosion of departmental boundaries. From the first, they opposed any attempt to introduce 'generic workers', staff who would straddle departments. NALGO has argued that a move in this direction is not feasible and that the existing departmental structure must remain. NALGO initially opposed even the sharing of administrative support amongst departments within the neighbourhood office. The unions have also insisted that existing lines of accountability must be retained so that social workers are supervised by senior social workers and estate managers are supervised by senior estates managers. They have been partly

205

responsible for minimising the role of the neighbourhood officer and ensuring that he or she does not exercise direct line authority over specialist staff.

The unions have also expressed alarm at the council's attempts to reconstitute the relationship between the workforce and the client population. There has been successful opposition to the introduction of flexible opening hours. According to a NALGO branch official the council's request for this was "a legitimate demand .... but it creates problems over people's conditions of work".[21] There has also been concern "about open plan offices increasing the number of assaults on staff".[22] The unions are aware that the relationship between the dispensers and recipients of services is frequently characterised by tension and it is this which has led them to express disquiet at proposals to make staff more accessible and accountable to the public. In particular, there has been an insistence that elected neighbourhood forums should have no responsibility for the management of staff. The unions are alarmed at the prospect of members of the public pursuing vendettas against their members and are anxious to avoid local control leading to different conditions of service in different offices.

In general, then, the response of the unions in Islington to the council's policy has been sceptical and wary. NALGO, especially, has remained unconvinced that decentralisation will lead to improvements in services and has tended to adopt the view that these can only come through the deployment of more resources. In interview, a senior NALGO branch representative conceded that decentralisation might improve the housing and building repairs service but characterised the initiative as a whole as 'a fetish'. He stated that the policy might lead to the collapse of certain areas of the council's service in the future. Given this lack of positive commitment to decentralisation, the unions have devoted their attentions to minimising any adverse consequences for the workforce. This had had a number of results. In the first place, it has delayed the implementation of the policy. Negotiation has slowed the process of change. In the second place, it has increased the cost of the policy. The Whitley conciliators noted in September 1984 that, in order to secure the acceptance of decentralisation, the council had offered to the unions up to 100 upgradings for existing staff and in excess of 100 additional posts. A large number of these concessions were compatible with the council's commitments to improve services, create jobs and combat low pay. The unions, however, have pushed the council further than they intended to go and further demands remain to be settled. According to the NALGO branch quoted above, the unions have enjoyed "considerable success in negotiation". A third consequence of the bargaining process has been to knock some of the radical edges off the council's proposals. The unions throughout have sought to minimise the impact of decentralisation on the conditions and working practices of their members. The view of a councillor heavily involved in drawing up and implementing the policy was that union influence had led to a "more rigid and more hierarchical" form of organisation than originally intended.

Trade union interests and bureaucracy

The policy initiatives of the GLC and Islington amount to attempts to refashion and partially withdraw from the conventional bureaucratic forms of organisation found in local government. The GLC's equal opportunities policy is an attempt to amend a particular form of bureaucratic employment relation, while Islington's decentralisation programme has at its heart an attempt to reform a complex of bureaucratic work relations.[23] Conflict has arisen with the trade unions because the bureaucratic forms which are the object of change incorporate important interests of local government workers. In defence of those interests workers and their representatives have resisted change.

In the GLC case the council set aside a system of agreed rules governing promotion and recruitment because this limited its ability to pursue a policy of 'positive action' for women and minority group workers. The GLC wished to redraw the rules governing promotion and recruitment in order to facilitate its political object of reducing the relative disadvantage of these groups in both the external and internal labour markets. One set of procedures which restricted the council's freedom to initiate policy, therefore, was replaced with another which enhanced it. This change was perceived as a threat by those who hitherto had been sheltered from competition and who were represented by the GLCSA.

In Islington the council developed plans for a flexible, task oriented form of work organisation. It envisaged replacing the existing extensive division of labour with a greater integration of functions at the point of service and wider discretion for front-line staff. These proposals were presented as an opportunity to increase job satisfaction. The reaction of the workforce, however, displayed an overriding concern with the quantitative impact of decentralisation on working conditions. There was widespread anxiety that the movement to neighbourhood offices would lead to an intolerable increase in workloads. This led the unions to attempt to negotiate guarantees that there would be no deterioration in working conditions and to demand compensation in the form of upgrading where they believed jobs were being expanded. It was clear that the existing framework of rules governing work and the relations between jobs were perceived as important defences by staff. They set limits on the exercise of managerial authority and provided the means for workers to cope with a demanding and occasionally hostile client population.

Bureaucracy, therefore, although it may originate as a structure of managerial control over work and workers, may simultaneously protect the collective interests of those whose careers and work routines are regulated. In local government, the case studies indicate, collective bargaining has led to the extension of trade union influence over the bureaucratic form. Career systems have been moulded to suit the needs of employees; job descriptions have been written to limit workloads. In addition to protecting the substantive interests of local government workers, however, bureaucracy can further the procedural goals of local government trade unions.[24] The detailed specification of work tasks, relations between jobs and methods of recruitment can function as base lines for negotiation. Attempts by managers to alter the structure can provide the unions with the opportunity to bargain over job descriptions, gradings and staffing levels. In the GLC and in Islington the attempt by the council to refashion part of the organisation initiated precisely this sort of bargaining process.

Trade union influence over bureaucracy may serve not merely to shield workers from the exercise of management control, it may also serve to shield them from the competition of groups beyond the employing organisation. Bureaucratic rules which incorporate the interests of local government workers may effectively exclude the interests of other, less advantaged groups. The unreformed grading structure at the GLC can be viewed as restricting the job opportunities of women and ethnic minority workers thus reproducing their disadvantage in the labour market. In Islington trade union restrictions on flexible working, workloads and office opening hours can be seen as similarly opposed to the interests of the borough's largely working class client population. Different appreciations of the function of union-authored controls have underlain the conflicts between left councils and trade unions. The councils, not surprisingly, have emphasised the consequences of union controls for groups beyond the immediate organisation and have accused the unions of a lack of concern for those who fall outside the ranks of those they represent. The unions, for their part, have emphasised the consequences for their members of abandoning existing procedures and have accused the councils of wanton managerialism.

Left Labour councils and the management of change

The Labour left has attempted to use local government to effect radical political change. In both the GLC and Islington it has revealed a commitment to rapid innovation and the development of novel, less bureaucratic organisational forms and practices. In order to realise its political strategy the left has attempted to create a much more unitary form of organisation. In pursuit of change it has striven to achieve tighter political control over all innovation and much routine local government work.

This can be seen in its attitude to local government managers. The left has been keen to subdue 'the bureaucracy'. Chief officers inherited from previous administrations, who were judged to be out of sympathy with present council policy, have been encouraged to leave and have been replaced by more supportive managers. In the GLC, for instance, the existing controller of personnel was declared redundant and managers with specific responsibility for equal opportunities were appointed at a senior level. There has also been a tendency for councillors to intervene in the running of departments and attempt a closer supervision of management work. In Islington the decentralisation of building works has been accompanied by the extensive involvement of councillors in the day-to-day operations of the department.

The desire to create a more politicised and unitary organisation can also be discerned in the Labour left's orientation to industrial relations. A notable feature of decentralisation in Islington and the GLC's equal opportunities programme has been the attempt to foster positive support from the trade unions. In both authorities the council has tried to bind the unions into the policy formulation process. The GLC invited the unions to sit on its equal opportunities monitoring group, a consultative body separate from the established collective bargaining machinery. Islington wanted the unions to participate in developing the details of its decentralisation programme. These attempts to secure the identification of the unions with policy have been combined with measures to build general employee support. Both authorities have used regular and well-designed information bulletins to explain their policies to staff. Islington has produced Neighbourhood News to communicate the details and rationale of decentralisation, while the GLC has published a magazine called Equals to serve a similar purpose for its equal opportunities policy. More radically, both councils have gone directly to staff to explain and seek their views on policy. Islington attempted to hold workplace meetings on decentralisation, while the GLC has organised mass meetings of ethnic minority staff in the GLC to generate debate about equal opportunities. It has been noted that in the private sector many managers have responded to the increased competitive pressures of the 1980s by trying to foster workforce co-operation through communication and consultation exercises.[25] The GLC and Islington cases indicate that Labour controlled authorities have responded to political uncertainty in a similar manner.

The response of the trade unions to these attempts to reconstruct industrial relations has been generally defensive and occasionally hostile. The unions in both authorities have been mindful of the possible costs of change for their members and loath to depart from the existing arm's length relationship. In interview, for example, an officer of the GLCSA stated that "We wouldn't regard them (the council) as anything other than employers when the chips are down". A representative of NALGO in Islington made a similar point. Commenting on the council's offer of consultation on decentralisation he argued that practices of this kind "tie you as a trade union to becoming part of the employers' machinery". These opinions have been mirrored in action. Islington NALGO declined the council's invitation to participate and the GLCSA has adopted a defensive posture in the equal opportunities monitoring group. The union's sharpest opposition, however, has been reserved for attempts to discuss policy directly with the workforce. These have been regarded as a threat to trade union representation itself and the unions have attempted to bring them to a close.

Faced with trade unions unwilling to grant open ended support for their policies Labour councils have tended to lurch towards a much harder position. Both the GLC and Islington, frustrated by what they considered to be unreasonable trade union opposition, decided to impose change. Unable to carry the unions with them they resolved to act without them. In both authorities there was a conviction that an electoral mandate gave the council the right to override the sectional interests of trade unions. The result of the GLC's decision to impose the new grading structure and of Islington's decision to advertise neighbourhood office posts without agreement, was to generate a crisis in industrial relations. Both decisions were effective, however, in quickening the process of change and once the initial crisis had passed 'normal' industrial relations re-asserted themselves. In effect, unilateral action by the authorities issued in a process of productivity bargaining in which the unions sought to extract compensation for change and to shield their members from its most adverse consequences. The strength of trade unionism in the two authorities and the ideological proclivities of the councils themselves ruled out any sustained attempt to manage without agreement.

The GLC and Islington, therefore, both tended to adopt unitary approaches to the management of change. On the one hand, they attempted to secure a fusion of their own and the unions' objectives by drawing the unions into the process of policy making. On the other hand, when hoped for co-operation was not achieved, they attempted to deny the union's influence and proceed without their agreement. Each of these ventures into unitarism, however, tended to collapse fairly rapidly into collective bargaining, and, through collective bargaining, the unions have been able to exert considerable influence over the details of both the GLC's and Islington's policies.

The disadvantages of collective bargaining, as far as the authorities are concerned, is that it can delay and moderate change and also increase its cost. This latter factor was not so important for the relatively wealthy GLC though alarm has grown in Islington at the financial implications of union requests for regrading and additional appointments in return for decentralisation. If the financial pressures on Labour controlled authorities continue to increase, then the costs of bargaining over change may come to be seen by councils as intolerable and excessive. Experiments with unitarism are therefore likely to continue. If the local government unions retain their present suspicion of participation and are unwilling to provide generalised support for local socialism then these experiments are likely to take the form of the unilateral imposition of change. Disputes between the two wings of what frequently considers itself a common labour movement are likely to continue.

Notes and References

1. **Sharron, H.** (1985) 'Overcoming trade union resistance to local change', Public Money, Vol 4, No 4; **Wolmar, C.** (1984) 'Divided we stand', New Socialist, December.

2. **Ingham, M.** (1985) 'Industrial relations in British local government', Industrial Relations Journal, Vol 16, No 1.

3. This is not meant to minimise the role of local government trade unions in the campaign against ratecapping and the abolition of the metropolitan authorities. My point is simply that industrial action has been initiated with greater frequency against Labour, and particularly left Labour, authorities than it has against authorities controlled by other parties.

4. **Ingham, M.** (1985) op cit, p 12.

5. **Ibid,** p 13.

6. **Ingham, M.** (1985) op cit, pp 11-12.

7. **Sharron, H.** (1984) 'Islington's legacy of bitterness', Social Work Today, 30 July.

8. Two examples are: **Blunkett, D. and Green, G.** (1983) Building from the bottom: the Sheffield experience, Fabian Tract 491, London Fabian Society, pp 20-22; and **Held, D. and Keane, J.** (1984) 'Socialism and the limits of state action' in **Curran, J.** (ed) The future of the left, London: Polity Press.

9. **Rose, H.** (1983) 'Property of the professionals', New Statesman, 30 September.

10. **Livingstone, K.** (1981) 'Interview with J. Rodrigues', Marxism Today, November.

11. A fuller description of Islington's proposals is to be found in **Heery, E.** 'Decentralisation in Islington', in **Hambleton, R. and Hoggett, P.** (1984) The politics of decentralisation: theory and practice of a radical local government initiative, School for Advanced Urban Studies, Working Paper 46, University of Bristol.

12. **Hain, P.** (1983) The democratic alternative: a socialist response to Britain's crisis, Harmondsworth: Penguin.

13. **Livingstone, K.** (1985) 'Fifth column', New Socialist, February.

14. **Gyford, J.** (1983) 'The new urban left: a local road to socialism', New Society, 22 April.

15. The two case studies are based on a series of interviews with councillors, officers and trade union representatives in the two authorities conducted between 1983 and 1985. Use was also made of internal council documents and trade union publications and of the considerable amount of material which has appeared on Islington and the GLC in the press and professional journals. I would like to thank all those who took part in the study for their help and co-operation. All views expressed in the paper, however, are solely those of the author.

16. **Livingstone, K.** (1983) 'Finding a role for the GLC -interview', Waterloo Sunset, GLC NALGO, June; 'Interview with J. Rodrigues', op cit.

17. London Town, the GLC staff magazine, which incorporates 'Staff Association News' and which has an editorial line generally supportive of the GLCSA, responded to the equal opportunities policy as follows: "It matters not one jot or tittle whether the council's or the ILEA's service is staffed one hundred per cent by black women or one hundred per cent by white men. What does matter is that they should be selected on merit alone without regard to bogus and irrelevant 'equality targets' or political leanings." London Town, September 1983.

18. The Staff Association wanted to preserve two separate streams, administrative/executive/clerical and professional/technical, 'Staff Association News', London Town, February 1983.

19. London Town was insistent that external recruitment "must be under strict control and safeguard", and must not lead to a situation "where the most attractive posts are likely to be filled externally", October 1982.

20. 'Staff Association News', London News, August 1983.

21. 'Decentralisation - the NALGO view', Neighbourhood News - Islington council's decentralisation bulletin, No 1, July 1983, London Borough of Islington.

22. 'Decentralisation - the MATSA view', Neighbourhood News - Islington council's decentralisation bulletin, No 3, October 1983, London Borough of Islington.

23. **Littler, C.** (1982) The development of the labour process in capitalist societies, London: Heinemann, p 38.

24. **Crouch, C.** (1982) Trade unions: the logic of collective action, Glasgow, Fontana, p 149. Crouch defines a procedural goal as "the right to control, to co-determine, or to bargain every detail of the work relationship".

25. **Edwards, P.** (1985) 'Myth of the macho manager', Personnel Management, April.

12

A FAREWELL TO MASS PRODUCTION? DECENTRALISATION AS AN EMERGENT PRIVATE AND PUBLIC SECTOR PARADIGM

Paul Hoggett

Well before we became involved in a recent study of decentralisation in Birmingham[1] our research and consultancy experience with a number of local authorities embarking upon programmes of decentralisation had convinced us of the need for caution - of the danger of being deceived by the disarming familiarity of a word which our experience suggested usually masked a multiplicity of prescriptions addressed to different symptoms. There is a sense in which decentralisation is an almost 'empty' term, a kind of camouflage behind which a diverse range (of often incompatible) political and organisational strategies can find cover. Our research on decentralisation in the London Borough of Hackney in 1982-83 certainly supports this interpretation. In this instance the word 'decentralisation' concealed a situation in which there were a number of competing initiatives with entirely different political and organisational factions lining up behind each one.[2]

In Hackney in January 1983 we found not one decentralisation initiative but four competing initiatives: a tenants'/building workers' initiative; a progressive managerial initiative being pushed forward by senior officers in the housing department; a pragmatic 'nascently Kinnockite' initiative;[3] and a radical libertarian initiative. Whilst in January the latter initiative appeared to be very much in the ascendancy (indeed it was councillors and officers aligned with this approach who were the initial sponsors of our research) by the beginning of March this particular faction had been essentially crushed. The first Hackney Redprint was thrown out without even having been disseminated beyond Labour Group, and a second pragmatically oriented initiative was being prepared. A year later the first two initiatives were to collide head-on resulting in the occupation of 'area bases' by tenants and building workers and their eventual removal by the guerilla tactics of housing management staff.

We felt that this experience was possibly an exception. That perhaps the hectic politicking of this local authority (correctly characterised by one witness[4] as Lebanese-like in its virulence and complexity) could be written off as an inner-London phenomenon.

Between November 1984 and March 1985 we had a second opportunity to study the emergence of decentralisation this time in Birmingham, a quite different local authority in terms of its culture and traditions. Whilst we found that the intensity of factionalising in Birmingham at this time was far more moderate than in Hackney, we were nevertheless surprised and relieved to find that in all other respects the route through which the initiative was developing closely resembled the one we had observed in Hackney.

As Chapter 5 explains in more detail we discovered three quite different conceptions of decentralisation within Birmingham's own Labour Group, each jockeying for position as the initiative unfolded. The dominant conception we described as 'enlightened bureaucratic' (a form of decentralised centralism) through which the main service departments were to be squeezed between an outer ring of neighbourhood shock-troops and the powerful chief executive function together with its political correspondent, the performance review committee. Many officers and councillors saw this as 'corporate management' in a new guise. Birmingham's Labour Group had experimented extensively with a tup down approach to corporate management in the mid 1970s, although the experiment foundered upon the sheer power of the 'service department empires'. A second conception, associated particularly with the Leader of the Labour Group, Dick Knowles, was essentially populist in character. It emphasised 'bringing the people' back into local government through decentralised forms of representative democracy (area committees and urban parish councils) but was profoundly suspicious of forms of community political organisation outside of the main party system (ie expressions of 'direct' as opposed to 'representative' democracy). The third conception, associated with a number of the younger 'educated' left wing councillors, appeared to resemble the pragmatic leftist initiative which emerged briefly in Hackney - it emphasised the localisation of service delivery across a number of the key public service departments and the encouragement of community development initiatives at the neighbourhood office level.

We do not wish to illustrate the process of intricate competition which took place between these differing conceptions; readers will find this retold in our final report.[5]   Suffice it to say that the competition appeared to assume a more amicable and decorous form than in Hackney and looks like resulting in over 40 neighbourhood offices which seek to contain both 'enlightened bureaucratic' and 'pragmatic leftist' conceptions (an uneasy and possibly unworkable compromise!).

I have recounted these two experiences in some detail because they serve to illustrate the way in which we have come to see decentralisation in processual terms.   We feel strongly that the study, let alone the evaluation, of decentralisation cannot be undertaken satisfactorily from within the research paradigm that presently dominates the sociology of organisations, a model that as some writers have noted recently:

> .... leads to research and theorising focusing upon organisations as wholes, paying rather more attention to organisational objectives and goals than to individuals and groups comprising the organisation.[6]

In contrast we advocate an approach which sees objectives as 'emergent' and 'shifting' rather than as 'givens', and which sees organisations as essentially political systems - that is, where issues of power, values and interests and their conflictual interaction are paramount.   It necessitates an approach to the task of understanding which is sufficiently free from preconceptions to allow for the possibility, for instance, that the 'decentralisation initiative' that emerges is actually a new form of centralisation. Hence our notion of decentralisation as an 'empty term' referring to a political and organisational space which can be filled by a whole range of initiatives masquerading behind this bland heading. Thus the term 'decentralisation' may actually obscure initiatives whose essential logic ranges from the centralisation of institutional power to managerialist cost cutting and rationalisation,[7] from the incorporation of urban social movements within the tentacles of the local state[8] to Eurocommunist and Libertarian Socialist strategies aimed at the transformation of state, economy and civil society.[9] Bearing in mind that the term 'decentralisation' may be used as much for the purpose of dissimulation as for understanding, we will use the term 'as if we knew what it referred to' until further notice.

217

Of course if one focuses only upon British local government it might seem that we are trying to read too much into what is, surely, a fairly narrow range of initiatives. The point is that our own parochialism as observers of British local government perhaps blinds us to the fact that the decentralist tide we have seen developing here over the past few years is no more than an echo of much wider and deeper social disturbances. Thus decentralisation hit the private sector in the mid 1970s and has proceeded with such vigour that in some countries - notably USA, Japan and Italy - it has now acquired the status of an emergent corporate paradigm.[10] Nor, as Chapter 3 indicates, is the experience of British local government particularly 'ahead of its time' when considered in the context of other European Social Democracies.

What might such 'wider and deeper social disturbances' be? Is it possible that the waves now crashing around the once tranquil civic offices of Birmingham and Islington are in some way an expression of subterranean movements almost beyond the conscious comprehension of the actors and factions involved? This draws us to the problem of the relationship between 'praxis' and 'process'. Theories of organisation which draw our attention to organisations as the site for fundamentally political relationships - the struggle between competing values, interests and objectives - are certainly an advance upon approaches which take goals, rules, power and authority as 'givens'. Nevertheless we must also recognise that organisational politics are as much a product of a prior determination as they are an expression of self-determination; actors and factions do have conscious and articulated purposes and values (ie praxis) but they may also be the empty vessels through which deeper social processes speak.

A new techno-managerial paradigm

The point has now been reached at which to dive deeper beneath the surface appearance of things to discover whether indeed some underlying social processes can be found at work. As previously mentioned, decentralisation hit the private sector some time before it found an echo within the public sector. We need to consider whether there might be some link between the two, whether decentralisation, far from being a passing fad, actually corresponds to a fundamental change in the organisation of productive processes throughout all advanced capitalist economies. Are the changes we are now seeing within the public sector in any way an expression of wider restructuring processes necessary for the capitalist economies to pull themselves out of this prolonged recession?

Crude Marxist analyses would answer this affirmatively. Rationalisation, speed-up, cut-backs and redundancies impacting upon public and private sectors alike are seen from this perspective as the necessary medicine to get profitable production going again. Of course in part this perspective is correct. Its limitations lie in the assumption that a resurgent capitalism of the 1990s would look very much like the resurgent capitalism of the 1950s. Such analyses assume capitalist development to be a continuous process, historical discontinuity only occurring with the revolutionary transformation of one mode of production to another (eg from capitalism to socialism).

More recently an alternative perspective has arisen propounded by both Marxist and non-Marxist economists. Often described as 'Long Wave' theory, this approach assumes that capitalism actually proceeds via a massive wave-like movement of alternating periods of growth and stagnation, each lasting decades. Each wave essentially corresponds to a revolution in the form of the capitalist mode of production. Capitalist development is itself therefore a discontinuous process, and whilst the discontinuities may not be as great as the passage from one mode of production to an altogether different one they nevertheless involve quite profound social upheavals.[11]

During the last few years a convergence has also occurred between Long Wave theory and less 'macro' research on economic restructuring. As capitalist firms attempt to reorganise themselves to cope with recession and to take advantage of technological innovations does the 'nature of the firm' change? When a factory becomes more automated does this shift its pattern of management and organisation in a certain direction? Increasingly research evidence does suggest the existence of such a shift, that approaches to the organisation and management of production that had been appropriate since the late 1940s are now being replaced by altogether new approaches. However before investigating these changes in more detail we need to examine more thoroughly the linkages that have been proposed between technology, organisation, economic development and social change.

For some time now Long Wave theorists have pointed to the association between periods of economic growth and revolutions in technology. Partly as a response to accusations of technological determinism models have emerged more recently which take a less technicist and more sociological view both of technology and its interaction with social and economic forces.[12] For example Peres has recently argued that each long wave of growth and stagnation corresponds to a new 'technological style' - a combination of changed technology and changed management and organisation. The postwar boom was based upon a 'technological style' combining Fordist techniques of mechanised mass production and Taylorist models of management and organisation. Moreover, she argues that each revolution in technological style necessitates a corresponding revolution in the 'socio-institutional' arrangements of society. Fordist mass production required arrangements for the rapid development of mass consumption (consumer credit, advertising and the development of mass communications industries etc), greatly increased state intervention in production and consumption (hence the Keynesian welfare state), decolonisation to overcome the limits to capital accumulation imposed by arbitrary international colonial boundaries, and so on. In a similar vein other writers have talked of successive 'social structures of accumulation' consisting of "all the institutions that impinge upon the accumulation process .... among the most important are the system ensuring money and credit, the pattern of state involvement in the economy, and the structure of class struggle".[13]

How then do these analyses help us to make sense of the changes which appear to be sweeping across the private and public sectors in the 1980s, changes that we argue correspond to a decentralist trend rather than a decentralist fad? The ascending movement of the post-war boom was based technically upon Fordist mass production. Production was geared to huge outputs of a few standardised products, economies of scale were paramount, flexibility of production was limited and quantity counted above quality. Managerially the ascending wave found expression through the Taylorisation of the labour process - the fragmentation and specialisation of work, the de-skilling of manual labour through the removal of discretion, knowledge and decision-making which became transferred to the 'medium layers' of company professionals, managers and technicians, and so on.

During the descending movement, all of yesterday's innovations become today's problems - the firm becomes fettered by its own massivity, economies of scale become diseconomies - both the previous techno-managerial paradigm and the socio-institutional arrangements necessary for its diffusion prove to be incompatible with the requirements of the new productive forces. The revolution in micro-electronics, robotics and information technology leads towards the flexible, automated production of a hugely diversified range of more custom-designed, quality products.

The recent book by Blackburn, Coombs and Green can help us understand these changes in more detail. They argue that mechanisation, far from being a unilinear process, has actually developed at different speeds in three distinctively different areas of the production process. Primary mechanisation refers to technological advances made in the way in which raw materials are transformed - ie it refers to the technical development of the tool (irrespective of whether this is a lathe or a typewriter). Secondary mechanisation refers to technological advances made in the way in which materials are transferred from one 'tool' to another - the automated assembly line in car manufacture and 'continuous flow' techniques of production in chemical and food processing industry being the most vivid illustrations. However both the transformation of materials and their transfer from one area to another have to be controlled in some way - targets must be set, materials ordered, production lines synchronised to avoid bottlenecks, output levels monitored - countless activities such as these are involved in the planning, design, supervision and co-ordination of production. Tertiary mechanisation therefore refers to technical advances made in the control of the production process through advances in information technology. The key point is that whereas the last great period of economic growth was based upon revolutionary developments in secondary mechanisation (Fordism) Blackburn et al argue that the current technological revolution centres upon tertiary mechanisation. Whereas Fordism revolutionised the horizontal organisation of work neo-Fordism promises to revolutionise the vertical organisation of work - that is, the hierarchy of control which rests upon the shoulders of the production workers. Not only will many tasks concerned with the control of production become fully computerised but the computerisation of management information systems will enable organisations to dispense with layers of managers. Moreover the integration of computerised control functions within the tools themselves (self programming machine tools etc) breaks down the separation of 'head' and 'hands' that was the hallmark of Fordism. Hence job enlargement, the delegation of inspection and quality control to workers, Group Technology, participative shop-floor practices, and so on can be seen as harbingers of a new techno-managerial paradigm rather than simply another fad. Management advances by dispensing with managers!

221

Thus the distinction between production and information technologies is an important one. Whereas the current technological revolution considered as production technology points towards the fully automated and decentralised factory, considered as information technology it points towards entirely new ways of controlling the labour process. As I have argued elsewhere:

> The vast 'middle layers' of managers, administrators, technicians and designers created by the impoverishment and de-skilling of manual labour under Taylorism now find themselves obsolete. Their planning and control function becomes usurped by the computerisation of financial and budgetary systems, materials ordering systems, performance targeting and monitoring systems, computer based design, and so on. With the removal of such middle layers, organisational structures become flatter and less hierarchical.[14]

Thus the emergent techno-managerial paradigm replaces bureaucratic supervision by delegation, participation and team work organised within a subtle framework of increasingly computerised control systems. Within this framework the exercise of authority becomes separated from its spatial location[15] - GEC in America can abolish company headquarters, radically decentralise to 50 or more 'cost and innovation centres' and in doing so can exercise greater control than it ever could under the old centralised system. This is what Aglietta[16] refers to as neo-Fordism. Thus under the new paradigm organisational decentralisation can actually facilitate the concentration of power.

Decentralisation as a 'progressive capitalist model' for the Welfare State?

What, then, have these theories of new developments in the private sector got to do with the welfare state? There seem to me to be two fundamental political objectives underlying socialist strategies for decentralisation within the local authorities. The first, dominant, objective is a concern to improve service delivery, the second objective concerns the redistribution of power between service providers and service consumers. The first then focuses upon the reform of local government, considered as an administrative and productive mechanism, the second focuses upon the reform of local government considered as a political system. The first objective seems to me to be primarily instrumental in character. It is concerned to defend local government and the principle of 'collective provision for public need' against the two-pronged attack of privatisation and centralisation. The second objective is more fundamentally ideological in character, its concern is both to extend and go beyond the existing limitations of representative democracy.

So far our analysis has focused upon possible changes in the private sector. Is there any way in which contemporary developments in the public sector (specifically those attempts to reform, through decentralisation, its administrative and productive processes), mirror what is going on in the wider economy? At first sight the parallels do not seem obvious. Secondary mechanisation does not appear to be a noticeable feature of the post-war state sector, one looks in vain for instances of Cowley-type assembly lines in the NHS or local government.

Looked at in another way however the parallels seem striking. The Keynesian welfare state has traditionally been concerned with the mass production of a few standardised products. Economies of scale have been constantly emphasised. Flexibility of production has been minimal. Production has in fact been organised on an 'assembly line principle', with professional and semi-professional 'people processors' replacing the material processing lines of mechanised factories. Unlike Fordist forms of organisation however the mechanisation of the transfer of information and resources between 'lines' has been inhibited by the power of professionalised departments to resist corporate approaches to problem solving.

The Keynesian welfare state therefore resembles Fordism without Ford. It resembles a kind of mongrel paradigm based on an uneasy marriage between a pre-Fordist craft (professional) productive system[17] and a Taylorised (rational-bureaucratic) system. Not surprisingly this mongrel form is neither efficient nor effective and it has been prone to constant reorganisations as attempts have been made to produce a coherent whole out of two contradictory elements[18] (the Griffiths reorganisation in the NHS being the most recent example).

The current crisis of the Keynesian welfare state is therefore not only a part of the wider crisis of all the socio-institutional arrangements of the declining long wave, it has also been generated by the internal contradiction at the heart of its own model of organising its productive forces. In addition this mongrel paradigm now has to contend, for the first time, with rapid changes in its own environment (sudden increases in local unemployment, inner city riots, etc) which cry out for speedy and flexible forms of state intervention.

Interestingly enough it is this 'mass production without Ford' which has been the main target of the critique developed by contemporary advocates of public sector decentralisation. Decentralisation has constituted an attack upon the massivity and remoteness, inflexibility, inefficiency and unresponsiveness of the welfare state. But the critique is not just an organisational critique, it is a political one also - it is a critique of certain collectivist ideologies for whom 'mass production without Ford' constituted a desirable model of socialism. The way in which programmed maintenance of council housing has been traditionally performed is a perfect illustration of the vindication of standardised, mass production by a political ideology in which collectivity was everything and individuality nothing. The design and maintenance of most council estates are a visible expression of a 'universalist conception' of the working class which has no place for diversity and difference. Considered politically this is 'Stalinism without Stalin'.[19] The social and political development which has thrown this ideology into crisis finds its expression today in the legitimate demand for a more differentiated state product. This demand comes directly from a new actor whose appearance over the last decade corresponds to another important change in the environment of most welfare state organisations - the 'differentiated consumer'. In contrast to the universal consumer the differentiated consumer presumes to enjoy certain distinctive characteristics - differentiated consumers may not be male breadwinners, nor white, nor able-bodied, nor even heterosexual, nor do they live in a 'universal area' but in a particular neighbourhood which has a particular name. Thus the development of more responsive forms of public service is a highly political issue as it offers the possibility of the development of a new form of collectivism, one founded upon the celebration of diversity rather than its disparagement.

In a strange sort of way I feel that things had come to such a pass in local government that it has required radical Labour councillors to show local government's 'managerial layers' what is best for them - it is almost as if councillors such as Brian Powell (of Walsall) and Maurice Barnes (of Islington) have dragged this layer 'kicking and screaming' into the latter part of the 20th century. Bearing in mind what has been said about the emergent techno-managerial paradigm of the private sector, I have been struck by the key role new technology has played in facilitating programmes of decentralisation, and particularly within housing departments. I have also been struck by the way in which In search of excellence has been adopted as the new managerial ideology in a number of key departments (eg Walsall, Glasgow) pursuing decentralisation.

If we leave aside the second, more ideological, principle underlying socialist approaches to decentralisation the 'service delivery' model of decentralisation appears to lead to new organisational and managerial forms strikingly reminiscent of the newer 'hi-tech' companies of the M4 Corridor: leaner and flatter managerial structures, decentralised 'cost and innovation centres' (ie district or neighbourhood offices with their own devolved budgets, powers over recruitment, performance indicators, etc) enlarged and more generic roles, team working, flexibility and informality, responsive back-line support to front-line staff, and so on. Aglietta[20] and others have noted how capitalism has had immense difficulty in developing the labour process within the service sector: as a consequence the 'productive forces' of this sector have remained highly under-developed. The distinctive feature of the current revolution in tertiary mechanisation is its applicability to precisely those areas - craft, small batch and service production - where Fordism made little headway. More important still, the uniqueness of local government compared with any other 'service industry' is the extent to which information has become one of its basic raw materials.

There are possibly three factors contributing here. Firstly, as Prottas[21] and others have noted, the exercise of management control over street level staff is an exacting task within welfare bureaucracies because of the enormous contingencies bearing upon the officer-client relationship. To get some glimmer of what is going on at this level, management has traditionally resorted to 'case files'. The information generated is perhaps more often a form of 'management reassurance' rather than 'management control' - no-one however can doubt the mountainous nature of case information built up within police, social service and housing departments. Secondly, unlike the private sector, the public sector is as much concerned with the management of need as it is with the satisfaction of need. Much of the work of local authority departments is concerned with the allocation of scarce resources and hence the mediation of consumption conflicts. Once more, information handling is crucial to the exercise of this task - information concerning resource availability (eg void control), the administration of waiting lists, the construction of complex eligibility criteria (more recently often involving equal opportunities considerations) etc. Finally the democratic process generates its own informational requirements; without facts and figures an accountable system of government is impossible.

Information is therefore one of local government's most vital raw materials: what poultry is to Kentucky Fried Chicken, information is to local government. I recently looked at the complete staffing structure of an inner London housing department and estimated that over 60% of the staff were primarily involved with storing, managing, manipulating or giving information! Perhaps the implication of this is that local government, more than any other public or private institution, is ripe for the current revolution in information technology.

The above has important political implications for decentralisation as a socialist project. As a number of writers have pointed out,[22] the revolution in information technologies is potentially also a revolution in control techniques. The establishment of what appears to be more autonomous neighbourhood and district units of organisation may have much more to do with the devolution of controls than with the devolution of powers. To my mind this is a crucial distinction. Decentralised systems could become a vehicle for the exercise of greater control over front-line staff, consumers and communities unless the secondary political objective (the redistribution of power between provider organisations and consumers) is given much greater priority than it has been so far. Without the development of such countervailing powers the decentralisation of service production will almost undoubtedly enhance the productive forces of the public sector but may do so via 'the centralisation of command'.

I would like to conclude by using the experience of Islington as an example of the dilemma facing the socialist project of decentralisation. Of all the decentralisation initiatives presently being undertaken within British local government at the present moment the Islington initiative[23] is certainly the most radical in terms of its scope, scale and complexity. Not only is the initiative multi-service, it has added new functions to the neighbourhood offices (community development and welfare rights), it has sought to integrate manual and white collar workers through moves towards a single-status workforce, it has fundamentally transcended the residential/fieldwork division within social services, reorganised central specialist functions such as architecture, engineering and construction on a new 'design and

226

construct basis' and it has helped facilitate the development of a neighbourhood forum alongside each neighbourhood office. Only the most begrudging and ungenerous person would fail to find this accomplishment considerable, but for those of us with a thorough grounding in the traditional assumptions of local government the experience of wandering around one of the new offices is positively breathtaking. Clearly during the next few years a whole range of adjustments and amendments will be made to the initiative as it accommodates to the contingencies of the Islington situation, indeed many of the initiative's more radical edges had already been knocked off during the complex employee negotiations which led to its implementation. Nevertheless, to my mind Islington stands closest to what I would see as a real socialist experiment within British local government. Personally I closely identify with what they are trying to achieve, there are precious few 'practical indications of socialism' emerging within our society to counterpose to the bureaucratic centralism of the Eastern Bloc nations. But here's the rub, the praxis of Islington's socialists may yet prove to be the vessel through which deeper societal processes find expression. For whilst this grand experiment may well prove to be a precious 'indication of socialism' it may, on the other hand, turn out to be a public sector expression of what Aglietta[24] terms neo-Fordism:

> .... a major revolutionisation of the labour process that tends to replace the mechanical principle of fragmented labour disciplined by hierarchical direction with the informational principle of work organised in semi-autonomous groups disciplined by the direct constraints of production itself.

As the trend towards decentralisation within the British public sector has broadened and deepened over the last few years so I have been impressed by the way in which its form has become increasingly managerialist and less overtly 'political'. In other words, if we consider decentralisation as an administrative and productive innovation then paradoxically as this innovation has undergone diffusion so it has become more diffuse, losing its original radical, political cutting-edge.

But perhaps this is how social systems normally change themselves. Perhaps the rule is that they are incapable of generating their own means of radical transformation from within. Perhaps innovators are always, and necessarily, 'outsiders' to such social systems, outsiders whose ideas at first seem crazy and heretical only later to become, in modified form, a new common sense. This then is the dilemma for any form of socialism which seeks to go beyond principled oppositionalism, that is, for a political practice which seeks to construct and innovate as well as oppose. As Daniel Cohn-Bendit is reported to have said to one of his liberal professors, "for you to be successful reformists, we have to be failing revolutionaries".[25]

The modern social democratic state is a remarkably complex phenomenon, a bizarre mixture of the modern and the pre-industrial, whose sophistication at times seems to be concentrated all in one area - ie in its ability to resist any fundamental forms of change. It is as frustrating to capitalists as it is to socialists; as Offe acutely observes, capitalism appears to be unable to live with it but nor can it live without it. A tradition of such pessimistic analyses has now built up, but this tradition has been based largely upon the experience of the Keynesian welfare state in 'normal times'. The point is that these are no longer 'normal times'.

The modern state emerged from the ashes of the last long wave during the years either side of the 2nd World War. Almost 50 years have elapsed since then. We are now in the depths of another grand recession. Our 'modern' state which was a part of the solution to the last recession is now part of the problem in this one. The role and function of the state is once more up for grabs. What kind of state will be necessary for the restructured capitalist economies to embark upon a new upswing? At the moment this is difficult to answer, not the least because the answer is not pre-determined. Peres, in particular, is at pains to point out that there is no one-to-one correspondence between an emerging technological style, and the socio-institutional arrangements necessary for its liberation. In the 1930s a wide range of scenarios for liberating the new productive forces were discernible from Hitler's Germany to Roosevelt's 'New Deal'. What is certain about such periods is that they are dominated by an atmosphere of political and cultural uncertainty. As Peres notes:

> The downswing is then a period of experimentation at all organisational levels of society, characterised by the proliferation of reassessments, proposed solutions and trial-and-error behaviour stimulated by the increasing gravity of the crisis. All this occurs in the face of the weight of tradition, of established ideas, of vested interests and other inertial forces which actively oppose the required transformations.[26]

228

That the current revolution in tertiary mechanisation provides an opportunity to vastly enhance the productive forces of the public sector there can be little doubt. The outline of the emerging techno-managerial paradigm, neo-Fordism, is now clearly discernible within the private and state sectors of production. I have argued that in some ways such developments in technique are peculiarly suited to the state sector given the centrality of information handling to its administrative and allocative functions. I have also suggested that the new developments should be welcomed to the extent that they provide more propitious conditions for the generation of a more differentiated state product and for the reintegration of many of the divisions which Taylorism has exacerbated within the public sector - between planning and implementation, design and execution, production and the supervision of production, etc. It would seem, then, that the technical conditions are beginning to emerge for a welfare state form which is more consumer-oriented, more efficient, less hierarchical and managerially more participative. Yet, as I have argued before, if it follows the private sector model it can become all these things yet still remain fundamentally undemocratic. If the welfare state became more like IBM and less like the Co-op its future would certainly become more secure but would it be any more recognisably socialist? I feel this brings us back to the point we have constantly reiterated within this collection of papers - the need to differentiate between the decentralisation of production and the democratisation of production. If the current wave of initiatives are to add up to something more than the welfare state acquiring a progressive capitalist image then consumerist and collectivist approaches to reform must be combined. This will require continuous effort as each advance becomes recouped and transformed by resistant forces into their own image. We need a kind of theory of 'permanent revolution' but one applied to changing our welfare state.

Notes and References

1. **Hambleton, R. and Hoggett, P.** (1985) Decentralisation in Birmingham. Report submitted to the ESRC Planning and Environmental Committee. See also Chapter 5 in this volume.

2. **Hoggett, P.** (1984) 'The politics of decentralisation in Hackney', in **Hambleton, R. and Hoggett, P.** (eds) The politics

of decentralisation: theory and practice of a radical local government initiative, Working Paper 46, School for Advanced Urban Studies, University of Bristol.

3. Interestingly enough the leading light behind this approach was Charles Clarke, the then Chair of Housing in Hackney, now Neil Kinnock's private secretary.

4. **Peters, G.** (1985) 'Different routes - same goal', Community Care, April 1985.

5. **Hambleton, R. and Hoggett, P.** (1985) op cit.

6. **Walsh, K., Hinings, B., Greenwood, R. and Ranson, S.** (1981) 'Power and advantage in organisations', Organization Studies 2.2.

7. Interestingly enough the decentralisation of Birmingham's social services department was first recommended by Price Waterhouse consultants during the brief 'Thatcherite' period of control of the city council between 1982-84.

8. **Ceccarelli, P.** (1982) 'Politics, parties and urban movements in Western Europe', in **Fainstein, N. and Fainstein, S.** (eds) Urban policy under capitalism, London: Sage.

9. **Evers, A.** (1981) 'Social movements and political power: a survey of a theoretical and political controversy', Comparative Urban Research 8(2) 29-47; **Castells, M.** (1983) 'Crisis, planning and the quality of life: managing the new historical relationships between space and society', Environment and Planning D: Society and Space 1.3, p 21.

10. See for example **Blackburn, P., Green, K. and Liff, S.** (1982) 'Science and technology in restructuring', Capital and Class, 18; **Murray, F.** (1983) 'The decentralisation of production - the decline of the mass-collective worker', Capital and Class 19; **Peters, T. and Waterman, R.** (1982) In search of excellence, New York, Harper and Row, provides the new managerial ideology for these structural changes.

11. **Mandel, E.** (1980) Long waves of capitalist development, Cambridge University Press; **Freeman, C., Clark, J. and Soete, L.** (1982) Unemployment and technical innovations: a study of long waves and economic development, London: Pinter.

12. **Peres, C.** (1983) 'Structural change and the assimilation of new technologies in the economic and social system', <u>Futures</u> 15.4.

13. **Blackburn, P., Coombs, R. and Green, K.** (1985) <u>Technology, economic growth and the labour process</u>, Macmillan; **Gordon, D.M., Edwards, R. and Reich, M.** (1982) <u>Segmented work, divided workers</u>, Cambridge University Press.

14. **Hoggett, P.** (1985) 'A long wave to freedom?' <u>Chartist</u> 106.

15. **Murray** (1983) op cit, describes this in terms of "the decentralisation of production" paralleling the "centralisation of command".

16. **Aglietta, M.** (1979) <u>A theory of capitalist regulation: the US experience</u>, New Left Books.

17. **Hoggett, P.** (1984) 'Decentralisation, labourism and the professionalised welfare state apparatus', in Hambleton and Hoggett (eds) op cit.

18. Heydebrand is one of the few writers to closely analyse this cleavage: **Heydebrand, W.** (1977) 'Organisational contradictions in public bureaucracies: toward a Marxian theory of organisation', <u>Sociology Quarterly</u>, 18:1.

19. **Polan, A.J.** (1984) <u>Lenin and the end of politics</u>, London: Methuen.

20. **Aglietta, M.** op cit, p 166.

21. **Prottas, G.** (1978) 'The power of the street-level bureaucrat in public service bureaucracies', <u>Urban Affairs Quarterly</u> 13.3.

22. **Greenwood, Onuf N.** (1984) 'Prometheus prostrate', <u>Futures</u> 16.1.

23. **Heery, E.** (1984) 'Decentralisation in Islington' in Hambleton and Hoggett (eds) op cit.

24. **Aglietta, M.** op cit, p 167.

25. Cited by **Castells** (1983) <u>The city and the grassroots,</u> Edward Arnold, p 322.

26. **Peres, C.** (1983) op cit, p 365.

ANNEX: DECENTRALISATION PROGRESS REPORT

The Decentralisation Research and Information Centre

Compiled by Danny Burns, Tim Kendrick, Kevin McGovern and Martin Tomlinson of the Decentralisation Research and Information Centre, School of Planning, Polytechnic of Central London.

This annex (correct at August 1986) provides brief profiles of decentralisation in:

Basildon	Lewisham
Birmingham	Manchester
Bradford	Newham
Edinburgh	Norwich
Glasgow	Sheffield
Hackney	Southampton
Hammersmith and Fulham	Tower Hamlets
Islington	Walsall
Lambeth	

Introduction

There are a number of different types of decentralisation although it is difficult to categorise absolutely, as there is a great deal of thematic overlap. The type of decentralisation which a local authority might adopt is determined by many factors. The most important of these is the political and managerial vision of what decentralisation should entail. This will have a bearing on what concept of 'neighbourhood' is being used, the services to be localised and the importance placed upon the devolution of political power.

There are also practical considerations such as the number of departments involved in the process, the existing organisation within these departments, the nature of the housing stock and any number of demographic factors.

These considerations often result in very different approaches. The following profiles highlight this fact. These councils vary in the degree to which they envisage devolving managerial responsibilities and political control. They by no means constitute a comprehensive list of local authorities which are going local or thinking about doing so, they are merely a sample of authorities which are presently implementing decentralisation proposals. Furthermore, while they are able to give an accurate picture of the most important decentralisation initiatives, because of their format they are unable to provide a more historical and thematic context. The following few pages attempt to fill that gap.

Historically it is possible to identify a few authorities such as Newcastle who were actively involved in area management initiatives in the mid-1970s. In 1974 Newcastle introduced a system of eight area housing committees. And in 1976 the council introduced a system of Priority Area Teams covering the more deprived part of the city (see Chapter 4 for more details).

The development of **patch social services** has been important. East Sussex County Council has had a 'patch' system in operation for about two years, each decentralised unit being a completely independent management entity. Likewise in 1984 Humberside social services department was extensively restructured. 48 neighbourhood teams were established which each served a population of about 18,000 and the high level of responsibility invested in the team managers has taken a great deal of the focus away from the director of social services.

The first political initiative came with the incoming Labour council in Walsall. Their manifesto displayed an overt link between creating a participatory democracy and sustaining a socialist local government. While their approach concentrated solely on housing it defined the areas of debate for many of the councils who were to follow. 80-90 'political officers' were appointed and 32 neighbourhood offices were set up offering a comprehensive housing service including housing management, housing aid, rent and rates collection, repairs and maintenance and information. Despite the fact that the Labour Party lost control in 1982 the initiative was sustained by the new administration. It should be noted that, at least in practice, this approach to participatory democracy was essentially passive; while it involved more people in the process of service delivery through dramatically increasing the demand for repairs etc, it did not develop any system of popular decision-making. Lambeth and Newham were to follow with **housing led programmes** which built on the 1982 manifesto commitments. The idea of consumer centres and new computer based communications systems were pursued.

The development of particular service led programmes concentrated on either housing or social services. However some authorities developed programmes for a **comprehensive decentralisation** of services. Islington, Manchester, Hackney and Birmingham were amongst them. While Hackney Council was at the forefront of these proposals, they soon became bogged down in a dispute with NALGO who boycotted all work on decentralisation for a year. Since then Islington has had the most success in implementation, having established 24 neighbourhood offices within half a mile of each resident. These offices involve decentralised social services and housing departments, as well as environmental health, welfare benefits and soon planning. Each office has its own neighbourhood forum.

Amongst these early decentralising authorities were authorities such as Camden and Haringey who have run into varying degrees of trouble, partially due to a waning in political enthusiasm after the 'honeymoon period' of 1982. Haringey has started completely afresh with new manifesto commitments in 1986. Camden's future is uncertain, the early decisions of the new council will determine how far Camden's programme gets off the ground at all. Other councils slowly began to build on the experiences of the earlier authorities to go local. Basildon, Greenwich, Edinburgh, Norwich, Renfrew, Kirklees and Wigan (amongst others) started to develop programmes. Some of these are still developing slowly, others such as Edinburgh have been accompanied by fresh manifesto commitments in 1986 which have injected new enthusiasm.

1986 has also seen a large number of new councils on the scene, either considering or starting to enact decentralisation programmes. These councils include:

> Ealing
> Gloucester
> Hammersmith and Fulham
> Isle of Wight
> Kingston
> Waltham Forest

This list is by no means exhaustive.

Since the 1986 local government elections perhaps the most significant development has been the election of the Liberals in Tower Hamlets. Having presented themselves to the electorate under a radical manifesto of decentralisation they very quickly introduced a new form of **decentralised control.** They have abolished all the central committees except the policy and resources committee, the statutory social services committee, a housing sub-committee and the newly created decentralisation committee. Following on from the first steps of Liberal Richmond, they have created seven area committees as full committees of the council. These committees are comprised of local ward councillors, and deal with all services within each of the individual 'hamlets'. Tower Hamlets has already reached the budgeting stage after only three months, but have not yet faced the crucial issue of industrial relations. It is worth bearing in mind here that this model of decentralisation is not unique, it was Basildon which first developed the concept of local all-purpose committees with primarily member representation. This is a significantly different approach to that of Islington for example, where there is more central control over resource distribution and where the maintenance of centrally determined policy such as equal opportunities is seen as important, but where there is also a greater degree of popular control in neighbourhood forums (even if at this stage they only have small independent budgets). The question of popular control has been important, and it is useful to further contrast the approach of Islington and Manchester. Islington has gone ahead very quickly with an idea and put it into practice, leaving the problems to be resolved in the actual situation, and Manchester has conducted a very far reaching consultation programme which has delayed implementation but may iron out more of the problems before implementation. Birmingham's parallel development of parish councils may also provide an added dimension to these (what must be seen as, at this stage) experiments with popular control.

Before completing this summary of the developments to date, it is essential to give some indication of the somewhat anomalous development of Glasgow Council who appear to have developed an extremely comprehensive devolution of housing services outside the processes which have stimulated other decentralisation programmes. Glasgow has 15 area housing offices which have complete control of their own budgets (this is likely to increase to 24). They are moving towards a system whereby each district would bid for budget allocation in a similar way to a local council's bid for rate support grant of Block Grant allocations. There are a variety of co-operative housing developments, where control has effectively been devolved to the tenants but the council retains ownership, as well as an increasing number of ownership co-operatives. There are various decision-making and consultative committees and even such developments as repairs co-operatives. It seems that these initiatives have not developed out of a single co-ordinated strategy, but are rather part of a continuous evolution towards participation in housing since 1956.

Above is an outline of the major developments of the last decade or so, but it must be stressed again that the list of authorities decentralising is not exhaustive, and inevitably this update will go out of date. It is hoped however that it is a useful summary.

BASILDON

Party in control:	Labour
Date of initial proposals:	1984
Total population:	160,000
Number of decentralised areas proposed:	Seven
Average population of decentralised areas:	23,000, however the defined areas are determined by the location of estates, not by population figures
Average number of dwellings in decentralised areas:	No figures available

Services to be decentralised:

Housing, including:

- Repairs
- Applications and lettings
- Rents and rates payments
- Estates management

Community services
Environmental health
Leisure and recreation
Planning (information)
Advisory and community services
Welfare rights
Information on all council services

Financial resources allocated:

Cost has been limited because no new staff have been recruited. Of the local offices now operating three required rehabilitation work costing around £100,000. Other costs such as new information systems are not available.

Number of staff in decentralised offices:

Ranges between 8 to 14

Organisation within decentralised offices:

Local area officer
(Town clerks dept)

Area assistant

Other officers still working within original division, eg housing assistants etc

Receptionist

Form of devolved control:

Joint estate management committees on council estates. Work on devolving decision-making to seven local committees is progressing. By September informal meetings will have taken place, by October the committees will have been formalised. Within 12 months there will be no service committees, and within two years there will be full area budgeting. The committees will consist of local elected members, members of JEMS, community representatives, and observers

Current state of play:

Six offices are open along with the central information office. The possibility of 20 sub offices is being considered. Environmental health officers should be located in offices within the next two months

239

BIRMINGHAM

Party in control: Labour

Date of initial proposals: 1983

Total population: 1 million

Number of decentralised
areas proposed: 45 at present

Average population of
decentralised areas: 22,700

Average number of   Ranges between 500 to 5,000
dwellings in   (council)
decentralised areas:

Services to be   Housing, including:
decentralised:
                                           -    Estates Management
                                           -    Advice on Housing Benefits

                                           Environmental health
                                           Social services
                                           Debt counselling
                                           Racism awareness

Financial resources
allocated: Figures not available

Number of staff in   Can vary greatly depending on the
decentralised offices: number of 'back up' staff. Ranges
                                           from seven to 116. In general, there
                                           are between five and 11 front-line
                                           staff

Organisation within   Front-line staff:
decentralised offices:
                                           Neighbourhood co-ordinator

                                           Neighbourhood assistants
             Chief   (one or more)
             Executives
                                           Clerical assistants
                                           (one or more)

Also:

Housing advisers (1-3)
Social service adviser (1)
Environmental health adviser (1)

Back-line staff:

Divided into teams including:

Housing
Environmental health
Social services (not always)

Form of devolved control: 12 area committees; one in each of the city's constituencies. These are advisory only and have small revenue budgets

Current state of play: 19 offices are open, another eight are due to be open by the end of 1986

The 12 area committees have been established. The council is presently discussing setting up 90 urban parish councils that will take decision-making down to units of an average of 10,000-20,000 people

See Chapter 5 for more detail on Birmingham.

BRADFORD

Party in control:	Labour
Date of initial proposals:	1982
Total population:	464,000
Number of decentralised areas proposed:	34
Average population of decentralised areas:	13,000
Average number of dwellings in decentralised areas:	1,000-1,500 (council)
Services to be decentralised:	Housing Also environmental health to be reorganised in 4-5 areas
Financial resources allocated:	Each office allocated £25,000 capital and a total revenue budget of £400,000
Number of staff in decentralised offices:	6-7 (max 10)
Organisation within decentralised offices:	Each office has a neighbourhood manager who reports to the area manager, of which there are seven
Form of devolved control:	Repair budgets will be decentralised with local committees to decide priorities
Current situation:	Nine offices opened so far, with a political decision to be fully decentralised by the end of this financial year

EDINBURGH

Party in control: Labour

Date of initial proposals: 1984

Total population: 439,000

Number of decentralised
areas proposed: 30-40

Average population of
decentralised areas: 12,000-15,000

Average number of
dwellings in
decentralised areas: Figures not available

Services to be   Probably 'all services where
decentralised: appropriate'

Financial resources
allocated: Figures not available

Number of staff in
decentralised offices: Not determined

Organisation within
decentralised offices: Not determined

Form of devolved control: The likelihood is that they would
                             follow the Basildon model, control
                             would be given to the people after
                             confidence had been gained in service
                             provision

Current situation: Six full-time and six part-time
                             workers seconded to work on
                             decentralisation. There have been
                             political guarantees

GLASGOW

Party in control: Labour

Date of initial proposals: 1956

Total population: 750,000

Number of decentralised areas proposed: 15 (considering increasing it to 24)

Average population of decentralised areas: 50,000

Average number of dwellings in decentralised areas: 2,500-18,000

Services to be decentralised: Housing

Financial resources allocated: District housing offices are completely in control of their own finance, and bid for budget allocation in a similar way to block grant or RSG allocations (this is the main role of the central housing dept)

Number of staff in decentralised offices: 13-100

Organisation within decentralised offices: -

Form of devolved control: Varies greatly, with tenant management co-ops, repairs co-ops, ownership co-ops, various committees

Current situation: As above: but paper on decentralisation to be presented soon

HACKNEY

Party in control:	Labour
Date of initial proposals:	1982
Total population:	183,000
Number of decentralised areas proposed:	30 (six districts)
Average population of decentralised areas:	6,000
Average number of dwellings in decentralised areas:	Ranges between 1,300 to 2,000

Services to be decentralised:

Housing, including

- Estates management
- Some local repairs (based on estates)

Rents and Transfers remain at district level

Financial resources allocated: No figures available

Number of staff in decentralised offices: Normally about eight

Organisation within decentralised offices:

Area officer

(3 or 4) Estates managers

(2) Area management assts

(1) Area clerk

A rota system operates for reception involving all staff

Form of devolved control: There are about four area forums per district which meet every two to three months. These are made up of tenants/residents representatives, ward members, district housing staff and community workers. They discuss a wide range of issues but are advisory only. Their recommendations are passed on to district housing committees

Current situation: Nearly all the local offices are operating. The new council is due to take early decisions on any future proposals for comprehensive decentralisation

HAMMERSMITH AND FULHAM

Party in control:	Labour
Date of initial proposals:	1986
Total population:	140,000
Number of decentralised areas proposed:	Possibly 8-10 but undetermined. Distribution of areas on a ward basis has already been rejected
Average population of decentralised areas:	-
Average number of dwellings in decentralised areas:	-
Services to be decentralised:	As yet undetermined, it may be comprehensive, social services and housing are likely to be the priorities
Financial resources allocated:	There is money available although amounts are undecided, local budgets may be introduced later
Number of staff in decentralised offices:	-
Organisation within decentralised areas:	-
Form of devolved control:	Area forums with devolution of money and responsibility are being considered
Current situation:	A decentralisation unit is currently being set up. As yet there are no definitive proposals. There will be an open forum for members, staff and unions. There are proposals for a large survey, possibly with as high as 10% sample. The council would like to see proposals by autumn. Various options are currently being discussed

ISLINGTON

Party in control: Labour

Date of initial proposals: 1982

Total population: 163,000

Number of decentralised
areas proposed: 24

Average population of   7,000
decentralised areas: (Ranges from 4,500 to 8,000)

Average number of
dwellings in   Ranges from 2,000 to 4,000
decentralised areas:

Services to be   Social Services
decentralised:
                                     Housing, including

- Rent payments
- Estates management
- Housing benefits
- Repairs

Environmental health
Planning
Welfare benefits

Financial resources   £9.8m is the final anticipated capital
allocated: expenditure for all neighbourhood
                                     offices between 1983-1987. The
                                     average cost per NO is £400,000. The
                                     council is also spending £3.5m on
                                     setting up a computer system in the
                                     borough based on a five year plan

Number of staff in   Average of about 40 staff per office
decentralised offices: plus about eight to 10 local repairs
                                     operatives where appropriate. (There
                                     are 16 local repair teams)

Form of devolved control: 24 neighbourhood forums are to be set up. The constitution of each forum will, as far as possible, be determined locally within guidelines established by the council. Initially they will have authority to spend a proportion of Islington's Partnership money (£1m in 19 86/87) on estate security and environmental improvements. Forums will also be allocated a 'community budget' of £2,000 for publicity purposes and social activities. It is envisaged that forums will eventually exercise a full range of decision-making powers with the exception of lettings and staffing

Current situation: 21 offices are open, the last ones are due to be operational by the end of October 1986. At present two Neighbourhood Forums have been fully constituted, seven others are in the pipeline and the rest are at various stages of development

The general political approach to decentralisation in Islington is outlined in Chapter 2. The neighbourhood forums are referred to in a discussion of ways of infusing representative with direct democracy in Chapter 4.

249

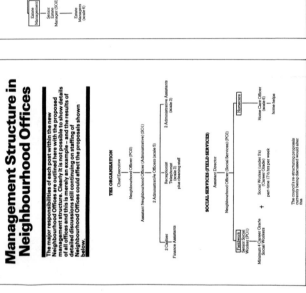

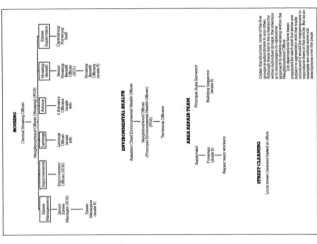

LAMBETH

Party in control:	Labour
Date of initial proposals:	1982
Total population:	248,000
Number of decentralised areas proposed:	32 (five districts)
Average population of decentralised areas:	7,750
Average number of dwellings in decentralised areas:	1,500 (council)

Services to be decentralised:

Housing including:

- Estates Management
- Repairs (16 teams)
- Housing benefit (at district level)

Financial resources allocated:

Figures not available

Number of staff in decentralised offices:

15 to 20. In some areas each neighbourhood housing officer is responsible for about 600 dwellings, in areas of greater stress this figure is 350

Organisation within decentralised offices:

All work on reception desk

Senior neighbourhood officer

Neighbourhood housing officers

Permanent Admin/Clerical staff (2), (there is a pool of admin staff that can be deployed to different offices)

Form of devolved control:

Local consultative estate strategy meetings which resolve minor issues, eg repairs delays. There are also five district housing committees which have tenant representatives from Tenants' Associations and the Lambeth Federation of Tenants on them. The DMCs deal with broader policy matters

Current state of play: All 32 local offices are open and the 16 local repairs teams are operating. Future plans include: decentralisation of housing benefits (public and private) within two years, decentralisation of rent accounts, housing development and other housing services within 18 months.

There are also plans to set up three Housing Aid Centres each with 40 staff

LEWISHAM

Party in control: Labour

Date of initial proposals: 1982

Total population: 232,000

Number of decentralised areas proposed: Not finally determined, initially five offices being built (joint housing and social services), possibly there will be 20-24 neighbourhood offices in the long run

Average population of decentralised areas: -

Average number of dwellings in decentralised areas: -

Services to be decentralised: Housing, social services, repairs (20 local repairs teams are operating), advice and information. Decisions on other services will be made later

Financial resources allocated: First five offices - £2.1 million capital. Revenue for the first five years is estimated at approximately £1 million

Number of staff in decentralised offices: Not finalised, but at least 36 plus repair team operatives

Organisation within decentralised offices: A management team of three plus a neighbourhood repairs officer oversees three teams within the office. These are the housing, social services and chief executive (headed by the information officer) teams

Form of devolved control: Not determined

Current situation: Three offices will be opened by the end of 1986, two will be opened early 1987. Discussions on further progress are currently at member level with important decisions to be made towards the end of September 1986

MANCHESTER

Party in control: Labour

Date of initial proposals: 1984

Total population: 455,000

Number of decentralised areas proposed: Not finally determined, but will be between 50 and 60

Average population of decentralised areas: 7,500 to 9,000 (varies greatly between areas)

Average number of dwellings in decentralised areas: Ranges between 1,500 to 6,000 in those areas so far declared

Services to be decentralised: Not finally determined, but will include elements of:

Housing
Social services
Environmental health
Building
Street cleansing

Financial resources allocated: No figures available

Number of staff in decentralised offices: Not determined, but it is expected to be 40-50

Organisation within decentralised offices: Not determined

Form of devolved control: Not determined

Current situation: The council carried out a consultation exercise in four areas of the city in October/November 1985. Consultation is presently being carried out on a city-wide basis. It is planned that the first five neighbourhood offices will be open by Summer 1987 (with

255

site starts this year) and a further 16 site starts are planned for 1987. To date 19 neighbourhood areas have been declared as part of a rolling programme lasting until 1990

NEWHAM

Party in control:	Labour
Date of initial proposals:	1982
Total population:	210,000
Number of decentralised areas proposed:	12
Average population of decentralised areas:	17,500
Average number of dwellings in decentralised areas:	3,000 council, 3,000 private

Services to be decentralised:

Housing

- Estate management
- Allocations
- Rents and benefits
- Cash functions
- Admin backup
- Private sector grants and improvements

Financial resources allocated: No figures available

Number of staff in decentralised offices: 28-35

Organisation within decentralised offices: Four area co-ordinators responsible to the director of housing. Three district managers based in area offices report to area co-ordinators and are reported to by area team leaders

Form of devolved control: Four area sub committees report to the housing committee. Each committee is made up of councillors, and Tenants' Association, resident group and minority group representatives

Current situation: Phase 1 - 3 districts (completed)
Phase 2 - 6 districts (to be completed by the end of this year)
Phase 3 - 3 districts (to be completed in about a year's time, presently there are problems in site identification)

At present only white collar staff are located in district offices, the next priority will be to bring in local repair teams

NORWICH

Party in control: Labour

Date of initial proposals: 1983 (working party set up)

Total population: 123,700

Number of decentralised areas proposed: Seven local housing offices, the larger areas having three sub-offices

Average population of decentralised areas:
Five offices = 2-3,000
One office = 4,200
One office = 6,200

Average number of dwellings in decentralised areas: -

Services to be decentralised: Housing

Financial resources allocated: Small capital budget for area committees (environmental works)

Number of staff in decentralised offices: 15-23

Organisation within decentralised offices:
Area offices

1 senior assistant (outside staff)
1 senior assistant (internal staff)

Each office also has a technical officer

Form of devolved control: There will be area committees, with the first elections in September. Two reps from each patch (600 dwellings) on area committees

Current situation: A decentralisation sub committee is being set up. One office has been opened since March, one will open in September, with two opening next year, and three the year after

259

SHEFFIELD

Party in control:	Labour
Date of initial proposals:	-
Total population:	540,000
Number of decentralised areas proposed:	15 (housing)
Average population of decentralised areas:	11,000 in pilot neighbourhood forums
Average number of dwellings in decentralised areas:	-
Services to be decentralised:	Essentially housing, social services are organised on an area basis anyway
Financial resources allocated:	Figures not available
Number of staff in decentralised offices:	40
Organisation within decentralised offices:	Five area office managers are responsible to the assistant director
Form of devolved control:	Two neighbourhood forums were set up as a pilot scheme in June 1985, they include ward councillors, council department officers, reps from tenants' associations, residents .... Advisory only. Decentralisation is seen very much in terms of increased public participation and consultation
Current situation:	As above

SOUTHAMPTON

Party in control:	Labour
Date of initial proposals:	1984
Total population:	204,000
Number of decentralised areas proposed:	11
Average population of decentralised areas:	18,000
Average number of dwellings in decentralised areas:	2,000-3,000 (council)

Services to be decentralised:

Housing, including:

- Rent payment
- Housing benefits
- Estates management
- Repairs requests

Financial resources allocated:

Capital : £491,000 (1984/87)
Revenue : £641,00 - includes:

- Employees
- Running costs
- Capital finance costs

Number of staff in decentralised offices:

Ranges between seven and 10

Organisation within decentralised offices:

Typical office organisation would be:

Area housing manager (PO6-9)

Local housing manager (SO1-2)

Four housing officers (S 5)

One technical assistant (S4/5)

Two cashiers/receptionists (S1/3)

Form of devolved control: Still not determined.   However, the council have been setting up 'Local Project Schemes' in various parts of the city.   Each project has a local forum made up of local groups which has the power to spend a capital budget.   The council is presently looking at how this idea might be expanded to decentralisation

Current state of play: Five local offices are now open

TOWER HAMLETS

Party in control:	Liberals
Date of initial proposal:	1986
Total population:	144,600
Number of decentralised areas proposed:	Seven
Average population of decentralised areas:	20,000
Average number of dwellings in decentralised areas:	-

Services to be decentralised: Most of housing, community services, 'field' social services, technical services (with the exception of transport, waste disposal and building control). Financial and strategic control will mostly remain central.

Financial resources allocated: No figures available

Number of staff in decentralised offices: Not determined

Organisation within decentralised offices: Not determined, but seven chief officers have been designated 'neighbourhood executives' to control local services

Form of devolved control: Seven neighbourhoods based on existing ward boundaries, with neighbourhood committees composed of ward councillors controlling all decentralised services in their area. NCs presently have a small budget based on population (£0.5m total)

Current situation:
All service committees were abolished overnight except for policy and resources, social services, housing sub- and special decentralisation committees

Neighbourhood committees are now working, with three controlled by Labour. The decentralisation team of seconded chief officers has drawn up an initial report on which services are to be decentralised. This has been agreed. Most housing and social services are to be decentralised, environmental health is to be partially decentralised. The director of finance has been asked to investigate banks and building societies re funding for neighbourhood offices. Staff training programmes are to begin. Implementation is planned to be largely completed by January 1987

264

WALSALL

Party in control:	Labour
Date of initial proposals:	1981
Total population:	264,000
Number of decentralised areas proposed:	31
Average population of decentralised areas:	8,000 (although this varies greatly)
Average number of dwellings in . decentralised areas:	Ranges from between 200 to 5,000 (both public and private)

Services to be decentralised:

Housing, including:

- Rent payments
- Improvement grants
- Lettings
  Repairs
- Mortgages

Welfare benefits
Social services, including:

- Home helps
- Meals on wheels

Earlier proposals to fully decentralise social services have been halted since Labour lost control in 1983

Financial resources allocated: No figures available

Number of staff in decentralised offices: Ranges between five and 20

Organisation within decentralised offices:	Neighbourhood officer
	Assistant neighbourhood officer
Urban renewal units	Neighbourhood assistants
Community care officer	Mobile technicians
	Neighbourhood rent collectors

There is no receptionist, each member of staff carries out this function. The key feature of the offices is the promotion of generic working

Form of devolved control: Grass roots representatives have access to housing committees via the neighbourhood offices. This has proved much more successful in some areas than others. Progress on devolving political control has been halted by the Tory/Liberal coalition, which took control of the council in 1983 but which was defeated in the last round of elections

Current state of play: All 31 offices are operating

GUIDE TO FURTHER READING

Many useful sources have been cited in the references provided at the end of each chapter. Here we group some useful texts under a series of headings covering different aspects of decentralisation and democratisation.

Overviews of decentralisation and democratisation

Gyford, J. (1986) 'Diversity, sectionalism and local democracy' in The conduct of local authority business (Widdicombe Committee), Research Volume IV, Cmnd 9801, June, London: HMSO.

Hambleton, R. and Hoggett, P. (eds) (1984) The politics of decentralisation: theory and practice of a radical local government initiative, Working Paper 46, School for Advanced Urban Studies, University of Bristol.

Smith, B.C. (1985) Decentralisation. The territorial dimension of the state, London: Allen and Unwin.

Central/local relations in Britain

Hambleton, R, (1986) Rethinking policy planning. A study of planning systems linking central and local government, SAUS Study 2, School for Advanced Urban Studies, University of Bristol.

Jones, J. and Stewart, J. (1983) The case for local government, London: Allen and Unwin.

Europe

Evers, A. (1981) 'Social movements and political power: a survey of a theoretical and political controversy', Comparative Urban Research, 8.2.

Pickvance, C. (1985) 'The rise and fall of urban movements and the role of comparative analysis', Society and Space, Vol 3.

Castells, M. (1983) The city and the grassroots, Edward Arnold.

America

Yates, D. (1973) Neighbourhood democracy. The politics and impacts of decentralisation, London: Lexington Books.

Yin, R.K. and Yates, D. (1975) Street-level governments. Assessing decentralisation and urban services, London: Lexington Books.

Political perspectives on the welfare state

Ascher, K. (1987) The politics of privatisation, London: Macmillan.

Beuret, K. and Stoker, G. (1986) 'The Labour party and neighbourhood decentralisation: flirtation or commitment?', Critical Social Policy, September.

Hain, P. et al (1976) Community politics, London: John Calder.

Hoggett, P. (1984) 'Decentralisation, labourism and the professionalised welfare state apparatus' in Hambleton and Hoggett, op cit.

Organisational learning and change

Agyris, C. and Schon, D.A. (1978) Organisational learning: a theory of action perspective, London: Addison-Wesley.

Landry, C., Morley, D., Southwood, R. and Wright, P. (1985) What a way to run a railroad. An analysis of radical failure, London: Comedia.

Personal social services

Beresford, P. and Croft, S. (1986) Whose welfare. Private care or public services?, Lewis Cohen Urban Studies Centre, Brighton Polytechnic.

Elcock, H. (1986) 'Decentralisation as a tool for social services management', Local Government Studies, July/August, pp 35-49.

Hadley, R. and McGrath, M. (eds) (1980) Going local: neighbourhood social services, NCVO Occasional Paper 1, London: Bedford Square Press.

Means, R. (1984) 'Decentralisation and the personal social services' in Hambleton and Hoggett, op cit.

Housing

Power, A. (1984) Local housing management: a priority estates project survey, Department of the Environment, London: HMSO.

Area management in the 1970s

Hambleton, R. (1978) Policy planning and local government, London: Hutchinson.

Harrop, K.J., Mason, T., Vielba, C.A. and Webster, B.A. (1978) The implementation and development of area management, Institute of Local Government Studies, University of Birmingham.

RECENT PUBLICATIONS FROM SAUS

OCCASIONAL PAPERS

OP 21 Pub drinking and the licensed trade: a study
of drinking cultures and local community
in two areas of South West England
Adrian Franklin (1985)   £4.30

OP 22 Implementing an inner city policy: a review of
the London Borough of Hammersmith and Fulham
Inner Area Programme
Gill Whitting (1985)   £5.45

OP 23 Shutting out the inner city worker: recruitment
and training practices of large employers in
central London
Tom Davies and Charlie Mason (1986)   £4.30

OP 24 Milton Keynes - the best of both worlds? Public
and professional views of a new city
Jeff Bishop (1986)   £6.55

OP 25 Educating about alcohol: professional
perspectives and practice in South West England
Robin Means, Lyn Harrison, Lesley Hoyes and
Randall Smith (1986)   £6.55

OP 26 Building societies: the way forward
Derek Hawes (1986)   £4.75

OP 27 Centralisation and decentralisation in England
and France
Stephen Garrish (1986)   £6.55

SAUS STUDIES

SS 1   An unreasonable act? Central-local government
conflict and the Housing Act 1980
Ray Forrest and Alan Murie (1985)   £6.55

SS 2	Rethinking policy planning: a study of planning systems linking central and local government	
	Robin Hambleton (1986)	£7.65

SS 3	Managing health services: health authority members in search of a role	
	Christopher Ham (1986)	£7.15

WORKING PAPERS

WP 45	Women's committees: a study of gender and local government policy formulation	
	Sheila Button (1984)	£4.60

WP 46	The politics of decentralisation: theory and practice of a radical local government initiative	
	Paul Hoggett, Robin Hambleton et al (1985)	£4.50

WP 51	Grant Related Expenditure and recreation	
	Glen Bramley (1985)	£2.15

WP 52	The treatment of capital in Grant Related Expenditure	
	Glen Bramley and Philip Leather (1985)	£2.15

WP 53	Grant Related Expenditure: public transport revenue support case-study	
	Andrew Evans (1985)	£2.15

WP 59	The restructuring of the defence industries and the role of the state	
	John Lovering (1986)	£2.00

WP 60	Homelessness in London	
	John Greve and others (1986)	£2.20

All prices include postage. Please make cheques payable to the University of Bristol.

For a full list of SAUS publications contact:

The Publications Officer, School for Advanced Urban Studies, Rodney Lodge, Grange Road, BRISTOL BS8 4EA. Telephone: (0272) 741117